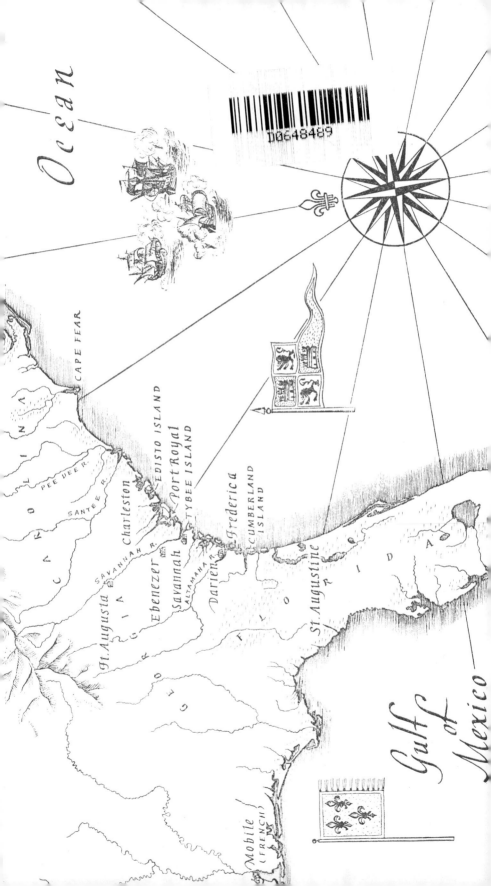

Ocean

CAPE FEAR

CAROLINA

PEE DEE R.

SANTEE R.

St. Augusta

SAVANNAH R.

Charleston

EDISTO ISLAND

Ebenezer

Port Royal

TYBEE ISLAND

GEORGIA

Savannah

ALTAMAHA R.

Darien R.

Frederica

CUMBERLAND ISLAND

St. Augustine

FLORIDA

Gulf of Mexico

Mobile (FRENCH)

"My country 'tis of thee,
Sweet land of liberty,
Of thee I sing,
Land where our fathers died,
Land of the pilgrims' pride . . ."

These famous lines from an American
patriotic anthem are the source for the
title of this chronicle of one of the most
engaging periods of American history.
Marion Starkey has used many contemporary sources to discover much new and
exciting material for this account of the
settling of the Eastern Shores from
1607 to 1735.

These were the colonies which later became
the original thirteen States of the Union.
Their settlers were men and women who
by any standards would be remarkable,
forceful, and creative. Here their characters
are brought to life by extracts from
diaries and letters which fill in some of the
gaps of familiar history. They were
individuals of widely varying tempera-
ments: the visionary Anne Hutchinson
from Boston; Stuyvesant famous for his
silver-embossed wooden leg and the
vigour with which he fired the Dutch;
Penn trying to organise his Utopia from
prison; people from different nations with
different dreams, some of whom even
so early, dimly perceived that they were
the founders of a great nation.

To bring all this history within the scope
of one book is an ambitious project but
Miss Starkey, herself a native of Massachusetts, has succeeded with flair and
distinction. She writes:
"Across the 'cruel Atlantic' our fathers
came in crowded little cockle shells of
ships, often uncertain of their destinations
and blankly ignorant of what they would
find when they got here. They came for the
noblest of reasons, to shape in the new
world a commonwealth dedicated to God's
goodness: and they came in the simple
hope of bettering themselves. They came
of their own choice, forsaking their homes
and their kin; they came because they
were made to, seized for the purpose on
the Guinea coast of Africa or in the
teeming slums of London. But whether
they came willingly or in bitter protest,
each of them helped build what we
have today."
For any English-speaking person this
introduction to the early history of that
magnificent adventure will be valuable and
exciting.

LAND WHERE OUR FATHERS DIED

Land where our fathers died

The Settling of the Eastern Shores 1607/1735

Marion L. Starkey

CONSTABLE / LONDON

For my friends in the best of "colonies," Connecticut. More specifically, for my students and colleagues at the University of Connecticut, from those I knew in the resounding days of the G.I. rush at Fort Trumbull, in summer school at the "Main Farm" at Storrs, to my friends on the lovely little campus at 1280 Asylum in Hartford.

62-15936

First published in Great Britain in 1964
by Constable and Company Ltd
10 Orange Street, London WC2
Copyright © 1961 Marion L. Starkey
Printed by Thomas Nelson (Printers) Ltd
London and Edinburgh

PREFACE

Tʜɪs is my story of the first settlements in what became the United States of America. In describing the colonies I have tried to find the diversities of the colonial experience. New Sweden on the Delaware gets a chapter not because it was more important than New Jersey or Connecticut, but because its story contained elements not found elsewhere. Plymouth, overrun with children, little resembled womanless early Jamestown; the Puritans of Massachusetts, the Dutch on the Hudson were very different people. Among other diversities was the startling disparity in the degree to which the settlements were given or seized for themselves self-government. There were also vast differences in their relations with the earliest settlers of all, the Indians. Universal problems included adjustment to climate and the heroic task of breaking and taming virgin soil; but even here the later comers profited greatly by the experience and the propinquity of prior settlements.

There was another factor in forming the pattern of narration. Historians, being fact-bound, have to depend on available documents. One reason that tiny Plymouth, historically so much less important than Massachusetts Bay, looms so large in the imagination of Americans is that it had the best human-interest account of any colony. It is William Bradford's simple, heartfelt eloquence more than mere priority of settlement that has immortalized it. The Massachusetts story is actually better documented, though not even Winthrop's wonderful journal has the popularity of Bradford's history; but other early colonies have been unfortunate in their intimate records. What a pity that no one in Thomas Hooker's congregation kept a journal of the journey to the Connecticut, that the first comers to the Hudson, the Delaware, and to Carolina did not put their experience on paper, or above all that the Indians had no means of making a permanent record of their observations of the white men. Probably some such records have been lost, as was Bradford's history for nearly two centuries. There is always the hope that in some tangle of files here or in Europe there are narratives as moving as Bradford's that some archivist will have the patience and good fortune to discover.

Contents

Contents

Prelude

Across the "cruel Atlantic" our fathers came in crowded little cockleshells of ships, often uncertain of their destinations and blankly ignorant of what they would find when they got here. They came for the noblest of reasons, to shape in the new world a commonwealth dedicated to God's goodness; and they came in the simple hope of bettering themselves. They came of their own brave choice, forsaking their homes and their kin; they came because they were made to, seized for the purpose on the Guinea coast of Africa or in the teeming slums of London. But whether they came willingly or in bitter protest, each of them helped build what we have today.

"Our fathers were Englishmen," one of them wrote. He put it too narrowly; at the least he might have included the Irish, the Scotch, the Welsh. But our fathers were also, from the very first, Dutchmen, Frenchmen, Germans, Poles, Swiss, Swedes, Finns, Portuguese Jews, Angolans, Congolese, Gambians, and all of them together laid the foundations of a great nation which a few of them, even so early, dimly perceived.

This is their story, and as Americans it is ours. Even for those of us who came in a later generation, on a smooth ship equipped with radar, or who skimmed over the Atlantic by plane, these are our fathers.

CHRONOLOGY OF SETTLEMENTS

1584–7   Sir Walter Raleigh, with a patent from Queen Elizabeth, establishes the first English colony in North America on Roanoke Island in territory he called Virginia. On 18 August 1587 Virginia Dare was born in this settlement, the first English child born within the limits of the present United States. What happened to this settlement is not known; when the site was revisited in 1590 it was found deserted.

1603   Death of Queen Elizabeth and accession of James I.

1606   The London and Plymouth Virginia Companies are chartered.

1607   Ships of the Virginia Company of London reach Virginia and establish Jamestown.

1619   The first Virginia Assembly meets, consisting of the Governor and Council, and twenty-two Burgesses representing the settlers. This is the first legislative body in North America.

1620   The Pilgrim Fathers, a group of separatists from the Church of England who had been living at Leyden in Holland, sail in the *Mayflower* and establish a colony at Plymouth in New England. Their settlement was made under patent from the Virginia Company of London, though in fact they settled outside the territory of the Company.

1620   A charter is granted to the Council for New England, the successor of the Plymouth Virginia Company. The chief member of the Council is Sir Ferdinando Gorges. The extensive grant to the Council later caused difficulties to the New England colonies. Gorges himself concentrated on establishing settlements on the Maine coast.

1621   The Pilgrim Fathers obtain a new patent for their settlement from the Council for New England.

1624   The charter of the London Virginia Company is revoked, and Virginia becomes a royal colony.

1624   The Dorchester Company with a patent from the Council for New England attempts to establish a fishing settlement in New England.

1624   The Dutch establish a colony on the Hudson River. Later New Amsterdam is founded on Manhattan Island. The Dutch also make settlements in the Hudson Valley, on the Connecticut River and on the Delaware.

1625   Death of James I and accession of Charles I.

1626   The Dorchester Company abandons its attempt to found a fishing settlement, but some of its settlers, under the leadership of Roger Conant, form a colony at Salem (Naumkeag).

1628   The New England Company is formed, in part as the successor of the Dorchester Company. It is largely under Puritan influence. It reinforces the Salem settlement. John Endicott is appointed Governor.

1629   The Massachusetts Bay Company, superseding the New England Company, receives a royal charter.

1630	Voyage of John Winthrop, Governor of Massachusetts.
1632	A royal charter is granted to the Catholic Lord Baltimore to establish a colony, Maryland, north of Virginia.
1635-6	Roger Williams is driven out of Massachusetts and settles at Providence. This is the beginning of the colony of Rhode Island.
1636	Massachusetts allows a migration to the Connecticut River and the establishment of a separate government for Connecticut.
1636	A Puritan colony is established at New Haven.
1638	Sweden founds a colony on the Delaware.
1642	Outbreak of the Civil War in England.
1643	Formation of the United Colonies of New England, comprising Massachusetts, Plymouth, Connecticut and New Haven. This union was virtually terminated in 1664.
1644	Rhode Island obtains a charter.
1649	Execution of Charles I.
1655	The Dutch take New Sweden.
1660	The restoration of Charles II.
1662	A royal charter is granted to Connecticut; Connecticut absorbs New Haven.
1663	A charter is granted to proprietors to establish colonies south of Virginia. Two settlements are made, one becoming North Carolina and the other South Carolina. South Carolina becomes a royal colony in 1719, and North Carolina in 1729.
1664	The English capture New Amsterdam, and bring to an end the Dutch colony. It had been granted in advance to James, Duke of York—the future James II—and is rechristened New York. The land between the Hudson and the Delaware is granted to proprietors, and, having been divided for a period into East and West Jersey, is eventually reunited to form the colony of New Jersey.
1680	New Hampshire is separated from Massachusetts.
1681	William Penn, the Quaker, founds the proprietary colony of Pennsylvania. With Pennsylvania is associated the small settlement of Delaware, which after 1704 has a government of its own.
1685	Death of Charles II and accession of James II.
1686	James II appoints Sir Edmund Andros as governor of the new Dominion of New England, which ultimately included New York and New Jersey as well as the New England colonies.
1688-9	The Glorious Revolution. James II loses his crown and is succeeded by William III. The Dominion of New England is abolished.
1691	Massachusetts receives a royal charter, and incorporates Maine and Plymouth.
1732	A royal charter is granted to trustees to establish the colony of Georgia. The charter is surrendered in 1752, when Georgia becomes a royal province.

I PASSAGE TO AMERICA: 1630

1

On April 12, 1630, the flagship *Arbella*, followed by her three consorts, passed Land's End and plunged her bow into the boiling Atlantic. It was the Sabbath, and the passengers should have gathered to hear the Reverend Mr. George Phillips commemorate the occasion in sermon and prayer. But the minister lay ignominiously ill in his cabin, and so in their quarters, cabins for the gentry, 'tween decks or gun room for the simple, lay most of his flock.

Only three days earlier this miserable company had faced mortal peril with stout hearts. Eight sail had been seen aft, coming as if from Dunkirk where the Spaniards were, and though outnumbered, the little convoy, the *Arbella, Ambrose, Jewel,* and *Talbot,* had readied for battle. Women and children were hustled out of the way, such "bed matter" as might take fire cast overboard. The longboats were lowered, and the men, armed with muskets, took posts behind the colored screens of "waist cloths."

One shot was fired, "a ball of wild fire," which the captain fastened to an arrow and sent into the water. It burned there a long time, and the people watched, as if it were a sign, and held themselves steadfast. In the hold the children did not weep and the women did not panic. They trusted in the Lord, and old England lay to the starboard. Would the enemy dare give battle within sight of Portland?

It did not, for this was not the enemy. Most were fishing craft, peaceably bound for Canada and the Grand Banks off Newfoundland. "Our fear and danger were turned into mirth and entertainment," observed Governor John Winthrop on the *Arbella*. The musket shot was used to salute each ship as it passed; the children scrambled back to deck to cheer and wave.

But the same women and children, the same men, who had braced themselves to meet the enemy with fortitude, did nothing of the sort when they met the Atlantic. It came at them head on in the teeth of a gale, and there was no arming against a sea of such troubles. They could not hold their footing on a deck that dipped away or rose to smite them; there was no point of rest for the eyes now that the last rock of Scilly was under a horizon where mountains skipped like young lambs. On deck the very livestock bellowed its dismay, and in their cabins, in their bunks and hammocks, the people heaved and moaned.

Now they knew themselves irrevocably committed to the unknown. They were voyaging into outer space, and though they could claim no priority in this venture, so many having gone before, they were none the less entering a way of life as remote from their imagination as if they were voyaging to another planet.

They had been on their way since March, hovering off the coast of England, tarrying here for supplies, here for a favorable wind. For those in authority, like John Winthrop and Captain Peter Milborne of the *Arbella*, those who had to concern themselves with provision and water, the delay had been onerous. For others it had been good to have England beside them so long. There had been no sudden break with the known and loved; merciful providence had been weaning them by degrees. Sometimes Lady Arbella and her gentlewomen had visited ashore. There had been sport for the children at Cowes when an ox and wethers had been fetched aboard, the beasts lowing and bleating as they were heaved to deck.

But these easy, reassuring days were now forever gone. They had done with England, which with all its iniquities had been a green and pleasant land. Now they remembered that the bravest accounts of life in the Americas had been punctuated with death. Women big with child recalled that the first English child born on American soil, little Virginia Dare, had been lost with all her

colony, leaving not a trace behind. Other settlers had survived
only after starving times, corn planted on graves so that the enemy
red men could not number the dead; they had heard of felons
offered a choice between America and the gallows who grate-
fully chose the gallows.

For death they could prepare themselves, and prayerfully in
England they had done so. But the humiliation of this particular
misery had been outside their reckoning. So on the wild Sabbath
when the convoy entered the Atlantic, even Mr. Phillips lay in
his cabin and had no heart, or rather no stomach, to lift up his
flock with exhortation.

2

Shortly after midday on Monday, Governor Winthrop went to
his cabin for a look at his two young sons. Stephen was twelve,
and Adam had just observed his tenth birthday aboard. "Our boys
are well and cheerful and have no mind for home," he had written
to his wife, who had remained behind. "They lie both with me
and sleep as soundly in a rug (for we use no sheets here) as they
ever did in Groton." But that had been written from Cowes, two
weeks ago. There was no health in them now and no cheer; Adam
could not control a puppy-like whimper when he saw his father.
"Up with you," said Winthrop. "I need you on deek."

The lads stared at him glassy-eyed. What he asked seemed no
less than what Abraham had asked of Isaac; but though this was
a kind father, he was firm, and feebly they obeyed. The deck still
lurched, but less heavily, and once they were out of the cabin
they were in the sun. The waves rushed to meet the dipping bow-
sprit, but under a blue sky they looked sportive, like dolphins.
Adam retched once more; then he felt better and looked to his
father for orders.

"Fetch your playmates. Tell them the governor wants them."

Grim to enter the stuffy quarters 'tween decks with their smell
of sick and of the necessary tubs, but gratifying to use the imperative and invoke "my father, the governor." At this command

the children straggled up to deck and dumbly looked to the re-
vered figure for orders. They were unexpected; he was calling
them not to pray but to sport; they were to have a tug of war.

A rope had been rigged, under Winthrop's direction, from steer-
age to mainmast, and as the young people came he told them to
lay hold of it, some on one side, some on the other. Some children
stared blankly, asking leave to die in peace, but a governor is
obeyed. They pulled on the rope, rather after the manner of
women easing their labor pains. They pulled halfheartedly at first,
then with a will as those on the other side yanked it away. The
sun shone warm on their backs and dispelled the chill that had
struck to the marrow. Presently they shouted as gaily as if they
were home on the village green, and their mothers, hearing mirth,
ventured out, and as the governor put it, "They soon grew well
and merry."

The crew looked on with various feelings. There were among
them profane fellows irritated to be in the service of a "praying
company" like these Puritans, and inclined to sneer. But the sport
was in the spirit of the merry England of the late Elizabeth, and
more of them relished it than not. Some seamen undertook to
teach the children and the young men some of their "harmless
exercise." "Some would play the wags with them," the governor
remarked, but did not interfere since it "did our people much
good."

Thomas Dudley, Winthrop's second in command, looked on
without comment. Already he suspected that of which he would
soon have much to say, that the governor was given to "lenity."
They were here embarked on a venture of high moral emprise;
if they were to hark back for health's sake to idle merriment, surely
there should have been seemly preliminaries of admonition and
prayer.

Winthrop had not forgotten prayer. Later in the afternoon,
when he heard two bells struck, he remembered that this was
Monday and drew apart to his cabin to commune with God and
his wife. "Monday and Friday at five of the clock at night, we
shall meet in spirit till we meet in person," he had written his
Margaret. She was remaining in their Groton home with the

younger children until she could give birth. She was his third wife, and he loved her as dearly as he had loved them all: the first for whom he had at seventeen interrupted his studies at Cambridge; the second whose holy dying soon after childbirth he had recorded with pious awe in his journal. "I will only take thee now and my sweet children in mine arms and kiss and embrace you, and so leave you with God," he had written her.

There would be times, as he would confess from America, when under the pressure of business he would let the hour of sanctified rendezvous go by unremarked, but this first day on the Atlantic was not one of them. He came out of his cabin restored and refreshed and joined the society that he had known so long at Tattershall.

3

On the flagship the gentlefolk were already old acquaintance, and not from the voyage alone. Most were of the company who at Tattershall, seat of the Earl of Lincoln, had for months been planning this adventure. It was to be the firmest planting that America had yet seen—eight vessels were to follow this convoy—and the practical details had been multitudinous. Not the least had been convincing Winthrop, already a settled man well along in his forties, and so an elder statesman in this young company, that he should lead it.

With him was the earl's young sister, lovely Lady Arbella, who recently and proudly had taken the prosaic name of Mrs. Isaac Johnson. None addressed her thus. She would be Lady Arbella to the last, and in her honor the old name of the flagship, *Eagle,* had been painted out and hers substituted. As for her husband, no one considered him prosaic. As ardent in his devotions as her ladyship, he had dedicated much of his substantial fortune to make this migration possible.

There were two of Lincoln's former stewards, Thomas Dudley and Simon Bradstreet. With the latter was his impressionable young wife Anne, who at eighteen was an old married lady. In

her two years of happy marriage to an adored husband, the union
had not yet been blessed with children, and this was a grief to
the girl. Sometimes she consoled herself by writing verses, but
not just now; there was too much motion on the *Arbella*, too little
privacy. It was the governor who recorded the odyssey of the
voyage in prose in his journal.

Not of the Tattershall elect, and unmarked by them except
perhaps as a boisterous tomboy engaging in the tug of war, was
the ten-year-old who later became Anne Pollard. She may not
have been on the *Arbella*, but if not she was close by on the
Jewel or the *Ambrose;* she had to be, for Anne was to lay undisputed claim to being the first settler of Boston. First, by virtue
of a flying leap from the bow of a longboat; undisputed, because
she was to survive Lady Arbella, John Winthrop, Simon and
Anne Bradstreet, and everyone else who might say her nay.

She was to live beyond the turn of the century, past her own
century mark, and celebrate this feat by doing on her best lace-
edged cap and bib to sit for her portrait to a limner. She was
toothless by that time (the early Americans' teeth were not their
most durable part) but her deep-set eyes were alert, and doubtless the obscure sign painter who took his name from her (Pollard
Limner) listened as he painted, to the story that had delighted
her children, grandchildren, great grandchildren, and the generations of publicans who visited her tavern in Boston, which she
had first known as a place of swamps and hollows, covered with
blueberry bushes.

But there were uncounted leagues to travel before Boston could
be thought of. One gale was past; there would be others, and not
gales only but full storms. Sometimes the little fleet was driven
back farther than the distance it could gain in a day's sailing,
and the other ships which had been left behind came near. The
voyage was long, but it was prosperous. On the *Arbella* there were
no deaths. After the first gale most passengers found their sea
legs. Once, a maidservant feeling the motion took "hot waters"
for her stomach's sake, overdid it, and fell seriously ill. But she
recovered. Mr. Phillips came out to catechize the children and
preach his Sabbath sermons; and though the deck dipped and

soared, and congregation and divine alike received an asperga-
tion of spindrift, the folk stood steadfast from "firstly to tenthly."
For most of his life, like his father Adam before him, John
Winthrop had kept a journal. In it he now recorded the wonders
of the great Atlantic, which he observed as eagerly as his young
sons. Once a whale came straight at them and "would not shun
us, so we passed within a stone's cast as he lay spouting up water."
Even when there was no land within two hundred leagues there
were fowl, flying and swimming. At night Winthrop remarked the
steady declining of the North Star and that the moon, especially
when new, was smaller than the moons of England. By day he
discovered that in these southerly latitudes the sun "did not give
so much heat as in England."

Nor was the journey devoid of human encounters. It was, after
all, more than a century since the new world had swum like a
new planet into Europe's ken, and many nations were launching
expeditions to probe its contours and to fish the fecund banks off
the northern shores. Often the *Arbella* hailed such fellow travelers
and spoke them in passing, or tried to. Sometimes a small craft
plying lonely shunned them, taking them for the Spanish, who,
since the Pope had awarded them all the Americas, the bulge of
Brazil excepted, were not disposed to extend the right hand of
fellowship to trespassers.

Apart from such wayfarers there were the other members of
the convoy. Sometimes they lost each other for a day or two, but
so far as wind and wave permitted they kept within sight of each
other's sails, each taking its turn to carry a light in the mizzen-
mast after sundown. On a "still calm" in fair weather there was
visiting between ships. Once the *Arbella* sent her skiff to the *Jewel*
for a hogshead of meal "because we could not come by our own,"
and the skiff returned with not only the neighborly loan but the
Jewel's master and John Revel, part owner of the *Arbella*. So a
feast was prepared, and Captain Lowe on the *Ambrose* was signaled to come share it. There were several such dinner parties, the
officers dining in the roundhouse, the ladies apart in the great
cabin. When the officers returned to their own ships, the *Arbella*
fired a salute of three shots.

One shot was fired (and the sails dipped) for other cause. A woman on the *Arbella* was in travail, and the nearest midwife was far ahead on the *Jewel*. At the signal the *Jewel* trimmed her sails and stayed. When they were within speaking distance, the midwife hiked up her skirts and got down the swaying Jacob's ladder of one ship and up again to the next, where she safely delivered the child. (Child and midwife were nameless; the governor did not anticipate posterity's greed for exact information.)

He had much to do besides watch whales and feast with visiting captains. If the captain was in charge of the ship and crew, he was in charge of the landsmen, and when there was division between them he had to intervene. Not long after the first gale the captain conducted the governor to the gun room to see for himself what a mess the men quartered there had made of the place. "It was so beastly and noysome with their victuals and beastliness and would endanger the health of the ship." The governor retired for prayer and then gave orders: fatigue detail for the landsmen. Four would clean for the first three days, another four for the second, and so in rotation so long as they remained on the ship.

Once it was a passenger who complained of abuse from a petty officer, and the captain had the latter hung up by his hands with a weight about his neck. Distressed by such severity, the governor persuaded the captain to lenience. But he himself ordered similar punishment for a servant he caught cheating a child. The servant had sold the child a threepenny box for the promise of three biscuits a day. At the time he was caught he had received forty biscuits and had sold most of them to other servants. This was capital enterprise on a small scale, but the governor was no student of the theory that Puritanism and capitalism went hand in hand. He had a basket of stones hung about the servant's neck and stood him with his hands tied up to a bar for two hours.

4

The ocean was a foretaste of eternity. It was as if the ocean
had no end; it became a way of life. Yet even the Atlantic was
finite. By early June they were off the Grand Banks, that rendezvous of fishermen from Europe over. Lines were cast from deck
and cod jigged up, "very great fish," some one and a half feet
long, and this was God's mercy, for aside from their weariness of
eating salt fish, the supply was running out.

It was eerie going on the Banks. The fog lay so thick on the
water that the ships lost each other, yet overhead the sun shone
bright. The captain had soundings taken, and finding them shallow, fitted the *Arbella* to another mainsail lest she be driven on
the shoals. On dark nights he would not risk retiring to his cabin.

On Tuesday June 8, overpowering the rank odors of the ship,
they caught the scent of land, "so pleasant a sweet air as did much
refresh us, and there came a smell offshore like the smell of a
garden." Before them the horizon steadied at last; land was in
sight, the hills about Penobscot Bay.

It was only a four days' sail down the coast to their provisional
destination, Salem, or Naumkeag as it was still called, and there
they had a holiday. Some were set ashore at Cape Ann, where
the children scrambled about picking strawberries. Lady Arbella
and the other gentlefolk enjoyed the hospitality of John Endicott,
governor in these parts until Winthrop came, and in his sturdy
frame house supped on venison pastry and good beer.

Their troubles were over. Their troubles were just beginning.
Even Endicott's house (which he had commandeered from its
builder, Roger Conant, and floated down from Beverly for his own
use) was no Tattershall. The common sort there still lived in
makeshifts; some had made dugouts in the banks, shoring up the
dirt walls with timber and covering the ground with reeds; some
lived in still ruder arrangements of poles, brushwood, sailcloths,
and skins.

Their plantings were nondescript. They were hungry, and living in expectation of this "supply" of provisions already nearly exhausted during the long voyage. There had been many deaths, among them Francis Higginson, whose lyric accounts of the new land had impelled many to follow.

Little Anne Bradstreet looked on this sorry way of life and clung to her husband while her heart sank within her. The Lady Arbella held herself valiantly and made no complaint. But for her the journey had been hard; before the summer was over she would be dead. "She stopped at New England on her way to Heaven," as Cotton Mather would put it; her stricken husband would survive her only a month.

Not all the ships of this "great migration," nearly a dozen of them, had made so prosperous a voyage as the flagship. On the *Talbot* an infection had come aboard while she hovered off England, and fourteen had died of it. Governor Winthrop's son Henry, a scapegrace but beloved, was not one of these, but the day after the *Talbot* came in he drowned in an attempt to swim a creek. Heavily the governor turned to the task of finding a place for the "sitting down" of all these people and a means of building and planting before winter should close in on them.

5

This passage to America in 1630 was far from the first; on its scale, and better provided than most, it was not even characteristic. No two voyages, even of ships traveling in company, were alike. Nevertheless the *Arbella* may stand as a symbol of the thousand and one migrations to America in the seventeenth century.

The migrants had been coming to Virginia since 1607 (or 1587 if you count the lost Colony of Roanoke). A little group of English exiles had been settled out Cape Cod way for a decade. The Dutch had posts on the Hudson and Connecticut. A group of settlers already in Newfoundland, unhappy at the long winters, were looking down the coast to Chesapeake Bay. In Sweden the great Gustavus Adolphus was listening to estimates of fortunes to be made on the Delaware. Presently Swedes and Finns would be planting along the river; Germans were to follow, Huguenots, Portuguese Jews.

The migrants came not from Europe only. Already Africa had sent a handful of settlers to Virginia. In England's Sugar Islands, including Barbados, founded while the concept of Massachusetts was evolving, planters would find their lands too narrow and look to the southern coast.

The migrants came as they had come on the *Arbella,* and for few was it a pleasure cruise. Some voyages would be swift, counted in weeks, some would stretch over long months. On some ships quarters would be kept sweet with washings of vinegar and the burning of herbs, and the provisions would be wholesome and ample. On others passengers endured filth and sickened on rancid rations. Some would come without the loss of a passenger; some would become plague ships. Children would be born on other ships, some to early death, some to live to hale old age.

And ahead of all lay the brutal task of breaking ground and building shelter.

II FIRST SETTLEMENT: JAMESTOWN

1

THE strawberries that had so delighted the passengers of the *Arbella*, giving them the illusion that in this happy land they would be nourished like the children of Israel by manna from God, ripened earlier in Virginia. They had been ripe late in April (Old Style) in 1607 when the men who had sailed with Captain Christopher Newport finally picked the Jamestown peninsula for their settlement, and young George Percy, eighth son of the eighth Earl of Northumberland, led a small expedition inland and came upon a "plat" of them, "fine and beautiful strawberries, four times bigger and better than ours of England."

Bigger and better. Already Percy was making a noise like a Chamber of Commerce. He was young, the age of his fellow passenger John Smith; though at a time when the average life expectancy did not reach forty, his twenty-seven years might not have been accounted youth. Like many of the thirty-six "gents" in Captain Newport's company of 105, he was a veteran of the Lowlands campaigns, and since his expedition was exposed to attack from the enemy, it went armed. Percy doubtless had a pistol, and the men with him had their muskets, but being of knightly heritage, he also wore his sword and his light armor. So accoutered and bearded, as were all manly men in his day, he not a little resembled one Don Quixote, hero of a book published in Spain a year before he set sail from England. In setting forth to give battle to anachronistic dragons, Don Quixote was no more ill-informed about current reality than was young George Percy in Virginia.

In a few short months he would be much better informed, but as of the day, he was all boyish enthusiasm. His high spirits had begun in the West Indies, which Newport's little fleet had reached late in March, after a long and trying voyage around by the Azores. Now in Virginia he was delighting in the new-found world. First there had been the majestic capes, named forthwith for the two English princes, Henry and Charles; then they had come upon the spit of land they named Point Comfort, and hard by found the pleasantly situated village of the Kecoughtans, who in their own fashion had made the strangers welcome. There had been a voyage up the broad river, which they named James for their sovereign, through a land as nobly beautiful as any county in England, where there were parklike forests and meadows made for the grazing of fat cattle, though only the deer had them now.

The cypresses stood to their knees at the water's edge; the forest, much of it surprisingly clear of underbrush, was of beech, cedar, the fragrant sassafras, and oak, among the latter the splendid live oak, still in youth after a thousand years of growing. From the very treetops hung grapevines, at the roots often thicker than a man's thigh. Here in the woodland and clearings was a smother of honeysuckle and a delicate riot of wildflowers—when they got a church built at Jamestown the worshipers would deck it with them—and here on the ground were the first fruits, to be had for the plucking.

So many flowers, so many fruits, even so many trees whose names were unknown. It was as with Adam in the unspoiled Eden; they would assign them their names.

So Percy went in joy, startled sometimes by Indians, who, however, after one rude attack from a band on the south shore of the James, were more likely to offer gifts, including the fragrant weed called tobacco. And this was only a taste of the richness of the country. Ropes of what looked like pearls were observed on the necks of some Indians; gold they seemed not to possess, but this, or so the Englishmen gathered, was only because in their ignorance they preferred the lowly, utilitarian copper. But gold surely abounded in this country. Presently the ships would go home laden with it, and the gentlemen themselves, having served their terms in this outpost, would return to England, their fortunes made.

In this expectation Percy and others of his ilk were mistaken. He himself would endure most unwillingly five grim years in this smiling country, and then take unauthorized leave when he was given charge of a pinnace for a quite different mission. Any number of other highborn gentlemen would not return at all, being felled by an invisible enemy with which by August they were all too well acquainted.

2

That the London Company of Virginia had been organized and this expedition sent out was largely due to the tireless prose-lytizing of Bartholomew Gosnold. Ever since he had explored the New England coast in 1602 he had been extolling the advantages of the country for permanent planting and the patriotic desira-bility of doing so before the Spanish, already in Florida, engrossed the entire continent.

It was partly due to Gosnold's practical experience that the company had been sent with realistic advice on planting. The colonists were to deal warily with the Indians, avoiding conflict so far as possible, and in this interest representing themselves as visitors rather than permanent settlers. This policy, considered treachery when encountered among the heathen, but diplomacy when practiced by Christians, was followed with fidelity. Captain Smith, at the moment immobilized by the fact that he had been under arrest since the West Indies, would become expert in di-verting Indian suspicion by his plausible tales.

Other instructions directed the choice of site as far up a naviga-ble river as a bark of fifty tons could sail, on well-drained ground, free of marsh and forest. Marshes were to be avoided for health's sake; forests, because aside from giving cover to the Indians, the labor of clearing and planting would require undue effort. And these stipulations were, over Gosnold's vehement protest, disre-garded.

The James was navigable as far up as the falls, and offered a quantity of high ground, clear of forest, and furnished with sources of sweet water. The place called Jamestown lay low, was set about by marshland and forest, and had no natural water supply except the river itself. But it had one advantage that no one had the wit to find elsewhere. The channel came close to the shore and ran so deep that in all stages of the tide not only the little *Goodspeed* and *Discovery*, but the 100-ton *Sarah Constant* could be lashed to a tree and unloaded with no tedious business of transshipment in longboats.

Gosnold, least quarrelsome of men, contested long and urgently with Edward Maria Wingate, newly elected president of the Council, against allowing so transient an advantage to outweigh such grave deficiencies. This colony was his baby, the answer to his prayers, the fruit of years of hard work. Many of the stockholders of the London Company had risked their investment on the basis of his experience and judgment. He could not bear to see it given so dubious a start.

But Gosnold was talking into the wind. To exhausted men, their numbers already depleted by the sicknesses and hazards of a voyage of more than four months, the manifest convenience of the channel at Jamestown outweighed objections which seemed academic. They made their choice and stayed with it, and for a time, while the spring breezes were still fresh and invigorating, before the heat pressed down and the miasmas rose and the mosquitoes swarmed up from the marshlands, Jamestown entered into such a period of lusty enterprise as it was perhaps not to know again until pious descendants came to raise "reconstructions" and memorials to that which many of these men might consider better forgotten.

May and June were good months. The unloading of supplies completed—thanks to the wisdom of President Wingate it was child's play—the laboring men under the direction of their betters set to work with a will. By mid-June, Jamestown had a fort "which was triangle wise, having three bulwarks at every corner like a half moon, and four or five pieces of artillery mounted in them. We had made ourselves sufficiently strong for these savages." The

higher land, "two mountains" Percy called it, had been cleared
and sown with corn which already in this virgin soil "sprang a
man's height from the ground." Newport was back from a "discovery" up the James and was preparing to sail the *Sarah Constant* back to England.

A payload had been assembled, for the "adventurers," or stockholders in England, had a right to some return from even so
early a voyage. The load, assembled with great toil, was rather
disappointing: cedar clapboarding and sassafras roots dug from
the swamps. It seemed odd to fare so far and hazard so much for
so prosaic a cargo; however, it was the best that could be done in
a hurry and there was promise of better things. Beyond the falls
of the James the discoverers had found rocks "of a gravely nature
interlaced with many vains of glist'ring spangles." This news
would be received with excitement in London and govern the
choice of personnel aboard the first supply, which Newport promised to have back in Jamestown within twenty weeks.

Young Percy and Captain Smith had been on Newport's expedition. In Virginia a sealed box containing the London Company's instructions had been opened and Smith was therein
named as one of the Council. Appointment to such eminence did
not give him immunity from wrongdoing; before the year was
out another councilor, George Kendall, would be shot for conspiracy. Furthermore, Wingate, elected president perhaps on
grounds of seniority, since at forty-seven he must have been nearly
the eldest of this youthful company, was the one who had charged
Smith with "mutiny." But if Smith had enemies, he also had
friends. He was released, and this discovery up the James became
the first of a notable series of Smithsonian expeditions.

It had been discouraging to discover the navigation of the river
blocked by the falls hardly one hundred miles inland. Always in
these days and for long after it was hoped that whenever a broad
river was found it would lead to the South Sea, or Pacific. Though
the breadth of the land mass in Mexico was well known, the continent was believed to narrow again in these latitudes as it did in
Central America. Captains sent to Virginia would be regularly
charged with finding the passage to the west coast, and when

charters were drawn up, lands were often granted from the Atlantic to the Pacific without anyone's having an inkling of how much real estate was being so grandly bestowed.

The explorers made one find which might have been of immense interest had they taken it more seriously: "a savage boy about the age of ten years, which had a head of hair of a perfect yellow and a reasonable white skin." The lad might well have been a child of someone from the lost Colony of Roanoke, which later expeditions were expressly charged to find. But Captain Newport had as yet apparently received no such orders, and Roanoke Island being to the south and east, one would hardly expect to find a remnant of it here. No one seems to have tried to question the boy, and Percy wrote him off as "a miracle amongst all savages."

3

When Newport sailed back to England on June 22, he left behind him a Council divided and men already despondent. He promised to return within twenty weeks, but voyagers acquainted with the length of the course by the Azores and the prevalence of contrary winds in the Downs knew better than to take that promise at face value. Besides, he had left rations for only four-fifths of that time; the supplies which had seemed ample had been sadly depleted before they reached the Virginia capes.

There was provision to be had in this country—berries, sturgeon from the river, the corn ripening on the little "mountains." But berries and sturgeon came only in their season, and the cultivation of the corn had been interrupted, just before Newport returned from upstream, by a foray of Indian warriors, an estimated four hundred of them. The attack was a great surprise; the settlers had permission from the Paspahegh tribe to plant here, and no one had taken seriously an earlier episode when a group coming to pay a social call had left in anger after one visitor had been beaten for making off with an ax. The arms of the working men still lay in their packing cases, and the attack was repelled only by firing the ordnance from the ships.

After that the fields had been neglected while the men palisaded the fort, and when that was done, men had to watch and ward against scouting parties which skulked among the trees and through the tall grasses of the marsh. And now the heat was settling down on them, as tangible as a heavy, moist blanket; one would have supposed that they had landed on the Guinea coast, close to the Line instead of in a latitude adjudged temperate. There was no assuaging their thirst except from the river, for President Wingate kept a tight hand on his stock of aqua vitae and sack, and the river was brackish at flood tide and full of slime at the ebb. The cool of the evening brought no relief, for it was then that the mosquitoes rose in whining clouds from the swamps.

Left largely to their own devices, for their betters were falling prey to fluxes and "calentures" or fevers, or taking peevish sides in the garboils that rent the Council, the laboring men bestirred themselves very little. They had not even constructed durable shelters; all that clapboarding cut with such labor in the spring had gone into the stockade or into the hold of the *Sarah Constant.* The men took what ease they could under tents of sailcloth, or in rude huts, or simply under the shade of the live oaks.

By July much of the company was sickening, though how seriously was not yet apparent. A common symptom was a dreary sense of indirection. It seemed a poor thing merely to lie here and wait for a ship to come back from England. The gentlemen should have been fulfilling their mission as conquistadors, conquering and looting the local halls of Montezuma. They were restrained by company orders to avoid picking quarrels with the Indians and by growing suspicion that there were no halls to loot. Some had had a glimpse of Indian longhouses, full of curiosities indeed, but poor in treasure. Copper instead of gold, and at least some of the ropes of pearls were already known to be strings of sea shells.

The laborers, men like John Laydon, John Dods, William Garret, noteworthy because they alone of this group would survive the colony's first fifteen years and go on to better things, might have pulled themselves together to work at the fields even through agues and calentures if they could claim any part as theirs. That they could not was also a Company order. The fruits of their planting would go into the common store, from which the idle would share equally with the provident. In the meantime no one fared well. The daily ration was one can of barley "sod in water" to each five men.

There had been only one death, that of a boy slain in the Indian attack. But on August 6 John Asbie succumbed to the "bloody flux," or dysentery, and it was as if his death were a signal for which these men had been waiting. There was, after all, one way out of this pointless venture. George Flower took it the third day after, when he died "of a swelling," and the next day William Bruster, gentleman, died of a wound. On August 14 there were two deaths, and from then on there was a kind of stampede into Lethe, forty-six according to Smith's reckoning by September 10.

"Our men were destroyed with cruel diseases, as swellings, fluxes, burning fevers, and by wars," wrote Percy. "And some departed suddenly, but for the most part they died of mere famine. There were never Englishmen left in a foreign country in such a misery as we were in this new discovered Virginia. . . . If there were any conscience in man, it would make their hearts bleed to hear the pitiful murmurings and outcries of our sick men without relief, every night and day, for the space of about six weeks, some departing out of the world . . . three or four in a night; in the morning their bodies trailed out of their cabins like dogs to be buried."

Captain Gosnold did not live to say "I told you so." He sickened with the rest, and on August 22 he died, heartbroken at the fate of the colony of his dear hopes. But a member of the Council was not dragged out of his cabin to be buried like a dog. In spite of the illness of most of the Council, even Wingate and Smith, they managed to honor Gosnold like the good soldier he was; volleys of small shot were fired, and all the ordnance in the fort was mustered for a salvo.

September brought a change for the better. Apparently cold weather came early, for on the 18th one Ellis Kingston was reported to have "starved to death with cold." Chill nights deterred the mosquitoes and set winged armadas of wild fowl on the move down from the north. Clouds of them darkened the sun, and the beating of their wings was a soft thunder overhead; when they alighted on the river the starving men of Jamestown shot them and feasted.

Very wonderfully the Indians came to the rescue. There was among them an ambivalence about the Jamestown men. Now they hunted them down as enemies; now they accorded them a courteous welcome as guests, to be pitied and helped when they showed themselves inept in wilderness ways. Or else different Indian bands felt and did different things. In any case some of what Percy called "these vild and cruell pagans" now came in mercy; they brought corn bread baked by their women, maize, fish, and flesh, and the survivors of the summer sickness ate of it and revived.

The Council got on its feet, ousted the troublemaker George Kendall, deposed the unpopular Wingate, and made John Ratcliffe president. Captain Smith, bouncing back from what came to be called the "seasoning," took over the job of cape merchant or keeper of the stores, and chivied the laborers into profitable endeavor. With cold weather coming they could no longer lie under the live oaks, or even in the sailcloth tents, which were already rotting. He set them to housebuilding, to felling timber, raising frames, and thatching roofs.

Late in the fall Smith set out on what was to become his chief object in the new world, further voyages of discovery, carrying with him odds and ends to trade with the Indians for corn. He had a knack for returning at dramatic junctures. In November he was just in time to prevent two Council members from taking flight to England on the little *Discovery*. In early January he returned from his most famous and controversial expedition, the one when he made the acquaintance of the emperor Powhatan and his lively daughter Pocahontas, the day before Newport came back with the first supply. This timing was particularly fortunate, for Smith, having lost the rest of his party in an Indian attack, was under vehement suspicion, and might have been shot but for the intercession of Newport.

4

The adventurers of the London Company had received Newport with mixed feelings, especially when they examined his cargo
and found nothing more valuable than clapboarding and sassa-
frass. However, it was early to expect bullion and precious stones,
and Newport had brought promise of better things. Above the
falls of the James he had seen with his own eyes those "vains of
glist'ring spangles" (Smith's spelling, and all too appropriate as it
turned out), and Indians had pointed out to him beds of mussels
from which pearls could be extracted.

Given this encouragement, the Company gave careful attention to the personnel sent with the supply. They shipped 105 men
with the usual top-heavy proportion of gentlemen, also six tailors
and one perfumer to enable them to keep up appearances. But
they included artisans, two apothecaries, one tobacco-pipe maker,
a surgeon, a cooper, a blacksmith, and most important of all, five
men fitted by the mystery of their crafts to assess and mine Virginian resources of precious stones and metals. They sent Daniel
Stalling, jeweler, two refiners, two goldsmiths.

The jeweler apparently found little of interest in the mussel
bed; he was next heard from as in charge of a relief expedition
to fetch fish from New England. The goldsmiths cannot have been
very busy, except as their craft included the working of metals in
general. But the refiners, William Dawson and Abraham Ransack,
made history.

They were the most indefatigable workers that Jamestown had
yet seen, and their zeal infected the colony. Inspired by "golden
promises," the most listless roused themselves to join the gold
rush. They dug for ore, washed the findings in the river, toiled
to load the ship with what Smith disrespectfully dubbed "gilded
dirt."

This ship was going back with a real payload. Instead of unloading and sailing for England at once for further supplies, it
remained fourteen weeks. With exasperation Smith watched the

inroads on the provision intended for the colony; with fury he saw
the crew profiteer by exchanging what ship's stores they could
lay their hands on for whatever the colonists could offer in exchange, furs, gold rings, sight drafts on kinsmen in England.
There being no clear distinction between ship's stores and what
was allotted the settlers as provision, it became possible for men
like George Percy, who had rich relatives in England, to hoard
private stock against the next period of want.

Meanwhile the refiners practiced their mystery, admitting none
to the assaying of the ore, and others than Smith (who held out
for loading the ship with clapboarding) suspected them of practicing alchemy. "One mad fellow desired to be buried in the sands
lest they should by their art make gold of his bones." Skeptics
remarked that the colony was required to impress the mariners
by building a golden church.

The ship sailed at last with its "gilded dirt," and the supplies
were replenished in April when the *Phenix,* which had been blown
off course, came in with an honest captain, who recognized the
colony's need, stinted himself to supply it. In the meantime Newport reached England, where the rumor of his cargo raised de-
lirious hopes. But not for long. When more expert refiners set to
work on the ore, they found it was what Smith had called it; the
gilding in the dirt was not gold, but iron pyrites or fool's gold.

The Company was slow to give up on its golden promises. Captains were to be regularly charged not to return without nuggets.
But its members also tried hard to find a more dependable source
of profit in Virginia. Since mulberries grew there, they would ship
in silkworms and men skilled in their care. Not that it worked;
they were the wrong kind of mulberry. They imported vignerons
from Languedoc to train the tangle of vines and make wine. That
didn't work either; the wild vines resisted cultivation. They
ordered the setting up of ironworks, saltworks, glassworks, none
of which came to much. They ordained the building of cities,
which Virginia was not to see for a century. And partly because
of King James's emphatic prejudice on the subject, they discouraged the cultivating of the weed which some Virginians
showed more disposition to plant than corn, the noxious tobacco.

Their efforts, however unfruitful, did not derive from the uto-
pian dreams of irresponsible men. There was high intelligence in
the London Company among such men as the Richard Hakluyts,
senior and junior, who had devoted their lives to the study of
America, the merchant prince Sir Thomas Smith, its first head,
and Sir Edwin Sandys, who succeeded him. They acted on the
best knowledge available, and if they often seemed obtuse to
conditions in America, that was in the nature of things, given the
time lag in communication.

They were also men of stubborn courage, holding on to their
venture for years without return on their investment, meeting as
best they could demands for more and more. Though their purpose was patriotic in their determination to save something of
North America for the English, against the Spanish who had
settled St. Augustine in 1565 and the French who founded Quebec
the year after Jamestown, they had no help from the Crown
beyond their charter.

To found a colony wholly by private enterprise was a super-
human undertaking, though that was something they learned only
by experience. As bad news came from Jamestown, as the cargo
of "gilded dirt" became the stock joke of London comedians, many
stockholders defaulted on their later payments. Yet the Company doggedly persevered, sending out what supplies it could
manage.

They were also working without real precedent. The Spanish
had long been in America, but their achievement was misleading.
They had worked in a different climate with different peoples,
and they had not in the English sense founded colonies. One
might expect some guidance from the colony planted on Roanoke
Island by Sir Walter Raleigh in 1585, and it must have been partly
for this reason that Virginians were perennially charged with the
duty of finding out what had become of it. But no one ever succeeded; no instruction came from silent Roanoke Island.

They were bedeviled with very bad luck. The most notable
example occurred in 1609 when the Company made its most
splendid effort and sent a whole fleet of colonists and supplies.
It was almost as great a migration as the *Arbella* would lead to

New England two decades later: nine ships and six hundred passengers. Now at last Virginia was to be firmly planted. But the fleet sailed under a dark star and disaster befell it.

Seven weeks out, close to the Virginia shore, an August hurricane battered and separated the fleet, and though eight ships and four hundred passengers got to Jamestown, they had suffered an irremediable loss. Their capital ship, the *Sea Venture*, had disappeared, and with her all the leaders of the expedition, Admiral George Somers, Governor Richard Gates, Colonial Secretary William Strachey, and Captain Christopher Newport.

Thus the settlers arrived without leadership, without instructions. Smith was now president of the Jamestown colony, but his commission was due to expire in September, and without clear authority he was unable to control the newcomers. Some of his old enemies had returned on the surviving ships; among the other passengers there was an incorrigible element, for in their zeal to people Virginia the London Company had picked up the scourings of the slums, and exasperated fathers had taken the opportunity to ship out unmanageable sons to see what the new world could do for them. Smith, who had been through bad times before, might have wrung some order out of this chaos, but he suffered a grave injury and had to go home. Thus the great migration, the most heroic venture that the London Company ever undertook, ended in the starving time.

These settlers too, the unruly with the docile, underwent their seasoning and died as miserably as those in the first summer. Stores were mismanaged, fields neglected; by winter there was such want that there was cannibalism. At least Smith, not a witness to be sure, reported with ghoulish relish that one man had "powdered" his wife and eaten her. When spring came, of a colony of five hundred there were only sixty survivors.

But in all Virginian tragedies there was an element of salvation. "God would not that it be unplanted," wrote Smith of this episode. Miraculously in spring the *Sea Venture* arrived; she was two ships now, the *Deliverance* and *Patience*, fashioned out of the *Sea Venture*'s stout timbers. And these brought leadership at last, Somers and Governor Gates.

A miracle had befallen the lost ship. When the hurricane subsided she was lodged unsinkably between two reefs off islands hitherto not much remarked, the lovely Bermudas. Not a passenger had been lost, and on the islands they found an abundance of wild hogs and fruits. They had lived on their stores and such provision, had salvaged the ship's timbers and built these little ships. When the story got back to England it would provide one William Shakespeare with a fable for his last play, and the London Company with a new and more immediately profitable investment. They would plant a colony there, and it was to prosper almost as signally as poor Virginia seemed to have failed.

For the miraculous arrival did not save the colony. Sir George and Governor Gates made a stunned inspection of the rotting timbers and haggard survivors of Jamestown, and agreed that there was nothing to do with this colony but evacuate it.

In their revulsion the evacuees wanted to burn tragic little Jamestown, stockade and all, but the leaders managed to restrain them; these poor sticks were Company property and the Company might have use for them again, as indeed it did. On June 7 they loaded the settlers aboard their craft and set sail. The first child born in the colony went with them, the daughter of John Laydon and Anne Burroughs. The mother had come in 1608 as maidservant to Mistress Forest, and as the first unattached English maid to reach the colony had been besieged by suitors. She and John may have looked out wistfully as the shores of the broad James slid by; for them this land had been home. Perhaps they alone were gratified by what happened.

Here was another miracle, another of the providential rescues of Virginia. While the fugitives were still within the capes, they were met by three ships. Their newest governor had come, Lord Delaware, and he ordered them back. They took what comfort they could in the fact that his ships were "exceedingly well furnished with all necessaries fitting." If they could not go home, at least they could eat.

Even his lordship did not stay long, and his report on the colony was largely a sick report, written to explain why his administration lasted not quite a year. He had suffered a "hot and violent ague," a flux, a cramp, the gout, and finally, he was embarrassed to admit, scurvy, "which though in others a sickness of slothfulness yet was in me an effect of weakness."

So he returned, leaving George Percy as his deputy. It was a bitter disappointment to Percy, for whom "strawberry time" had long since lost its charm; he wanted only to get out. Two years later when Sir Thomas Dale took over his duties and placed the colony under martial law, he got home at last. It was a bit irregular; he had been entrusted with a pinnace to fish the Chesapeake; when he got his catch he took it to England instead of to hungry Jamestown. There was a word and a mortal penalty for this sort of thing, but not for a son of the Earl of Northumberland. Runnygate or not, Percy kept away from Virginia.

The colony staggered on from one year to the next, with small sign that it was the true beginning of England's magnificent colonial empire. Eventually, after one final disaster, the bankrupt Company had to let it revert to the Crown while it concentrated on the luckier Bermuda venture. Yet it had not failed. It had somehow kept the colony alive until it could begin to send down taproots. And the very miseries of the first years would point the way to other later colonists.

1

Virginia's first and worst years were not wholly dismal. Once a man got past his seasoning, found his land legs as it were, he could find much to interest him in the forest. There was game to hunt, though in spite of their muskets Englishmen were for a long time inept in taking deer; curiosities like flying squirrels to trap and send home; above all there were the people of the forest. White men and Indians eyed each other in these years with a peculiar blend of fascination and repulsion.

A few tribes, probably those who had had rough handling from earlier white visitors, were hostile. Others like the little settlement of Kecoughtans were cordial and generous. Most adopted a policy of wait and see.

At almost any time during the first decade the Indians could have exterminated the whites simply by leaving them alone. It was years before the latter raised enough corn to meet their needs, and though there were always supply ships on the way, they came irregularly and never brought enough, especially as the ships always carried new colonists, few of whom would be of service until they too had been seasoned. The starving times were not one but multiple. Without the Indians' willingness to barter their own by no means abundant stores, Jamestown would have followed Roanoke Island into limbo.

For nearly two decades the Indians did not recognize the white men as a threat to their own way of life, though they could not have given serious credence to the white men's story that they

were here only for a visit. Even when the settlements expanded
to Henrico and Bermuda Hundred, even when the whites un-
ceremoniously dispossessed the kind Kecoughtans to take over
the smiling shores near Point Comfort, they were such feeble folk,
given to dying like flies in the summer heat, so utterly incompetent in providing for themselves or even husbanding what supplies they had (for rats from the ships and rot were always
destroying their stores) that it was frivolous to regard them as an
enemy who might one day be formidable.

At the same time they were fascinating. The ships in the river
were a great wonder to people who had only dugout canoes.
Naked trees grew from the decks, and when the white men spread
cloths on their branches they could work a magic whereby the
invisible wind would carry them where they wanted to go. Their
firearms were another marvel. One Indian visitor to Jamestown
engaged in rivalry at target practice with a white man, and when
his bow proved inferior to the musket was so wroth that he bit his
arrow. He and his like became covetous of both muskets and
ordnance; and though the white men preferred to barter blue
beads or bits of copper, there was often someone willing to boot-
leg musket and shot. In time many Indians got the wherewith to
become skilled marksmen.

Then there was the white man's livestock. At first little of it
aside from the rats survived very long, for in famine the settlers
would eat up what little they had. But the hogs presently multiplied, and the Indians found pork as palatable as venison. The
white men took issue with their cultivating such tastes, but as
the Indians pointed out, the colonists had been allowed to hunt
their deer, and the hogs were only a fair return.

One importation the Indians did not like at all: the dogs, noisy,
rushing at strangers with bared fangs and snapping at children.
However, as the acquaintance of Powhatan with John Smith
progressed, the old emperor did accept as a gift one small white
dog.

The settlers meanwhile were fascinated by the Indians. Their
letters home, their "true relations" and such, were full of anec-
dote and observation; indeed, a far clearer picture of Indian life

comes out of the records than of life in Jamestown itself. The writers made scant reference to the bits of armor, the laces and perfumed ruffles affected by the gentlemen, or the jerkins and hose worn quickly ragged by the laborers. Any fool knew what Englishmen looked like; the novelty lay in the way the Indians shaved half their heads, painted their bodies, and even in old age held themselves proud and straight. The prevailing mood was not admiration; they were recording curiosities, not attempting anthropological research. They used epithets like "vile and cruel," dismissed Indian religious practice by reporting them "at their idolatries."

That at least was the official attitude. Unofficially there were exceptions. Some settlers, both the English and some of the European artisans imported with them, yielded to the urge to go native. There was to develop one Indian-English romance without which the early annals of Virginia would have been dreary indeed.

2

One of the original Jamestown settlers, given hospitality when he lost his way in the woods, was the first to get an intimate view of Indian life. He was William White, a laborer and without the prejudices of a gentleman's education; he made sympathetic report of what he saw. What impressed him was that the Indians washed. "In the morning before break of day, before they eat or drink, both men and women and children that are above ten years of age, runs into the water, there washes themselves a good while till the sun riseth, and offer sacrifice to it, strewing tobacco on the water or land, honoring the sun as their god. Likewise they do at the setting of the sun."

When Newport returned with the first supply, he made formal presentation to Powhatan of an English "son," the thirteen-year-old Thomas Savage. The intention was to apprentice the boy, as it were, to Powhatan to learn the language so that he could serve as interpreter. The child was a quick study; within months Powhatan was entrusting him with a message to Jamestown. By the time

Savage was sixteen he had acted many times as go-between for
the English and the Indians, and had received from the former
the rank of ensign.

Another lad, well-connected, being the son and namesake of
Sir Henry Spelman, the antiquarian, also lived with Powhatan
until Pocahontas in a time of trouble sent him to the Potomacs.
He too became a notable interpreter, though there was in time
suspicion among the English that he had learned Indian ways all
too well, had "in him more of the savage than the Christian."
In 1619 one piece of business at the first sitting of the House of
Burgesses would be to accuse him of relaying to his Indian friends
information discreditable to the English.

If Savage was a good boy, serving his own people rather than
the Indians, if Spelman was of divided allegiance, there was no
doubt at all of four of the Dutch and one of the Swiss brought
in with Captain Newport's second supply in 1608. These went
wholeheartedly native.

Eight so-called Dutchmen, apparently all skilled artisans, had
come under such circumstances as disinclined them to dedicate
themselves to building the British empire. They spoke little English, aside from terms picked up from the crew, one recurrent
phrase being "those damned Dutchmen." Conditions at Jamestown did not impress them with English power and glory. When
late in 1608 four were sent on a good-will mission to Powhatan
(they were to build him a proper English-style house), they
stayed.

They may or may not have built Powhatan his house. Indian
chiefs were then and thereafter fascinated by possessing a door
that could open and shut, and would spend whole days playing
with it. Aside from this mechanical toy, Powhatan was in no need
of a house. His longhouses were better made than any in ram-
shackle Jamestown. "Finding his plenty and knowing our want,"
the Dutchmen contentedly settled down. It was good to be among
people who lived in modest comfort and who washed; the Indian
language was no stranger than English, and if, as was probable,
they took Indian maidens as bedfellows, they learned it fast. They
became Powhatan's willing subjects, instructed him in what they

knew of English plans, and conspired with him to get what tools and arms he wanted from Jamestown.

The supplies were arranged through their compatriots, and they used as depot a glassworks conducted by some Poles a mile out of the settlement. They worked with such address that though the implements were promptly missed, no one suspected the cause until Smith investigated. He caught one of the fugitive Dutch, "a stout fellow" named Francis, who had been sent "disguised savage like" to the rendezvous. Under duress Francis gave Smith to understand that he and his friends had been detained by force, that he alone had escaped "with the hazard of his life," and at the time of his capture "only walked in the woods to gather walnuts."

Francis and a king of the Paspahegh taken with him were put in irons, the latter as hostage for the return of the Dutchmen. Powhatan protested to Smith that they were staying of their own will, and to "bring them fifty miles on their backs" was more than his people could do. The hostage king escaped, irons and all, and the three remaining Dutchmen continued to enjoy Powhatan's hospitality.

Later a Swiss, William Volda, was sent to reclaim the Dutchmen and an English fugitive named William Bentley. But Smith's strong point was not judgment of character. He had once had entire faith in the leader of what he now called "the damned Dutchmen." In relying upon Volda, "this wicked hypocrite," who had professed disdain for "the lewd condition of his cursed countrymen," he was equally deceived. Volda also stayed with the king, and not only conspired to enrich Powhatan with arms and tools but induced other Jamestown malcontents to desert.

What alarmed Smith about such defections was his suspicion that the Spanish had a hand in them. There was always fear in Jamestown of the Spaniards, whose ships could be dispatched from St. Augustine far more swiftly than help could come from London; and indeed in 1611 a Spanish caravel did visit Point Comfort and succeeded briefly in planting a spy in the colony. But that was after Smith's time. The present fugitives might prefer Indian company to English, but they were innocent of Spanish connections. While Smith "wrastled" with the situation he was badly hurt in a gunpowder explosion and had to leave Virginia, never to see it again.

Presumably the Dutchmen, the Swiss, and perhaps William Bentley lived happily ever after, and if later explorers ran across fair-haired Indian children, there need be no talk of "miracles."

But if Europeans went native among the Indians, there was one Indian who went the other way. There was Pocahontas, "the unbelieving creature," favorite daughter of Powhatan, a wood sprite, who like Undine of legend got herself a soul by marrying a mortal.

3

Smith had his first and most famous encounter with Powhatan, "the great king," in December 1607. Since early fall the captain, who was cleverer than anyone else at this sort of thing, had been entrusted with foraging and trading with the Indians for provision. He had begun with the Kecoughtans, who by this time had lost their awe of the beggarly settlers and at first scornfully gave him scraps. Smith was, however, a persuasive visitor; the natural kindliness of the little tribe reasserted itself, and Smith went home with nearly thirty bushels of corn.

The expedition sufficed neither the colony's need nor Smith's restless itch for action. He was allowed to take the pinnace with a crew of five sailors and two landmen up the James on a voyage of discovery and trade. His first voyage, early in November, was a success. But when in December he took the pinnace upstream again, his passion for discovery brought on disaster. Coming to a branch of the James which his craft could not enter, he hired an Indian canoe and two Indian guides and penetrated the interior with his landmen, John Robinson, gent, and Thomas Emory. In White Oaks Swamp the party separated and never met again. Robinson and Emory were surprised and killed, and Smith was captured.

He was treated kindly enough. Smith was a personage, like Don Quixote an end-product of medieval chivalric combat, an institution that stirred fellow feeling among the forest folk. He was received with due courtesy by one forest king after another, passed from hand to hand until at last he stood before their emperor, the aging Powhatan.

The terms *king* and *emperor*, as used by Smith, were of course relative, a matter of semantics. The forest kings were only local chiefs, their status closer to that of the judges in ancient Israel than that of James of England. Powhatan's position more resembled that of a feudal overlord than anything in imperial Rome. However, his influence was not confined to Virginia, as known to John Smith; his father had probably been forced out of more southern territory by the intrusions of the St. Augustine Spaniards, and Powhatan still had influence in Carolina. Had Smith thought to question him about the fate of the Roanoke Colony, Powhatan could probably have told him.

That Smith used such resounding terms as *king* and *emperor* when he came to write his memoirs was due to his English pride. The Spanish had conquered authentic emperors, Montezuma for one, and the English could not be content with less. Smith's semantics would be of importance when one of Powhatan's daughters visited England; the child of a man designated as emperor would command a very different reception from the child of one designated only as chief.

This emperor's "werewocamo," or capital, stood across the peninsula from Jamestown, on the north bank of the York, about fourteen miles from present West Point. Powhatan received the captive "with such a grave and majestical countenance as drove me into admiration to see such state in a naked savage." "Naked" was a relative term. Powhatan, reclining on a great bedstead piled with mats, lay under a coverlet fashioned of racoon skins and wore about his neck "many chains of great pearls." Two of his principal wives sat at the head and foot of his bed respectively; several young women, perhaps other wives, perhaps his daughters, including little Pocahontas, sat at a distance, and on either side of the fire were ranged ten of his chiefs.

So young Smith, bearded, blue-eyed, and probably wearing light armor, since in the recent combat most arrows had glanced off him harmlessly, came before the old forest king, and to a small girl watching with wide dark eyes from the background, he looked exotic.

At first the reception was kind. Smith was feasted—"fattened" was his word for it—given a chance to explain himself and to get acquainted with the court, including eager little Pocahontas and her brother Nantaquas. It was only after some time that the amenities abruptly ended in a sentence of death.

Such a conclusion to so much cordiality was a barbarous shock to Smith; however, it represented no caprice on the part of his majesty. Smith was, after all, technically guilty of murder; he had resisted arrest, and his pistol had killed one of the men sent to take him. The concept of an eye for an eye prevailed here as in ancient Judea. The delay in pronouncing sentence had probably been caused by Powhatan's sense of justice; he must have sent emissaries to the villages to ascertain the facts. Smith had, without knowing it, faced trial; now he faced death.

He had faced it before and he was no man to be easily disposed of. Three Turks had so learned long ago in Transylvania, when one by one they had challenged him to knightly combat, and Smith had come out of it with their several heads as trophy. The Prince of Transylvania, a spectator, had been so impressed that he had conferred on Smith, who being lowborn had not had one before, a coat of arms featuring the three heads on a shield.

He might have given as good account of himself with Indian heads, but his sword and pistol had been taken. It was an occasion for merciful providence to intervene, and providence did so in the person of the ten-year-old girl who had been hovering in the background. When Smith was put on the ground and his head placed on a rock, she flung herself upon him, put her own sleek head beside his, and claimed him for her own.

The gesture was impulsive, but not at all eccentric. As the daughter of a king, Pocahontas was acting within convention in claiming the captive. It may be that like Brünnehilde with Wotan she was responding to her father's secret wish. Powhatan himself was fascinated by the young man, and must have deplored the legal technicality that required him to die. His daughter's action relieved him of the necessity. Smith was released, the conversation resumed, and for the time Smith and Powhatan were friends.

In his progress among the lesser forest kings to Powhatan's court, Smith had already, to hear him tell it, delivered a series of lectures on astronomy, the use of the compass, and English history. Considering that at best he was speaking only a kind of pidgin Indian, and that the Indians this far inland knew no English at all, his fluent communication of such details was more remarkable than his rescue by Pocahontas. Dignity may have required everyone concerned to deliver the rolling periods recorded by Smith in some of his various accounts, but real communication was dependent upon ingenuity of gesture.

It was Powhatan's first opportunity to question an Englishman directly about what was uppermost in his mind. What, he asked, were the English doing in his country? In reply Smith improvised on the official version that the English were here only on a visit, and adapted it to cover the situation in which he had been caught. The expedition had been forced into the Chesapeake by bad weather and a fight with the Spanish, and had come up the James in search of fresh water. There most of the company had stayed in order to mend a leak in the pinnace; soon Captain Newport would return to fetch them home.

Why, Powhatan then inquired, did some members of the company go so far? Why Newport's trip to the falls, and why Smith's voyage inland, a kind of trespassing, since it was far from the place where the English had permission to squat? Smith had two answers. One spoke of the death of an English boy in the attack on Jamestown, which must be avenged, and the other was the English desire to find the "back sea on the other side of the main where there was salt water."

Powhatan rested on his mats under his warm covering of fur, and eying Smith, reflected for a long time. How far was this young man to be trusted? He was daring, he was intelligent, achieving glibness without language, but was the truth in him? Smith's project of getting to the "back sea" seemed harmless, especially as Powhatan had enemies in those parts, including a "fierce nation that did eat men." So he described the salt seas that lay back of the falls at a distance variously estimated as a journey of five to eight days.

It was wonderful news for Smith. The loss of his two landmen was nothing, all the misery of Jamestown was naught if this were true, if he were so close to the "South Sea." Both he and Powhatan were, however, victims of semantic confusion. In describing the journey from the falls to a place where the rivers were brackish, Powhatan probably referred to a roundabout way of getting to the head of the Chesapeake. Neither could have grasped what the other was talking about.

Smith in his turn gave another of his lecture courses. He described the countries of Europe, the might of the English king, "the innumerable multitude of his ships," and the "noise of trumpets." What Powhatan followed of this inspired him with visible respect and, or so Smith thought, with not a little fear.

Powhatan kept his guest for several weeks, entertaining him royally, and when in early January he sent him on his way, he provided four men to guide him and carry his own personal effects and the provision sent with him. He had sufficiently made up his mind about Smith's integrity to extend to him a warm invitation to settle on his river at a place still called Cappahowasick, where provisions would be exchanged for hatchets and copper and "none should disturb him."

Smith returned in triumph only to find himself in disgrace when he got to Jamestown. He had come in that condition in the first place, under arrest "for mutiny." Members of the Council were congenitally suspicious of each other; George Kendall had recently been shot on the charge of conspiracy. Now they prepared to do the same with Smith, whose expedition away from the James had been unauthorized, had cost two lives, and whose entertainment at the courts of so many forest kings gave him the appearance of a renegade.

He was not shot. Newport came in the nick of time, carrying among other supplies a crown (copper, since the Indians preferred it to gold) wherewith to seal Anglo-Indian amity by crowning Powhatan. Smith's services were needed to guide Newport and a suitable cortege, and even if they had not been, it would be strange to bring the emperor tidings that the Englishmen had executed the man he had honored.

So Smith, with rather ill grace seeing that his life had been spared for this purpose, attended the coronation, a rite that rejoiced neither him nor Powhatan. Smith was irritated because he thought that the gesture, like the gold rush, was a waste of time; Newport should be sailing back for more supplies instead of ranging the forest to confer incomprehensible honors on a savage king. Powhatan was baffled, disappointed, and finally outraged. He valued copper indeed, but this trinket they wanted him to wear seemed a singularly pointless use to put it to. He made plain his disappointment that Newport had not instead brought him firearms and ordnance. Newport did give him some muskets, but protested the difficulty of hauling cannon through the woods.

Finally, Powhatan, ignorant of the Christian ritual of coronation, wasn't having it. He would not kneel to have the crown placed on his head. The English, intent on their own notions of royal propriety, finally compromised by giving Powhatan a shove on the shoulders that made him bend forward a bit, and then thrust the crown in place. It was this indignity that outraged the old man. He was wise, he was forbearing, yet even Pocahontas might not have been able to save the English from his anger, but for his wary respect for their firearms.

Powhatan and Smith were to meet again, but their friendship was already undergoing corrosion. When Newport, far from removing the Jamestown settlers, more than doubled their number, Powhatan knew Smith for a liar, or what was nearly as damning, as a youth not received into the councils of the elders of his tribe. Nor did Smith ever accept the invitation to move into Powhatan's neighborhood. The emperor had to content himself with the boy Thomas Savage, and presently with the four Dutchmen, the Swiss, and the occasional English fugitives who sought the more abundant life at his court.

Smith went his own way, never treacherous according to his own lights, never bloodthirsty in his dealings with the Indians, but subscribing to a no-nonsense policy that sometimes impelled his compatriots at Jamestown to call him cruel. He never killed an Indian except in fair contest, but he sometimes did what was worse, subjected them to a chivying that destroyed their dignity. What might have happened had Smith been a different sort of man, a Roger Williams for instance? Might not Powhatan in a situation of mutual trust have been trustworthy? Might John Smith, the first Englishman to open diplomatic relations between the English and Indians, have instituted a policy which could have changed not only the history of the colony but of the United States? But Smith was what he was, admirable in courage and resourcefulness, an eager observer, but not imbued with respect for ways of life which he, though no model of piety, dismissed as "pagan." And even if he had had some of Williams' vision, what could he have done about it? A man who returns from establishing a genuine *entente cordiale* with the local sovereign only to be threatened with execution for his pains is in no position to enforce a policy incomprehensible to his fellows. He would have been damned with the Dutchmen.

The real intermediary between the two worlds was not Smith but the little girl who had saved him. Pocahontas had not given her faith lightly; she was faithful unto death. Like a forest goddess, like a little Pallas Athene taking favored mortals under her shield, to the best of her ability the girl watched over the colony.

4

She was eager to visit her protectorate, and her favor with Smith gave her the freedom of the little city. She climbed into the rigging of whatever ship was moored to the landing tree, explored the fort, and once organized a tumbling act. Finding lads of her own age in the stockade, she led them out to what was called the market place, set them to turning cartwheels, and then joyously matched them. She was dressed for this exercise in nothing but her tawny skin.

Older men looking on remembered that her name meant Little Wanton. However, the phrase as used by Elizabethans connoted mischief rather than depravity. By now they knew Indian customs well enough to know that the girl's nakedness was testimony to her innocence. When girls had seen the "return of the leaf" twelve times, they had to dress, at least to the extent of wearing a "kind of semicinctum leathern apron . . . before their bellies and were very shamefaced to be seen bare." Pocahontas was just under that age when Smith met her; soon she would wear her apron and take on the dignity of her real name, which was either Amonate or Matoaka. To the English she would always be Pocahontas, Little Wanton. Even when years later she received a Christian name, they remembered to call her by it only to her face.

A few months after Smith's visit Powhatan sent his daughter to Jamestown on an embassy. She was accompanied by his official messenger, the misshapen but redoubtable Rawhunt, and several men to carry gifts of venison and bread. To Rawhunt was entrusted the mission of asking the return of the boy Thomas Savage, "which he loved dearly"; to Pocahontas the more delicate diplomacy of negotiating the release of three men imprisoned at the fort.

The occasion was too ceremonious for cartwheels. Instructed by her father, the girl waited in self-effacing quiet for three days, paying no attention to the prisoners, before she ventured to "entreat their liberty." The Englishmen could not refuse the child. The prisoners were brought to prayer at the little church, then "we gave them their bows and arrows . . . and sent them packing." Pocahontas had gifts, "such trifles as contented her."

Smith treated her with playful affection. In his notes he called her the "nonpareil" of Virginia; in the little phrase book he was compiling he had one for her beginning, "Kekaton, Pocahontas . . ." which being translated in full means "Bid Pocahontas bring hither two little baskets, and I will give her beads to make a chain."

His fellows gossiped about the relationship, saying that Smith would marry the girl and so make himself king. Perhaps it was what Powhatan expected of him, as the conventional response to what Pocahontas had done for him. But Smith was not of the marrying kind, and as he ungallantly remarked, marriage with a king's daughter would not put him in line for the royal succession. That he did not suggest marriage, even when the girl put on the apron signifying her nubile state, may have been one factor in the chilling of Powhatan's feeling for him.

But nothing chilled the loyal Pocahontas. When she could she visited the colony "with her wild train" to bring provision, and early in 1609 when the "Dutchmen" were stirring up the old king against Smith, "the dark night could not affright her from coming through the irksome woods, and with watered eyes gave me her best advice to escape his fury." At the risk of her life she was warning Smith of an ambush.

In the fall of that year Smith was dangerously hurt and sent to England to recover. Pocahontas was told, perhaps by her father, that he was dead, and was supposed to have been married to one Kocoum. But Kocoum, whatever his merits, was to play little part in the life of Pocahontas. Though she could not come to Jamestown as freely as before, she did not lose her interest. In April 1613 she was induced by one Jazapaws to come to a feast on an English ship, where she was seized and made prisoner. She was sold to the English for a copper kettle; Captain Samuel Argall had arranged the betrayal in order to have a hostage for his dealings with Powhatan. The old emperor, though grieved for his daughter, refused the English terms for her surrender. The freeborn Indian girl endured life in the colony for more than a year, or until she met an Englishman of the marrying kind and was released under a new name, the Lady Rebecca, or Mrs. John Rolfe.

5

Rolfe, a man of twenty-five, had been doubly bereft before he met the lonely Indian girl. He had set out for Virginia in the great migration of 1609 with a young bride already advanced in pregnancy. They were on the famous *Sea Venture*, which went aground in Bermuda, and their child was born on and named for the enchanted island. By the time the *Deliverance* and *Patience* had been constructed from the salvage the child had died, and the mother, reaching Virginia in 1610, did not survive her seasoning. Rolfe was alone, as most Englishmen were in Virginia.

Once he shook off his agues he found comfort in hard work. Almost Puritanic in his religious bent, while he steadied his soul to accept the providence that he must begin life in the new world a childless widower, he experimented with the cultivation of tobacco. He had already made progress in curing it for export, so laying the first foundation of Virginia's economy, when he found a young woman as lonely as he, the betrayed, unransomed Pocahontas.

She was still a girl just past her mid-teens, shapely in spite of the tedious inactivity forced upon her, lovely in spite of her inability to perform the rites of purification at daybreak and sundown. Once he had seen her, it was all up with John Rolfe; "such passions and sufferings which I have daily, hourly, yea and in my sleep endured, even awaking me to astonishment," he wrote. He searched his heart. Was what he felt mere "carnal affection," an urge to satisfy an "unsavory palette"? In prayer and holy meditation he found assurance that he was guiltless of "unbridled desire . . . so far as man's weakness may permit," that what he felt was a divine call to save her soul.

The girl was responsive, "adding hereunto her appearance of love to me, her desire to be taught and instructed in the knowledge of God." Was it God's will that they marry? Rolfe studied scriptural references to "the heavy displeasure which almighty God conceived against the sons of Levi and Israel for marrying strange wives." But if she became a Christian, she would be no strange wife. When Rolfe confided in "honest and religious persons," they agreed with this conclusion. So Pocahontas was baptized and received into holy church, and pagan Little Wanton became the Christian Lady Rebecca. She was already Mistress Rolfe when her husband wrote a long, touching letter to his governor, Sir Thomas Dale. He did not therein ask permission; humbly, reverently, he announced a *fait accompli*.

Sir Thomas was a martinet, engaged in imposing a harsh mili-

tary code on a colony grown unmanageably disorderly since the
importation of so many recreants, ordaining any number of capital crimes, one of them a third unexcused absence from church.

Had such a man been infected by notions of racial purity,
Rolfe would have received short shrift, but as it happened, Sir
Thomas had been moving in the same direction. Report had it
that he had considered an alliance by intermarriage with local
royalty, and disregarding his own wife and child in England was
asking Powhatan for the hand of a young daughter. His suit
was unsuccessful. Powhatan had given his consent to Pocahontas'
marriage, but he was not parting with any more of his daughters.
He put off Dale with the excuse that he had just sold the girl to
one of his braves. But Dale was in no position to rebuke Rolfe
except on grounds that must have startled the latter. He denounced Rolfe as a commoner presuming to marry above him.

It was a charge that the honest tobacco man was to hear later
when he took his wife and their son Thomas on an extended visit
to England.

6

Captain Smith, back in England after one "discovery" of the
New England coast, and about to embark on another, was enchanted to hear of Pocahontas' visit. She was royalty, and must
be royally received. To ensure this end he addressed a letter "To
the most high and virtuous Princess, Queen Anne of Great
Britain."

"Most admired Queen," he began, and went on to describe the
debt of gratitude that the colony owed "to this tender Virgin." It
was in this letter that he for the first time described the girl's
part in saving him from having his brains beaten out. Since then
she had rejected her "barbarous condition, was married to an
English gentleman . . . the first Christian ever of that nation,
and the first Virginian ever spake English, or had a child in marriage by an Englishman."

He "who never begged anything of the state" now begged

royal favor for the royal girl, asking that she be ceremoniously received, "her husband's estate not being able to make her fit to attend your majesty. . . . Seeing this kingdom may rightly have a kingdom by her means," a gesture suitable to her rank was not only an expression of gratitude but a stroke of diplomacy.

On this note the captain humbly kissed her majesty's gracious hand, dispatched his letter, and hurried off to Branford, where the Rolfes were staying. He had brought some friends with him, and was immediately sorry.

Until she reached England, Pocahontas had believed that the man was dead. She took one look at the beloved face of her childhood hero, made a wordless gesture of greeting, and turned away, covering her face with her hands. Not even her husband could induce her to speak, and the disconcerted Smith, wishing he had not vaunted her knowledge of English, had no choice but to withdraw.

When he returned a few hours later, the girl had mastered her emotions, laboriously arranged her thoughts into English, and was ready to speak not in the rolling periods which Smith usually ascribed to anyone, savage or Christian, who spoke at all, but in something like emotional incoherence.

"You did promise Powhatan what was yours should be his," she said, her mind going back to distant days in a distant court, "and he the like to you. You called him father, being in his land a stranger, and by that same reason, so must I do you."

Smith hastily demurred. "I durst not allow of that title, because she was a king's daughter." But Pocahontas, "with a well set countenance," was going on.

"Were you not afraid to come into my father's country, and caused fear in him and all his people (but me), and fear you here I should call you father? I tell you then I will, and you shall call me child, and so I will be forever and ever your countryman. They did tell us always you were dead, and I knew no other till I came to Plymouth. Yet Powhatan did command Uttamatomakkin to seek you and know the truth, because your countrymen will lie much."

Uttamatomakkin was a member of Powhatan's council, whom

the king had sent to England "to number the people here and inform him well what we were and our state." On landing at Plymouth the ambassador had begun his census by making notches on a long stick, "but he was quickly wearied of that task." In London he ran across Smith and directed him to show him "our God, the King, Queen and the Prince I so much had told him of." It had been beyond Smith's power to show him God, and apparently he undertook no presentation to the king, whom he presently convinced the guest he had already seen in a royal progress. The emissary was discontent. "You gave Powhatan a white dog which Powhatan fed as himself," he protested. "But your King gave me nothing, and I am better than your white dog."

It was important that Pocahontas not return to Virginia with a similar report, and thanks to Smith's intercession with the queen she did not. Means were provided to make the girl presentable. She was laced into bodice and stomacher to have her portrait engraved and be presented at court. And there she charmed everyone, courtiers, the Lord and Lady Delaware, their majesties.

Gaucheries might be expected of a young woman who had so recently entertained Jamestown by running naked into the market place to turn cartwheels, but none were recorded. Before a queen Pocahontas bore herself queenly. Again the only demur made to her marriage was that Rolfe had presumed. He was made to wait in anterooms while his wife footed the minuet with noblemen or sat in state to watch a masque by Ben Jonson.

But this brief glory was costly. The English climate also required seasoning of breeds not born to it. The fogs and stale airs of London made Pocahontas cough. By the summer of 1617 when the Rolfes embarked for Virginia, she was spitting blood. She died in Gravesend without seeing Virginia again, and her little son, left behind for an English rearing, also did not see his mother's country again until he was a man grown.

Again bereft, Rolfe returned to his tobacco planting, and was married for the third time, this time to Jane, daughter of Captain William Pierce. A pity he hadn't sat with Pocahontas for his portrait. A man who could so promptly find a wife in a land still nearly womanless (so far as the English were concerned) had something in carriage or countenance that would have been worthy of a Van Dyke. Or perhaps his beauty was only that honesty of soul which had won Pocahontas.

1

O N a bitter evening in early December 1620 a young woman stood alone by the bulwarks of the *Mayflower*, staring at the sands faintly glimmering in the wintry twilight. They had been there for her to stare at for twenty-four days.

It had been a merciful providence when they had rounded Cape Cod after more than two months at sea. The slender spit of silver-gilt sands had looked like home; and to Dorothy Bradford, whose father Henry May had belonged to the Ancient Brethren, first of the dissenters to emigrate from England, Holland was home.

There had been brief happiness. A quiet Sabbath aboard giving praise to God, and then a Monday of glorious labor ashore. The boats had been lowered and the women got into them, each carrying a great bale of bedding and small clothes to wash that which indeed was overdue for washing. Some women sang as they beat and scrubbed their clothes, and all the children clamored as they swarmed across the silver beach, or waded with the menfolk into the shallows to dig up shellfish.

There was a store of children on the ship, thirty if you counted the babes in arms: Oceanus Hopkins, born on the high seas, and Peregrine White, who would be born while the ship lay at anchor in the harbor. (But Peregrine still rode in his mother's womb that washday.) Many bore good English names like John and Elizabeth; others bore names that would have interested the late Mrs. Rolfe of Virginia, in that they expressed the hope and faith

of their parents. There were the little Brewster boys, Love and
Wrastle, whose sisters, Fear and Patience, had been left behind
in Leyden. The Allertons had a six-year-old girl Remember, and
the Whites a five-year-old son Resolved. (But no one, even in
jest, had named a child Little Wanton.)

It had been a happy day, but this was not friendly Holland,
and the land repulsed them.

There were beasts and beast-like men in the dark woods beyond the crescents of sand. Men put on their armor and carried
their muskets to guard the women while they scrubbed. Even
the first fruits of the land cursed them. The diggers in the flats
brought aboard soft-shelled clams and quahogs and mussels, and
all the company, starving for fresh food after weeks of hardtack
and dried fish, had fallen to and feasted. And then most were
like to die; even in the worst of the gales there had been no such
retching and recourse to the necessary tubs. Rightly or wrongly,
the victims blamed the succulent mussels for their affliction.

The illness was not, however, fatal. The company pulled itself
together, and the men looked for a place to land and plant. There
were two requirements: a safe harbor and a dependable supply
of sweet water. The tip of the Cape offered the one but not the
other. Corn Hill, which promised well at first, had nothing better
than dew ponds which might dry up in a drought. The men of
this company were acquainted with the mistakes at Jamestown;
they not only knew John Smith's writings on Virginia, but his
accounts of later explorations in what he himself had named New
England. They could indeed have had Smith's services as guide,
but his price had been too high for poor folk, who after scrab-
bling for a living in Holland had set out so meagerly provided
that in Southampton they had had to sell much of their store of
good Holland butter to find the cost of clearing port. They followed Smith's advice, but the man they left behind.

And now for nearly four weeks the women had been staring
blankly at the Cape while menfolk engaged in "discoveries." In
this time houses could be framed and roofs thatched, and Susanna
White could have borne her child by her own hearth. But it had
been as with the birth of little Oceanus; the children, including

frightened Resolved, were packed off to other parts of the ship, and Susanna wrestled for the new life on her hard bed in quarters so cramped that there was hardly space to attend her.

Snow was on the ground when sixteen volunteers, among them Dorothy's husband William, set out on the second discovery. This time they made first contact with the savages, half a dozen of them who ran when they saw the white men, and an Indian burying ground and storage mound. The discoverers had brought corn back to the ships, where it brought cheer, but Dorothy was frightened. Now William was off on the third discovery, north to a place with the evil name of Thievish Harbor. There were sure to be savages there, resentful that the Englishmen had made off with their corn. Just the day before her husband had left with the party against her protest that he was not yet recovered from the chill he had taken at Corn Hill. Would she ever see him again?

She would not, but that was not William's doing. He was chilled indeed, and there were Indians near Thievish Harbor, which Smith had put on the charts as Plymouth; the Indians fired arrows, and from the thickets some men distinctly heard the roaring of lions. All this Dorothy could not know, but she could imagine it and worse as she stood by the bulwarks, too far gone in misery to know that she herself was chilled to the bone.

They had come this long way to this cruel land in order to worship God according to the faith of their own hearts, but had it been God's will that they do so? They had had freedom of worship in Holland. No one disturbed them. They had lived modestly, working at humble trades, but surely better than they could hope to live here. What was this talk that their children would grow up speaking Dutch rather than English? Could not God, who had spoken to His chosen people in neither tongue, but rather in Hebrew (which William hoped one day to learn), reveal His will as readily in Dutch? Might it not have been mere stiffnecked stubbornness that had sent them on this cold mission?

How many signs had God sent to warn them. Often after coming from Leyden the company had nerved itself to go, only to suffer yet another delay. There were obscure difficulties about a patent of sorts from the London Company of Virginia. There was the fund-raising, the dickering with Thomas Weston and Company, who finally agreed to finance the expedition on terms so exorbitant that the American settlement looked in prospect like a debtors' prison. These were poor folk, not a "gent" in the English sense among them, with no earls and lords to plead their cause and speed them on their way.

The *Mayflower*, a "sweet ship" which had carried wines in the Mediterranean, 180 tons, and so larger than any ship in Captain Newport's little convoy, had not set out alone. She had as consort the forty-ton *Speedwell*, designed to remain in America a year to serve in fishing. But whenever they were well at sea, the *Speedwell* began to leak. Twice they had turned back, the second time when they were three hundred miles out on the Atlantic, only to find in port that the *Speedwell* was apparently sound. Was not this a sign from God that their voyage was unblessed?

Many had taken it so. When in September, far too late in the season to hope for smooth sailing, the *Mayflower* had gone it alone, the necessity of splitting the company had offered no problem. Many accepted that it was God's will that they remain behind.

September was well along before the *Mayflower* sailed from Plymouth. It was late for a crossing; even the hardy fisherfolk who knew the wild coasts better than Smith himself were heading into home ports now. Yet for a time it was an easy passage, as if the animus of God had been directed at the *Speedwell* alone. The *Mayflower*, the tall ship—how Dorothy at Southampton had marveled at the towering height of the poopdeck, which she confounded with the beak, so that ever after she was never sure which way was forward—took the swells lightly, riding like a gay butterfly across the blue ocean.

But then God's wrath was manifest in gales so powerful that they split a beam and washed John Howland overboard when he went above for air from the long galley between decks where five-score passengers huddled and suffered. The people were stiff-necked yet. They found a heavy screw with which to mend the broken beam, and below the water line Howland clung to ropes

until he could be hauled up with a boat hook, and though he
was like to die, the fierce will to live that had given him his
clutch on the rope brought him through.

Now here was land, but it was lonely, forbidding land, and
they had no patent to plant where they were. Their destination
had been a subject of long controversy. Some had held out for
New Guinea, where living was easy and fruit could be plucked
from the trees. Others objected that their "English bodies" were
unfit for the tropics, and besides the Spanish, insecurely as they
held that coast, would be certain to oppose them.

There was thought of Virginia, but nothing they had heard
of Jamestown suggested a welcome for a praying company that
dissented from the Establishment. There had been a possibility
of their pioneering on the river that Henry Hudson had discovered for the Dutch. But the settlement would belong to Holland,
and "our fathers were Englishmen," said William, husband of
Dorothy. True, but how strange this loyalty to a land that had
mocked and imprisoned them and cast them out. They had come
at last with a patent for unsettled lands in northern Virginia,
and had not reached them. The discoverers were seeking a place
to plant on a shore where they had no explicit rights. Small wonder that God did not prosper them.

Meanwhile the ship swung at anchor in Provincetown Harbor,
and the crew was muttering about dumping the passengers ashore
and leaving them to shift for themselves. It was a profane crew,
given to mockery of devotions and to lewd eying of young girls
like Priscilla Mullins. For such reason even more than danger at
sea the women and children had kept to themselves in the narrow
quarters. Captain Christopher Jones was a good man; he respected
their religion and kept what order he could. But some of his
officers were no better than the men, and if officers and crew
banded together could even the captain save them?

It was a time to pray, and alone on the cold deck Dorothy tried
to lift her heart. But prayer was led by the menfolk; St. Paul
himself had commanded it. Her husband daily searched out
Scripture and in her hour of need could read the passages that
brought healing to the heart. Alone, Dorothy could bring to mind

only one bleak text: "Sing you barren that you did not bear."

The words came as if shouted into her ear and turned her mind to what was not to be thought of if life was to be endured, the cries of her child John when she had said good-by at Delft Haven. Let him be left, William had said, while his parents went on to prepare a place for him. Yet so many children had come, younger and tenderer than five-year-old John. Most had endured the voyage more stoutly than their mothers, adjusting themselves to life between decks as if it were another of the crowded tenements at Green Gate, differing only in that it had a sportive floor that rocked and rose to meet them.

A mother without her child was no woman at all. At an unimaginable distance beyond the waste of waters, Dorothy's child called and she could not hear; he wept and she could not comfort him.

Despair like this was a sin. She would go below where there were other children whose cries could be heard, whose griefs could be consoled. She would take little Oceanus in her arms or the newborn Peregrine. But first Dorothy bent over the bulwarks and looked this time not at the pale sands but at the shifting waters lapping the painted flanks of the ship. So she had looked on the rare occasions in mid-ocean when her husband had escorted her to deck. There had been something hypnotic about the sight; even on the Atlantic she had felt something drawing her to the water, and her husband, seeing her bemused, had pulled her away. Now the pull was very powerful and her husband was afield; when with a sudden movement she stumbled, there was no hand to steady her.

Four days later on a Monday morning the discoverers returned triumphant. They had found a place for their planting. Thievish Harbor, now Plymouth, would accommodate the *Mayflower*, it had a fine brook which would be proof against drought, the land was good, and much of it had been cleared for them. There was even the dry stubble of corn in the fields. Indians had planted and then providentially abandoned the place. There had been one attack from savages, but only from a roving band.

The uncertainties were ended now. The *Mayflower* could weigh

anchor, move down the coast a very little distance, unload the
stores, and the men could build.

As Dorothy had known he would, William had taken another
chill. His ankles were swollen and every joint ached as he stiffly
climbed the ladder and looked about for his wife. He didn't see
her, and it was as if those he met avoided his eyes. Then someone,
it must have been Elder Brewster, led him apart into the great
cabin and told him.

What was there to tell? No one seemed to know what had
happened. There was only one certainty, which Bradford mutely
rcorded under deaths in his notebook "December 7, Dorothy,
wife to William Bradford." More than that he never wrote, not
even that the girl—she was only twenty-three—had drowned.
Nor could he yet repeat the rubric beginning "The Lord hath
given. . . ."

He was too sick for composition, "vehemently taken with a
grief and pain." Only much later would he write of what had
been endured, and though he did not name Dorothy, something
of her informed his writing. "They had now no friends to welcome them, nor inn to entertain or refresh their weatherbeaten
bodies; no houses or much less towns to repair to, to seek for
succor. . . . It was winter, and they that know the winters of
that country know them to be sharp and violent. . . . What could
they see but a hideous and desolate wilderness, full of wild beasts
and wild men. . . . Summer being done, all things stand upon
them with a weatherbeaten face, and the whole country, full of
woods and thickets presented a wild and savage hue."

The men of Jamestown had not brought their women. A few
had come after the first year, but only after more than a decade
were there many. Say what you will about the Jamestown men,
their fecklessness, their inability to learn by experience; they had
pity on their women. Eighteen wives had come on the *Mayflower;*
when winter was over only five were left.

2

The *Mayflower* men, neither the "saints" of the Leyden congregation nor the "strangers" they brought with them, were not
people to lie under the trees like the first settlers of Jamestown,
even if climate and season had permitted. They reached Plymouth
by December 16, Old Style, and after a discussion as to whether
to build on Clark Island or the mainland, they applied themselves
on Christmas Day to the first labor of building. Christmas was
no holiday to them. Some felled timbers, some set up the pit
saw and applied themselves to riving, others to fetching and
carrying. Temporary shelters of sapling and turf were set up so
that they need not waste time by returning every night to the
Mayflower, anchored some distance from shore, and the foundations were laid and the framework raised for the first permanent
building, the Common House, which by January was serving as
hospital. All winter, luckily a mild one for these parts, though it
hardly seemed so to them, the able-bodied continued this work
on every fair day.

It did not, however, proceed very fast, for the able-bodied
became few. Sometimes less than half a dozen could be about,
and their services were required to tend the sick and bury the
dead. With all their godliness, with all their scorn of indolence,
these people underwent a seasoning as cruel as that suffered at
Jamestown. Their word for it was "the general sickness." The
deaths had begun while they still lay off the Cape, from scurvy,
and the drowning of poor Dorothy. Scurvy continued here, and
acute rheumatic pains such as Bradford suffered—now they centered in his "hucklebone"—and the chills that brought on pneu-
monia. Most of the men were cared for in the Common House;
the women and children, less crowded now, lay all winter as they
had lain all fall 'tween decks on the *Mayflower*. The tall ship with
her butterfly colors had become a hospital ship.

It had been no part of the plan that their transport remain
with them all winter. Pity might have impelled Captain Jones

to stay by them; he was taking the risk of having to drink water all the way back to England by breaking into his own stores to provide beer for the ailing, but he could not have kept the ship against the will of a mutinous crew. The fact was that the latter, stout fellows that they were, were as sorely stricken as the praying congregation. Half of them died, and not until April were the survivors sufficiently recovered for Captain Jones to risk taking his "sweet ship" into the teeth of the Atlantic gales.

Some of the crew, notably the profane bosun, came to appreciate the gentleness of the people with whom they had unwillingly traveled. The bosun, young and strong though he was, fell fatally ill, and marveled that the likes of Elder Brewster waited on him as tenderly as if he were one of the children. "You, I now see, show your love like Christians indeed one to another," said the bosun, "but we let one another lie and die like dogs."

In mid-January there was near disaster of another kind. Watchers on the ship saw flames lick from the roof of the Common House, and suspecting an Indian attack, launched the shallop against high wind and heavy swells and put ashore to the rescue. There were, however, no Indians. A blazing fire in the hearth had sent sparks shooting up the mud-and-wattle chimney to ignite the thatched roof. The building was "as full of beds as they could lie by one another," and also held some of the stores, including open barrels of gunpowder. It was an emergency that could not wait on rescue from the ship. Bradford, still racked with the agony in his hip, and others of the sick, dragged themselves from their pallets to move the explosives outside. The fire was extinguished before it could destroy the timbers of the roof, and the sick men went back to bed. But they had taken a further chill, and Bradford and Governor Carver had lost most of their clothing and personal belongings.

Half the company was dead by spring. Whole families were gone: Christopher Martin, the treasurer, his wife, and her stepson; John Turner and his sons; Thomas Tinker and his wife and son; Edward Tilley and his wife Anne. Captain Miles Standish lost his wife Rose, Edward Winslow his Elizabeth and the little girl Ellen More who had been their servant and charge. Few of the children died; many had sickened no doubt, but their mothers had ignored their own desperate weakness to care for them. So most of the children pulled through, but many of them were now motherless.

The general sickness had served the principle of natural selection. Most survivors would live into hale old age. Though the sea-born Oceanus Hopkins did not live beyond his sixth year, his nursery companion Peregrine White, fatherless by spring, inherited the staying power of his mother Susanna, and lived and prospered into the next century.

Sickness or not, there had been no idleness during the winter. Once able to be about, the men fell to with ax and pit saw. Land had been laid out in narrow strips and assigned by lot, and by the time spring came, and with it the new year as it was reckoned Old Style, shelters had been raised and thatched to house the company. They would live in quarters nearly as crowded as in 'tween decks: one room and a hearth, with perhaps a sleeping loft under the thatch. Orphans were redistributed, and single men assigned the families. William Bradford made his home with the Brewsters and their sons Love and Wrastle.

The exodus from the *Mayflower* was made on March 21. On April 5 the company watched the ship that had housed them so long spread her sails and point her prow to England. She left with a skeleton crew and no lading except their letters. She made a prosperous voyage and got a thankless welcome from the adventurers in London who had financed the enterprise. "That you sent no lading in the ship is wonderful and worthily distasted," Thomas Weston wrote. "I know your weakness was the cause of it, and I believe more weakness of judgment than weakness of hands. . . . A quarter of the time you spend in discussing, arguing and consulting would have done much more."

The letter was addressed to Governor John Carver, but he never saw it. Perhaps incompletely recovered from the sickness, he had been working to set seed under a sun hotter than April suns had any right to be. Suddenly he was taken with a blinding headache. He managed to get home to his wife, Mary, who made him lie on his pallet and fetched him damp cloths. But he died without speaking again, and not many weeks after, Mary, her life purposeless without him, for they had no children, died too.

It was a new governor who received the letter, William Bradford. He too had made a slow recovery, so that they had to appoint an assistant, Isaac Allerton. But he was well enough when Weston's letter came in on the *Fortune*, and replied with vigor. Carver, he retorted, "needs no apology, for his care and pains was so great for the common good . . . as that he oppressed himself and shortened his days; of whose loss we cannot sufficiently complain."

The little colony had taken precarious but stubborn root by the time he wrote. Though their English seeds had done little in strange soil, the Indian corn looted from Cape Cod had done well. They had made their first harvest, offered their first thanksgiving, and their government was in order. When the *Mayflower* had first sighted land, saints and strangers together had drawn up a compact "to combine ourselves into a civil body politic," and elected their first governor. The present governor was having troubles in "our better ordering and preservation" from some of the strangers, notably the "profane" Billington family, which had lost neither chick nor child in the general sickness; but there was order none the less.

During the spring there had been an unexpected social event; on May 12 Edward Winslow married Susanna White. Since Winslow had been only six weeks a widower, his precipitation might have caused comment under less difficult circumstances. Susanna had lost her husband in February, and the two White menservants had died earlier. Unthinkable for a widow still in her mid-twenties to cope singlehanded in this place with the care of the five-year-old Resolved and the suckling Peregrine. The two bereaved households were united, and the only recorded comment referred to the necessarily civil nature of the ceremony. Their pastor, John Robinson, was still in Holland, and though Elder Brewster was a skilled exhorter at Sabbath meeting, he was not empowered to administer the sacraments. However, a civil ceremony was a novelty only to the "strangers"; the theory that a marriage, which united property as well as human lives and so governed inheritance, should be civil, had already been accepted by the Leyden congregation.

So Susanna, governed more by duty and need than passion, became the wife of Edward Winslow, and arranged against the stark wooden walls of their one-room home the belongings that had come with her on the *Mayflower*. There was the hooded cradle of fine wickerwork that she had brought in anticipation of Peregrine's birth. There was her late husband's cabinet, painted black with a white floral design and bits of mother-of-pearl inlay. Into its six drawers she folded away Peregrine's baby clothes and blankets, and some of the pretties that she had with endearing vanity brought for herself. She had satin slippers to be married in, salmon colored, trimmed with galloon, and a tiny coquettish satin cape, bound with a bit of velvet ribbon mottled like leopard skin.

The baby's clothes were much in use. Only Peregrine's cap and bib survived to be cherished by his children and children's children. Susanna's little cape could be worn on fine mild days to meeting in the fort meetinghouse. The satin slippers were in this new rough life hardly more than a wistful memento. One got lost, but the other, faded to the faintest of pastels, was piously preserved by posterity.

Susanna, Spartan mother, would take hearty root in the new land, survive her second husband, who was to become eminent in the colony and die on a mission of trust to England in Oliver Cromwell's time. She would live to her eighty-sixth year, squired in her old age by the son she had borne while the *Mayflower* still rode the tides of Provincetown Harbor.

3

Like Jamestown, Plymouth owed much in the first years to the "savages." When the settlers could, they bought corn (and paid for that to which they had helped themselves from the buried stores on the Cape), and later they traded for beaver to ship home. They had bad luck with their first cargo, for the ship was seized by pirates, but eventually the furs, supplemented by laboriously cut and planed clapboarding, reduced their debt to the grudging adventurers.

They were never as generously provisioned by the Indians as Jamestown had been. Emissaries to Indian encampments, far from being feasted, nearly starved before they could get home. The Indians hereabouts were probably as generous by nature as those of Virginia, but they lived in a less generous climate and were ill-supplied themselves. Bradford laid this circumstance to the fact that they had been cultivating their corn without good English hoes, but there was a more cogent reason. The Indians here were in the process of pulling themselves together from the social disorganization of a plague.

European visitors to this part of the coast had noted the plague as early as 1612. It was a mysterious affliction, the more perplexing in that it seemed to be purely an "Indian sickness," to which the Europeans were immune. There were no trained medical observers, but the chances are that the Indians had picked up from the whites either measles, virulent among people who lack immunity, or a form of influenza which merely inconvenienced the Englishmen who carried it but killed the Indians. Later this unpremeditated form of biological warfare would include smallpox, recognizable as such by the English, but as of now it was only the "Indian sickness." Though the results hampered the white men in their search for provision, they were also a help in that the native population lacked the stamina to repel even so puny an invasion as that of the Plymouth settlers. The decimation of the Indians was to be a major factor in the choice of New England for the Massachusetts Bay settlement.

Around Plymouth and Cape Cod the plague had raged until recently. Going inland the settlers came upon whole villages of unburied dead, and that the cleared fields of Plymouth had been ready and waiting for them was due to this cause. The Indian whose protégé they became kept neighboring tribes at a distance by telling them that he had buried the plague in the ground near Plymouth and could dig it up whenever he chose to launch it against his foes.

This was their friend Squanto. Every early settlement needed an Indian benefactor. Jamestown had Pocahontas; Plymouth had the man whose full name, Tisquantum, they abbreviated to Squanto. He was no such figure of romance as the Virginia girl, effected no dramatic rescues, claimed no royal descent, and being well along in years, fluttered no maiden pulses. However, in his crabbed way he was more important to Plymouth than Pocahontas had been to Jamestown; he taught the settlers American husbandry, he became their ambassador to the Indians. All this came to him the more naturally because he was native to the place they had chosen.

Aboriginal Plymouth did have one survivor, and that because Squanto was abroad, receiving a cosmopolitan education, when the plague struck. In 1605 he had met an early explorer, George Weymouth, and had gone to England with him. He remained several years, long enough to acquire fluency in English and perhaps a cockney accent before he went home, this time as an aide to John Smith. He remained in America with Thomas Hunt, whom Smith had left to fish and trade for beaver. Hunt betrayed him. He seized twenty-seven Indians on Cape Cod to sell in the slave market at Malaga, and one of them was Squanto.

Already versed in white man's ways and probably a quick study in Spanish, Squanto was a man to land on his feet. He was taken in hand by local friars, given a Christian education, and watching his chance, found the means to ship to London. There he attached himself to a merchant's family until 1619 when he was allowed to join an expedition organized by Captain Thomas Derman, who set him ashore at his old home.

It was a desolate homecoming. He found only stubble in the remembered corn plots; his people lay in their graves, or if they lay unburied, Squanto, singing the death song, did what was necessary. It must have been at this point that he conceived the notion that the plague could be buried in the ground; from his viewpoint it was an honest magic.

The coming of the Pilgrims, less than a year after his own return, was a godsend to the lonely man. He, who had lost so much more than they, could understand their losses and their need, and Englishmen were no strangers to him.

He came first as interpreter for the Wampanoag sachem Massasoit toward the end of their first winter. Their time of helpless affliction had been complicated by the knowledge that there were Indians skulking invisibly about. Guards had to be set and, when there were enough able-bodied men to undertake such exertions, ordnance lugged ashore and set on the hill; and peppery little Miles Standish, known behind his back as Captain Shrimp because of his red hair and short stature, organized a training company. The ordnance was clumsy and inaccurate in aim, the muskets were rusted with damp, but it was possible to extract a resounding noise from the gear, and the racket impressed the Indians.

Early in spring one Samoset, whose home was on the Maine coast, where he had picked up a kind of pidgin English from the fishermen, came to announce that Massasoit was coming with his retinue to treat with the English. When the sachem came there was a great feast, a much greater feast than the English relished, for it was all at their expense, but the results were worth the inroads on their stores. Massasoit concluded a peace treaty with them, restored the tools that skulkers had been picking up, and when he left allowed his interpreter, Squanto, to remain with them. It was not wholly magnanimity of spirit that impelled Squanto to do so; he ate better with the English. But here also was his own home place, and here were people to plant it. He would help them.

They were already at their sowing, using English seed, and they would have starved if they had had to depend on it. Under Squanto's direction they set out kernels of the corn they had found on the Cape, in the only manner guaranteed to get results on this soil. First they must have fertilizer, Squanto explained; in each hill there must be placed three herring, the heads toward the center. He taught them how to trap the fish which in this season began their run up Town Brook. And while the English seed rotted in the ground or came up only to languish, the corn sent up its shoots and flourished. It was late summer before the ears filled out, and in the meantime the diet was often little more than shellfish and cod. But Squanto instructed them in these things too, and in the herbs, salads, and berries of the country; and most of those who survived the winter were hardy folk and able to gather in the fall to give thanks to their God when the corn was full in the ear and the waterfowl returned to the bay.

Squanto served them in other ways. He was their interpreter in delicate negotiations with the Indians, and helped launch them on the beaver trade, which eventually furnished their most valuable commodity to send back to England.

Though the Pilgrims, like other settlers, saw the Indians as "savages" from whom only the worst could be expected, they found in Squanto "a special instrument sent of God for their good beyond their expectation," and counted on him for a degree of integrity seldom found among Christians. They were the more shocked when in 1622 they caught him in doubledealing, in trying to impress the Indians with his power to make war or peace, with the result that Massasoit threatened to break his peace with the English.

Captain Standish and Governor Bradford were faced with an appalling dilemma. Massasoit demanded nothing less than the head of Squanto, and under the treaty which Squanto himself had negotiated, he had every right to it. Only a diversion, the unexpected arrival of a ship from England, saved Plymouth from this unthinkable necessity. Later in the year Squanto himself took on an "Indian sickness," and died of it, asking his friends to pray that their God admit him to the English heaven.

They mourned him, and this was a loss impossible to restore. He had taught them all he knew of agriculture, and without him they had lost the "ears" with which they listened to the Indians. How imperative such an intermediary was they had just learned in terrifying news from Virginia.

V WHITE MAN, GO HOME

1

MARCH 22 fell in 1622 on Good Friday. That this day had a solemn significance to the whites some Indians certainly knew. It was also the second day of the new year as it was reckoned Old Style, and in Virginia plowing had begun. In Bermuda Hundred near the junction of the James and the Appomattox, planted only three years earlier, and already showing the results of skilled management, a frightened servant told Captain George Thorpe that strange Indians lurking in the neighborhood were behaving suspiciously.

His master only smiled. If the Indians were lurking instead of inviting themselves in to share his breakfast, it could be only from shyness; being strangers they were unsure of their welcome. No seasoned Virginian in these happier days dreaded the approach of Indians, certainly not Thorpe, who was conspicuously their friend.

He was a man of complex responsibilities. The Bermuda Hundred plantation was, under his direction, experimenting with exotic seeds and making ambitious plans for producing rice, flax, wines, ship's stores, silk, and even iron ore. He was a member of the Governor's Council. But dearest to his heart was his work with the Indians. He had served Governor Francis Wyatt as ambassador to Opechancanough, one of the inheritors of the empire of Powhatan, who had died in 1618 before he could hear of the death of his daughter in England. Recently he had taken charge of the College Lands, whose profits were to be used to educate the Indians.

This project had taken form in 1618 when the new charter then issued to the Company directed that 10,000 acres be set apart at Henrico "for the building and planting of a college for the training up of the children of those Infidels in true religion, moral virtue, and civility." The idea was not new; farseeing stockholders like the Hakluyts had always had it in mind that the Indians be given an opportunity to share the benefits of English civilization. That nothing had been done earlier was due to the colony's hard birth, the extreme difficulty of conferring such benefits even upon Englishmen in Virginia. But the colony had established a foothold at last; starving times were over—or seemed to be; it was time to look forward to greater things.

Pocahontas had not died in vain. During her stay in England her dignity, her grace had convinced the most skeptical that her people were worthy of salvation. Soon after her death English bishops had appealed for funds for this purpose and in response received close to £2000 in cash and bequests, to say nothing of a communion set, a library, and a collection of maps. Enthusiasm extended even to India, where on a homebound ship a chaplain collected £70 from seamen and passengers. Now Thorpe was in charge of the College Lands in which the funds had been invested, and looked eagerly forward to founding a school in which his Indian friends could learn to read their Bibles and take up useful trades.

Meanwhile he was widely known for his adventures in friendship. He had taken pains to have a house built for Opechancanough, complete with a door and lock which had become the king's favorite mechanical toy. At his home, when Indians came by in the morning with venison or corn to sell, he had them to breakfast. When they were caught in his neighborhood at nightfall, he had a guest chamber prepared for them.

He listened to their complaints against his servants and neighbors, and when he found justice in them, punished the white men. One common complaint was against the huge English mastiffs that still frightened the Indians. Thorpe had shot one canine offender, and ordered that others be gelded to gentle them. The command gave offense to the colonists, not the less because Thorpe as a member of the Council had the authority to enforce

it. It is likely that he was more popular with the Indians than
with some neighbors. He had faith that such benign influence
would win the former to Christianity, and had no patience with
the views of the Reverend Mr. Jonas Stockden, who was convinced that "till their priests and ancients have their throats cut,"
there was no hope of converting the savages.

Recently there had been trouble. A petty chief whom the English called Jack of the Feather because of his taste in adornment
had been accused of murdering a white man, and in resisting arrest had got himself killed without being brought to trial.
Opechancanough had at first threatened to avenge this death.
But he received with courtesy a messenger sent by the English
and assured him that he "held the peace so firm the sky should
fall [before] he dissolved it."

On Good Friday the sky fell.

Thorpe's reassurance had not convinced his manservant. The
Indians he had seen were strange and their manner stranger.
Instead of returning to his work in the fields, he did some lurking
himself. From a distance he saw what happened. When Thorpe
came out of his house for a look at the weather, a savage came
on him from behind and neatly split his skull. Others fell on the
body and inflicted nameless indignities. By that time the servant
was running too fast to observe details; the mangling was discovered later by rescue parties, who, when they saw what was
left of Thorpe, friend and benefactor to the Indians, could take
comfort in that what had happened had happened so fast that the
victim knew nothing of it.

2

There had been nothing personal in this slaying. Judging by the
alarm given by his servant, his execution had not been entrusted
to his friends. And what was done to Thorpe was being done all
over the colony to men, women, and children at exactly the same
moment. The Indians had, as it were, synchronized their watches;

the massacre began at eight o'clock in the morning, and most of the 347 known dead died within moments of each other.

In some houses Indians sat with their white friends at breakfast, and then, having downed their hominy grits and received their signal from some obscure pulse, calmly rose and slaughtered their hosts with their own weapons. There was no need to seize the weapons; many white folk had already given them, glad to have the Indians, long skilled in their use, borrow them to fetch in fresh meat and waterfowl.

Sometimes there was more elaborate trickery. At Thomas Hamor's on the south side of the James, they set fire to a tobacco warehouse, and when his men came running to quench the flames, shot them full of arrows and beat out their brains. Hamor himself did not come at once. There were ships in the James and he was writing a letter that he wanted to send by one of them. It was not until he finished that he went to look at the fire. An arrow lodged in his back, but he was able to get back to his house, and when it was fired, to escape with several others to the Baldwin house half a mile away, where the master and a boy had put the Indians to flight by firing muskets at random.

This was the story all over the colony, far-flung now, for the settlers had grown careless and had been planting wherever they found good black loam, with small heed to the safety of propinquity. Kecoughtan, or Elizabeth City as it had been called ever since the English on a flimsy pretext had dispossessed the friendly little Indian colony to move in themselves, and Jamestown had been spared, and thither the survivors fled in panic.

Jamestown, site of so many disasters, owed its exemption from this one to the conscience of "one converted infidel." This man, unnamed, lived with one Pace, who had "used him as his son." On the night before, his brother had come to him to relay orders from the king for him to kill Pace and his family. The Indian informed Pace, who after setting a guard on his house, rowed to Jamestown to warn Governor Wyatt, who in turn warned as many plantations as he could reach. And wherever the colonists were fortified and took a stand, the Indians fled. Their strategy had been based on surprise; even more widely scattered in their vil-

lages than the whites, they were unprepared to give open battle
or lay siege to strongholds armed against them.

Yet in the panic that prevailed as more details of the disaster
were brought to Jamestown with each refugee, there was no
resolution to take a stand in the outer plantations. Householders
were ordered to abandon their dearly won estates and come to
the stockade. A few resisted, among them Captain Daniel Gookin,
who considered his thirty-five men and boys a sufficient army to
defend his newly planted Newport News, but one Mrs. Proctor,
similarly resolved, was not allowed to do so. One would like to
know more of this "civil, modest gentlewoman," remarkable not
only in her courage but in her single state in a woman-hungry
colony, where a maid could hardly reach her teens or a widow get
into her weeds without being snatched into matrimony. The officer had to threaten to burn her house and slaughter her cattle to
induce the woman to move, and when she did the Indians came
in to accomplish what the officer had only threatened.

The burning and slaughtering went on at Henrico Island, at
Charles City, at most of the "hundreds" in their turn, Berkeley's
at Falling Creek, Flowerdew, Southampton, Martin's, Brandon's,
and so up and down Virginia.

At Jamestown, its government disorganized, for six of the Council had perished, crowded with refugees unable to bring provision
and cattle with them, there was like to be another starving time.
It was weeks before the English could sufficiently master their
wits and resources to decide how they could resettle and go on
with spring planting.

3

In a sense the massacre was a tribute to Virginia. It was a
recognition that the English settlements were establishing themselves so firmly as to menace the whole way of life of the Indians.
Until then the English had seemed not worth the effort of whole-
sale expulsion; simpler, less wasteful of energy, to let them die off
in their own manner. Only now, fifteen years after the founding of

Jamestown, were they demonstrating real capacity for survival. Virginia had reached its nadir during the starving time. The London Company found it almost impossible to raise more capital, especially after Lord Delaware followed his providential rescue of Jamestown by an ignominious retreat. But for the new opportunity offered by Bermuda, the Company might have been forced to dissolve.

A gradual improvement had begun between 1611 and 1616 under the administration of Sir Thomas Dale. A seasoned old soldier of manifold campaigns in the Netherlands dating back as far as 1588, he became the most enduring of Lord Delaware's deputies, the most hated, but not the least successful. The hatred derived from his martial enforcement of what were called Dale's Laws, though Delaware had sanctioned them.

Survivors of the starving time included many unruly members of the great migration who could not be controlled by gentle persuasion. The Company having granted special authority to deal with them, the Council had evolved a code imposing capital punishment for such varied offenses as speaking against his majesty or the Lord Governor, refusing to be catechized or attend church, committing murder, arson, sodomy, or any theft at all.

The code, harsh even for contemporary England, tempted all but the most docile to watch their chance to run off to the Indians. Hangings and croppings of ears served the fields ill as fertility rites. But Dale was not without intelligent foresight. He supplemented the code with an experiment which was presently to have revolutionary effect: he allotted each laborer three acres of his own and time to cultivate them.

Before this, most of the land was the property of adventurers in London who had never set eyes on it, and its produce went into the common store in which all shared, the improvident with the industrious. Smith had once proclaimed a rule that he who does not work shall not eat, but this, even so far as it could be enforced, was negative, offering punishment rather than reward.

Now that the reward had substance, the industry of men of

firm will who had health and strength knew no bounds. Communal labor continued, and the released time was niggardly, one month distributed over the year with the provision that none be excused from planting and harvest. But it could be supplemented by work in the hours allotted to rest, and the incentive was tremendous.

Many of the laborers here, as in later English colonies, had in England been tenant farmers crowded off the land by the growth of the wool trade, which required extensive enclosures of land for sheep grazing. It was this economic revolution that had filled English jails with vagrants and the city streets with waifs, as landless men drifted to the cities with no means of employment but begging and thieving. To such as had not forgotten what they had known of husbandry, it must have been painful to see here good land in abundance and none of it for them. But now there was a change; those who had the will need be landless no longer.

Thus a subtle transformation began to work from the grass roots. It was not immediately apparent. The provident were still outnumbered by the unseasoned newcomers and the city-bred who had no knowledge of how to make the fields produce. Yet a beginning was made, and if the colony as a whole was not yet self-supporting, it contained individuals who were.

Gradually, Virginia became a place where those with the will could work to their own profit and enjoy life. A gentlewoman would report that in her Virginia home she fared better at far less expense than in England. John Pory, arriving with Deputy Governor George Yeardley in 1619 to serve as secretary, was at first shocked to find most Virginians drinking nothing better than water, and Jamestown still primitive, but he remained to write home "that we are not the veriest beggars in the world." The Jamestown cowkeeper went to church "accoutered all in fresh flaming silk," and the wife of one who had been a collier in Croydon "wore her rough beaver hat with a fair pearl hatband and a silken suit into correspondence." The governor, who at "his first coming . . . brought only his sword with him," had returned to England with a fortune of £3000 to spend. After five months the charm of the honeysuckle-scented Virginia countryside had won

John Pory: "Among these crystal rivers, and odoriferous woods I do escape much expense, envy, contempt, vanity, and vexations of mind."

There was even intellectual life; in 1621 Virginia acquired a poet, George Sandys, younger brother of the London Company's Sir Edwin, who brought his translation of Ovid with him. Neither the massacre, of which he made the first official report, his duties as treasurer of the colony, manager of the glass factory, nor his experiments in raising silk worms could distract him from composition. He went back to England with the translation completed, and it was a good one, applauded by Dryden and Pope.

4

The year 1619 had been a turning point. It saw the first introduction of African labor, the first importation of women in numbers, and the founding of the House of Burgesses.

The first of these events was of contemporary significance only to the principals. The settlers had no prescience that the buying of twenty "negars" from a passing Dutch man-of-war was the start of that which would eventually affect their way of life almost as profoundly as the Englishmen's presence was affecting that of the Indians. For many decades there was only a handful of Africans; slavery as such was a concept foreign to English law, and for a long time these new hands would serve as another kind of "duty boy," as privileged as the latter in becoming their own men when they had performed the prescribed term of service.

The coming of the women was more immediately revolutionary. There had been none at all until Anne Burroughs had come with her mistress in 1608. Happy had been the lot of the maidservant, who could queen it until she made her choice among so many men craving the company of an Englishwoman. What happened to her Mistress Forest? Had she and her husband Thomas succumbed to the miasmas of Jamestown, or was she, God forbid, the wife whose husband "powdered" her (with salt) and ate her during the starving time?

Other wives, sisters, daughters came little by little, some bringing children with them, but until 1619 most Englishmen had no feminine society except that offered by the Indian girls. These were not all unwilling; there had been one invasion of Jamestown by maids got up in horns and feathers, who whether in mockery or invitation cried out, "Love you not me?" Such invitations were not always spurned; when Smith reported that Pocahontas was the only Indian girl married to an Englishman, his tacit emphasis was on the word married. The penal code placed no explicit ban on informal alliance between the English and the girls of the forest.

But as a breed the English lacked the realism of the Latins in such a situation. Spanish, French, and Portuguese colonists, separated for most of their active lives from women of their own kind, took mates as a matter of course in America or Africa, and begot children whom they acknowledged as their own and reared to the best of their ability as Christians. In Virginia, John Rolfe had done this only after prolonged inner conflict about the righteousness of such conduct. Were the English so conscious of race, a concept still hardly known, or was this shamefacedness a part of the Bible-reading Protestantism? A cheerful Catholic Portuguese, currently engaged in setting himself up as a paterfamilias in Angola or Brazil, never troubled to examine what was said in Leviticus about taking strange wives.

Such English as were literate or took their catechism to heart worried about such things. In time they would coin words to convey their embarrassments: *squaw man, half-caste,* and eventually the ugly sounding word *miscegenation.* Eschewing the temptations of the Indian women, they ran into worse. When twelve years after the founding of Jamestown the London Company sent a shipload of women to them, it was high time.

Ninety "young women to make wives . . . handsome and honestly educated maids . . . being such as are specially recommended into the colony for their good bringing up" were sent out in one or another of the eleven immigrant ships dispatched to the colony in 1619. Their condition had something in common with the Africans on the Dutch man-of-war, for they would be "sold" in Virginia to defray the price of passage, for 120 pounds of tobacco, or an estimated $500 apiece, and they were committed for life. And like the Africans they did not necessarily come of their own volition.

The Company's honest, commendable intentions were nearly defeated by employees who used their inside knowledge for private gain. The clerk Robinson counterfeited the Great Seal in order to convince yeomen that he had a commission to collect their daughters "to serve his majesty for breeders in Virginia." He was caught at it, hanged, drawn, and quartered. Owen Evans also pretended to such a commission, and had "bred so much terror to the poor maids that forty had fled from one parish to obscure places, and their parents do not know what has become of them."

These had been illicit measures; still, it is plain that not all maids had come gladly. The passage to America was seldom a pleasure cruise. The way was too long, for though now most ships followed the great-circle route that the *Mayflower* took, the voyage was not necessarily quicker than the longer route via the Azores and the West Indies because winds were so often contrary and storms in the North Atlantic so frequent. And all immigrant ships were overcrowded.

The maids endured the stench and confusion between decks and wondered miserably about the sort of life they would find in Virginia. The colony still had no rosy reputation. Such disasters as the starving time were well known, and maids who hadn't heard the tale of the man who salted his wife to eat her, surely heard it on shipboard. Was it to this end that they were to be given in marriage, to serve as meat for their mates? In this fear too they were one with the Africans, who knew white men only as dwellers of their hollow ships and regularly believed on their transit to America that they had fallen into the hands of man-eaters.

But some girls had stout stomachs for the voyage and stout spirits for the long adventure ahead. They could shrug off the tale of the cannibal husband as a yarn sailors spin to daunt greenhorns. Dowerless in England, like to spend their lives in other women's service or in the stews, they looked forward to finding a proper man in America and ordering his household according to

their own notions. When the time came for bidding, they would
(again like some Africans) look about to catch the eye of a man
to their liking.

The enterprise worked well. Only the honest and industrious
were allowed to bid for the girls, and these made a point of considering the debt incurred as a debt of honor. The shipment was
profitable and others followed. Eleven maids and one widow came
early in 1621, and later in the year twelve on the *Marmaduke*
and thirty-eight on the *Tiger*. For the latter shipment the Company, needled by loose talk that it had been recruiting "maids"
from Bridewell, furnished "testimony of their honest life and carriage . . . for the satisfaction of such as shall marry them."

The House of Burgesses, the other memorable innovation of
1619, took the wives into account in granting patents for land,
"because in a new plantation it is not known whether men or
women be the most necessary."

5

A vital handicap of the Virginia colony, a factor that made it
"un-American" in contrast to its own subsequent history and the
early development of New England, had been its lack of self-
government. Governor and Council were appointed and the rules
drawn up by gentlemen in London, who were without practical
experience of local conditions and whose information was always
out of date. The first settlers had not even known who was on their
Council until in Virginia they opened their sealed orders.

This lack of real responsibility, compounded with sickness and
famine, must have played a large part in the unseemly rancors
that characterized the first men in Jamestown. They seemed to be
constitutionally bent on spying on each other, ordering each
other shot for one malfeasance or another, and when opportunity
offered, running home to England to report, like children tattling
to Teacher about the misconduct of their fellows.

They had had a bewildering multiplicity of governors, many
of whom seemed bent on ignoring or contradicting what had been

done before. Nominally, Lord Delaware had the longest administration, from 1610 to 1618, but during his lordship's absence after 1611 (and he died on his way back in 1618) the actual administration was in the hands of deputies, the feckless George Percy, the steely Thomas Dale, and after him Samuel Argall, whose principal achievement was making his fortune by questionable means from the fur trade.

In all this time there had been no opportunity for the real colonists, be they gents or laborers, to take a share in shaping policy or framing laws. The adventurous, the strong-willed, like John Smith, were their own masters only when they were off on their discoveries.

The inadequacy of such rule finally impressed the Company; in 1618 they worked out a new charter, and the following year, after Sir George Yeardley, the new governor, had arrived with "the great charter of privileges, orders and laws," the landowners elected twenty representatives, two from each of ten settlements, which, added to the six members of the Council, constituted the first House of Burgesses. They met with ceremony in the church at Jamestown, listened to an invocation from its rector, Richard Buck, who may have married the John Rolfes, took the oath of supremacy, and set to work on the details of America's first representative government.

Their first business was a dispute on membership, inspired less by the rancors of old than by a constitutional point. Martin's Hundred had sent two burgesses, though Captain John Martin, one of the original settlers, held his land under a patent which exempted him from the general rule. Should these be seated with the rest? The point was time-consuming; a copy of the patent had to be read and discussed, Martin himself interrogated. In the end his delegates were expelled.

Only then, in early August, while the heat grew daily more oppressive and the miasmas arose from the marshes, could the body set to work to frame its laws. It legislated against idleness, gaming, drunkenness, set a tax on excessive apparel, made rules for the Indian trade, ordained the regular reading of divine service, regulated the marriage of the maids.

It was a short session. The heat bore down too hard and too many burgesses fell ill for them to go into a long session. In instructing their speaker, John Pory, to send a copy of their deliberations to London, "the assembly doth most humbly crave pardon that in so short a space they could not bring their matter to more perfecting . . . hoping their courtesy will accept our poor endeavor." They recognized that their laws must wait on approval in England but asked that it "would please [the Company] not to take it in ill part if these laws . . . to pass current and be of force until such time as we may know their further pleasure out of England."

The "humble cravings" of this assembly were still an unimaginable distance from the spirit which would presently lead one Virginian to say, "Give me liberty or give me death." They were still dependent on the will of London. Not until after the London Company dissolved in 1624 and the colony went under a royal charter did the settlers approximate self-government. It was the Indian massacre that did this for them. The colony managed to survive it; the Company, bankrupt already, did not.

6

News of the massacre reached London in July 1622 and was received by the Company with something less than tender sympathy; the colonists were denounced for their imbecility in letting it happen. "To fall by the hand of men so contemptible . . . make[s] us to confess that it is the heavy hand of almighty God for the punishment of your transgressions." They were recommended to look to their souls and improve their manners, and cease the cowardly abandonment of outlying plantations. London had no provision to send them, but was shipping a large number of fresh emigrants, who must be received properly, housed, and fed until they could maintain themselves.

Never had the Company shown itself more blind to the needs of the colonists. The latter were threatened with a new starving time. Livestock had been slaughtered and stores burned or pillaged by the Indians. The best of the planting season had gone before the survivors could resume any planting at all, and then there were difficulties inconceivable to London. The best men had to hold themselves on the alert for new ambuscades. There was not land enough about such protected settlements as Jamestown and Kecoughtan to provide for the refugees. Corn could not be planted too close to any settlement, because as it grew it gave cover to the enemy. And the London Company in lieu of corn was sending new mouths to feed, and for arms was shipping out antique breastplates and cuirasses from the Tower of London, the sort of arms which, as Smith was pointing out (he was vainly petitioning the Company to let him return with picked men to take the field against the Indians), made it impossible for men so cumbered to maneuver against the fleet Indians.

Again settlers were tempted to abandon the star-crossed colony. "Oh that they were in England without their limbs, yea though they begged from door to door," a desperate boy wrote his parents, speaking for the newcomers. Some did go home. The population of the colony, estimated at 4000 in 1621, was down to 2500 in 1623, a reduction not wholly attributable to the massacre or the hazards of seasoning.

But one observer had written truly of Virginia. "I may fitly compare it to the growth of an infant which hath been afflicted from its birth with so grievous sickness that many times no hope of life remaineth, and yet it liveth still." Among the timid, the sick, and the homesick there was in the colony a hard core of settlers to whom Virginia, not England, was home. John Laydon, who had come in 1607 and so had lived through the worst, stolidly hoed the corn on his good acres near old Kecoughtan, and though he kept a wary lookout for interlopers, he had no disposition to return to a land where he had been landless. Neither did Anne his wife, who had exchanged servitude in England to be mistress of her own house here. As for the four Laydon girls—a pity there were no sons, but obviously God appreciated Virginia's need for women—England to them was merely something the old folks sometimes talked about.

Yeardley, who had begun his administration with the founding of the House of Burgesses, did not abandon Virginia. He had known what he was getting into, for he had first visited in 1609 and had shortly after served his first term as governor. In 1621, worn out with difficulties with the Company and by the situation in the colony, he had asked that his commission not be renewed, and relieved that summer by Sir Francis Wyatt, he was not in command at the time of the massacre. But the disaster did not drive him home. He had retired to his own allotment on Smith's Hundred above Jamestown, and lived a Virginian until his death in 1627. He who had started life nearly as humbly as Laydon— he had been apprentice to a tailor in youth—had been knighted after his removal to Virginia. It was as Sir George that he had taken up his second term as governor. It was as one of the landed gentry, subject to the rough and ready pioneering conditions, but still gentry, that he cast his lot with the surviving settlers.

The London Company dissolved in 1624 so far as Virginia was concerned; it was having better luck with Bermuda; and the colony went under the Crown. The pressure on its people for immediate commercial return was relieved; they began to work out their own destiny through the burgesses, and slowly arrived at order and the first beginning of prosperity.

In 1625 there was another beneficial change. The Crown to which they were subject was placed on the head of Charles I. The advantage was that James, and under his influence the Company, had implacably opposed the cultivation of the colony's one cash crop, tobacco. Charles, though expressing a personal prejudice against it, left the colonists free to work out their economic life.

John Rolfe had played an important part in the tobacco industry. While he was wooing Pocahontas, he had been experimenting with the culture and curing of tobacco. The latter was particularly important, since only properly cured tobacco was fit for export. Thanks to him exports had begun, and at last Virginia had a crop on which a substantial profit could be made.

James had vehemently disapproved a society "founded on smoke." His majesty had taken exception to the custom of "drinking tobacco" in England on grounds of morality and health; the

Company had protested that if the colonists spent half the time on their corn that they lavished on the "stinking weed," they would not be hungry so often or make such extravagant calls on London for stores.

There was justice in these protests. The healthfulness of tobacco "drinking" has been challenged by others than King James. The commodity did demand extraordinary care in its growth, and was to prove wasteful of soil, even the rich topsoil of Virginia. Planters were to consume land extravagantly, and the labor needed to break new ground, set the young plants, and cure the ripe leaves was to cause them to crave more hands from Africa than the score who came in 1619. Tobacco would become a monster, crowding future John Laydons from the soil almost as ruthlessly as the enclosures had crowded them out of England.

But the colonists could not be denied their one profitable crop. The nearest they had to a local monetary system was the certificates attesting to the weight of the "sweet scented" deposited to the planters' credit in the warehouses. The Company had recognized that fact in setting the price of the brides they exported not in pounds sterling but in pounds of tobacco.

Under the new regime tobacco became king. Now it was the burgesses who ordered the colonists to vary the single crop with corn and the nurture of mulberry trees, and to encourage a group of vinegrowers from Languedoc who were trying to tame the luxuriant wild vines and establish imported roots. Nor was corn neglected. In 1634 Virginia actually had some for export. A shipload was sent to Massachusetts Bay to supplement the stores of the newly arrived Puritans, and Governor John Harvey triumphantly announced that "Virginia is become the granary" of America. It had become nothing of the sort, but that Virginia after so many starving times had any surplus at all excused the boast.

VI MASSACHUSETTS: MOTHER OF COLONIES

1

Descendants prize priority. Americans take more pride in tracing their ancestry to the *Mayflower*, humble as were her passengers' origins, than to the *Arbella* and the ships that followed in her wake. It might have been different if Lady Arbella Johnson had been fruitful instead of dying untimely; even so she might not have been as popular an ancestor as the plebeian Peregrine White. She came too late. The ship that bore her name was not the first, the tenth, or even the fiftieth to reach this coast.

In ways more important if less picturesque, the *Arbella* and her consorts could claim priority. Massachusetts Bay was the first American success story. It was the first undertaken after careful study of the circumstances that had given predecessors such painful if heroic beginnings. It was massive migration; a thousand came in 1630, and thousands more quickly followed. There was in this venture a masculine thrust, a sense of direction, that no colony had known before. While Plymouth remained a feeble little settlement, while Virginia, settled more than two decades earlier, had only just established taproots and no one could yet foresee that it was to become "mother of presidents," Massachusetts became visibly, almost from the year of its founding, the mother of colonies.

Years had been spent in planning, and long before the *Arbella* led the great migration, tentative settlements had been made. Earlier in the twenties it had been learned from a modest experiment

on Cape Ann that fishermen did not make good planters or planters good fishermen. In 1626 Salem had been founded; if its
achievement was still inconsiderable, at least it was there to
provide a welcome for the travelers. It would not be written of
them as of the *Mayflower* people that there was no habitation to
receive them.

From the pioneers assurance had come of fertile lands, fine
stands of timber, ample sources of fresh water, and best of all,
very few Indians to bar the way. Francis Higginson had reported
the mysterious "Indian sickness" that providentially had destroyed
whole nations of savages, releasing their lands to the undisputed
use of the white men. The climate was at least tolerable; winters
were not too long or snows too heavy.

Their fleet took sail in a favorable season; it was not subjected
like the *Mayflower* to impossible delays and finally driven off
course. It arrived in the strawberry time that was to become
proverbial. ("He must have come in strawberry time," people
would say when they heard an implausibly optimistic report.)
There was time to make a start at building before they were
caught in the grip of winter that had nearly defeated Plymouth.

They had come well provided. The "great disbursement" for
which John Smith in Virginia had pleaded in vain was theirs
from the first. Few had the wealth that Isaac Johnson had placed
at the disposal of the company, but most of the leaders had at
least modest substance, and they had pooled their resources.

They had a sense of direction; they did not come like so many
early Virginians in the hope of making an easy fortune and going
home to spend it. Not that they disdained fortune; if gold was
here they would be happy to find it, and when Winthrop's eldest
son and namesake followed his father to the colony he would
spend much time prospecting and assaying. But they had come
primarily to build, to plant, to make homes, to found a commonwealth where they could order their lives and worship according
to their own lights.

They took the precaution of precluding remote control from
overseas. What had made life in Virginia so difficult, what would
hamper New Netherland and bedevil other colonies still un-

thought of, they avoided by bringing their charter with them. This move was not explicitly authorized. Certainly King Charles, in permitting them to hold four General Courts a year on their own soil, had no intention of granting them the self-rule that they attained. The conveyance of the Charter to the Bay was a sharp Yankee trick whereby for more than half a century Massachusetts would succeed in conducting itself almost like a sovereign state. It was no accident that when eventually the American colonies sought full independence, Massachusetts led the way.

2

Even so, beginnings are not easy. No disbursement is so great as to cover all contingencies. There would sometimes be hunger in Massachusetts. A new land exacts seasoning of its settlers. These people underwent their seasoning, and others besides the Isaac Johnsons died of it.

Governor Winthrop had no leisure to welcome his son Henry or give vent to his grief that after having safely come across the sea Henry drowned right after reaching shore. His responsibilities were too grave for him to have any real personal life.

It was strange that he was here at all, let alone as leader. His interest in the colony was not of long standing. Two years earlier he had dissuaded the younger John Winthrop from joining Endicott in the settling of Salem. When he himself agreed to go, many of his friends had been appalled. England hath need of thee, they said in effect. Men of his piety were wanted at home to purify the bishop-ridden church rather than abroad in the arduous task of founding a church in the wilderness. Such work was for younger men. Let him consider the welfare of his family and stay home to husband his estate.

Winthrop's reply had been a blend of the piety and practicality peculiar to the Puritan mind. Late as he was in taking an interest in the grand schemes being shaped at Tattershall, his imagination had at last been fired by the chance to shape a commonwealth on virgin soil after the desires of godly men. His personal participation was needed, for many would neither contribute capital investment nor join the migration unless a man of his stature were in charge. As to his family's welfare, everyone from his loving Margaret to the youngest child not only approved the venture but was eager to share it. Moreover, comfortable as was his estate in England, he had there by no means enough substance to establish his sons in life. As the psalmist said, sons are arrows in a quiver, and Winthrop had a quiver full of them. Their opportunity would be richer in the new world.

So for that matter would be his own. Puritans were finding one avenue of preferment after another closed to them in England. Charles had just dissolved Parliament in anger at its troublesome Puritan members, and Winthrop had lost his lucrative office under the Master of Wards. Living as a country squire in Groton was pleasant, but he had too much pride of place to relish seeing a promising career come to a full stop when he was in his prime. Thus the opportunity to help found and govern so vigorous a new colony did not present itself wholly as an act of self-denial. (Indeed, Winthrop was to become restive on those perennial occasions, afforded by Massachusetts' precocity in self-government, when his severest critic, Thomas Dudley, got the job away from him.)

Now that the crossing had been safely made, his first and urgent task was to find a place for the "sitting down," so that they could build and if possible plant before winter overtook them. Long before July 6 when his last ship came in, the *Success*, with a sorry tale of goats washed overboard and passengers "near starved," he had been exploring "Mattachusetts," by which he meant Boston Harbor, the Mystic, Noddles Island, Nantasket.

Charlestown on the Mystic was his choice, and his plan was for a compact settlement, the building of a "city on a hill." This plan he could not realize. Other men were energetically looking around and resolving to "make a pitch" at places to their liking. Some joined a small earlier settlement at Dorchester, some went across Boston Neck to found Rocksbury or Roxbury. Sir Richard Saltonstall, who had come "with some store of cattle and servants," chose Watertown up the Charles, "a fruitful plat . . .

watered with many springs," and took Mr. Phillips with him as pastor.

Some who had expected more than the crude and scattered hamlets that Massachusetts had as yet to offer, and foreseeing famine, found passage on the returning ships and went home. (The governor was to learn, not without wry satisfaction, that the Lord did not prosper this retreat; the *Ambrose* lost her masts and had to be towed; three other ships were set upon by the Spanish and badly knocked up, and on all ships there were deaths.) But the number of returnees was not serious. Many lacked passage money, and others preferred to bear what ills they had to facing the Atlantic again. Most settlers remained with Winthrop at Charlestown; at least they wintered there.

Charlestown had timber, but the building went slowly. Before his death Isaac Johnson had the happiness of seeing the meeting-house completed, so that John Wilson could preach under a roof instead of under the tree where the first congregations gathered. But most people managed nothing better than huts, and some were still camping in tents of sailcloth when on Christmas Eve winter blasted in on a powerful northwest wind.

Until then the season had been mild, with light frosts more refreshing than not after the sultry summer. (Winthrop had found that contrary to his early impression the sun gave off more rather than less heat than in England.) But now the river froze, and so did fingers. Rations ran short; even Indian corn was hard to come by, and some could or would not stomach it.

Now there was homesickness for England. Even the poor who had no estate there, who had been driven from their tenant farms and found no employment in the towns, reflected that if starve they must, it would have been better to starve in England, taking comfort from the homeliness of familiar ways.

There was sickness, especially scurvy. It was still considered to be of psychosomatic origin; it was not an optimistic affliction like some phases of "the consumption," and since it produced sluggishness and depression, it was deemed a judgment on the slothful and low-spirited. Winthrop remarked that those who despaired easily and "lingered after their former condition in England" were those who took it, whereas those who looked forward and worked with a will did not.

Some were cheerful. Regularly at low tide womenfolk bundled up their petticoats to wade out and dig at the clam banks "with much heavenly discourse of the provision Christ had formerly made for many thousands of his followers in the wilderness." Husbands walked all the way to Plymouth or into the woods to the Indians to dicker for corn. "Our last peck of meal is now in the oven at home a-baking, and many of our godly neighbors have spent quite all, and we owe one loaf of that little we have." They assured themselves that "in the miss of beer" they could still "rejoice in a cup of cold water." They said, "Methinks our children are as cheerful, fat and lusty with feeding upon these mussels, clambanks and other fish as they were in England with their fill of bread."

But these brave ones rejoiced as much as those of little faith when on February 5 the supply ship *Lion* came in, and shortly after the scurvy was on the wane. Along with the flour, "powdered beef," and small beer, the *Lion* brought a store of lemons.

It came by Winthrop's foresight. He had sent to Bristol for this supply late in July when he first saw the need. The provision that in England had seemed so ample had been largely consumed in voyage. The earlier settlers, enfeebled by illness, had small surplus. Given the magnitude of clearing the ground before planting could be made, there was no hope of crops this season beyond a little "garden sass." So Winthrop had contracted with Captain William Pierce to fetch provision from Bristol and had urgently written his son John to find the money to honor his bills of exchange, "for they can't stay." And he added, "People must come well provided and not too many at once."

Now the *Lion* was in. Lean stomachs were comforted with good beer and familiar English food; thanks to the lemons, scurvy was on the wane, depressed spirits were reviving, and people looked forward to spring and planting. Spring came early this year; indeed under the Julian calendar it usually came early in these times. Winthrop, who had found Charlestown's water supply unsatisfactory for so large a sitting down, looked about him again and hit on Boston. He had first mentioned it in his journal in October in connection with the death of a cow "from eating Indian corn." Now, though Charlestown was not abandoned and Winthrop kept as his country seat the farm he had already staked out on the Mystic, Boston became his "city on a hill."

3

The natural advantage of Boston, with its fine, island-girt harbor, was obvious. But as a place of first settlement for people whose immediate need was shelter, it had one drawback, lack of timber. Children like Anne Pollard might delight in the blueberry bushes, but they were hardly building material. Timber had to be ferried in from the islands, and the firewood supply would remain a perennial problem and a source of enrichment to the surrounding countryside.

Boston already had one resident, the Reverend Mr. William Blackstone, who had left England in 1623 to escape the rule of the "lord bishops" and two years later had settled on Boston Harbor. For five years he had enjoyed private possession, studying the books he had brought with him, working his garden and little orchard. The life suited his temperament. Yet when he heard that Charlestown was ill-suited to so large a press of newcomers, he cordially invited Winthrop to consider Boston. Three years later he was on the move again, to Rhode Island. Boston had grown too fast for one who liked isolation for his contemplations, and he was finding the rule of the "lord brethren" as irksome as that of the "lord bishops."

The phrase "city upon a hill" was pious rhetoric, and embodied no concept of city planning. It is possible that almost any other early town in Massachusetts, centered about the village green and the meetinghouse, had a more orderly plan than Boston in its first decades. Here too land was eventually reserved for a green, Boston Common, where cattle could be grazed. On one of its three little mountains a beacon was set whence outlying communities could be signaled of danger approaching by sea. But the village itself grew helter-skelter, its first buildings close to the waterfront, since that was where timber from the islands was most readily available.

Most of the first buildings were one-room structures of un-painted clapboarding, placed by roads which were trodden out at the convenience of the householders. Presently Boston town meeting and its selectmen would take a hand, regularly rein-forced by admonitions from General Court, which first met in 1631, and attempt to impose some regularity on the width and direction of its streets, forbid that chimneys be made of wood. Late in the day attempts would be made to restrain householders from dumping their rubbish into the streets, and the hogs from ranging at will, even thrusting their inquiring snouts into the sanctity of the meetinghouse during prayer.

Such measures were adopted slowly and enforced only gradu-ally. For the first decade there was always more to Boston than met the eye of the immigrant unsteadily descending from the latest transport. It in no way suggested that it was already the capital of a phenomenally expanding colony, that these crude dwellings housed energetic and highly intelligent men and women who as early as 1636 founded a university and a free school so that their young might be properly educated and their future ministers be given a grounding in Hebrew, Latin, and Greek, without returning to old England. The first reaction of most im-migrants was utter dismay. So stout a heart as Anne Hutchin-son's quailed when she first saw Boston, and she confessed that she would have turned home again but for her conviction that England was about to be destroyed by divine wrath. And she arrived as late as 1634, when Boston already had one house of proper brick.

Winthrop's beloved Margaret arrived in November 1631, and though she was fresh from the seasoned timbers and the creature comforts of her home in Groton, she loyally forbore comment on what met her eyes here. Winthrop had directed her to wait for the next return of the *Lion,* whose Captain Pierce he trusted above all others, and had left it to her as to whether she should bring baby Ann, the daughter whom he had never seen. "If thou bringest her, she will be more trouble to thee in the ship than all the rest." He had used the wrong deterrent. What mother in Israel begrudges care for her latest born? Margaret had brought her daughter, but only to bury her at sea.

The reunion of the governor with his family (for his namesake and several younger children had come, and the widow of the unfortunate Henry) was marked with affectionate ceremony. The *Lion* gave a salute of half a dozen pieces as the ship's boat took off for shore, and at the landing the waiting militia saluted again "with divers volleys of shot and three drakes." People not only from Boston but from the neighboring towns had taken the day for a holiday, and waited with gifts, "fat hogs, kids, venison, poultry, geese, partridges . . . the like joy and manifesting of love had never been seen in New England. It was a great marvel that so much people and such store of provision could be gathered at so few hours' warning." So Winthrop wrote in his journal, and publicly proclaimed November 11 as a day of thanksgiving.

4

Whatever Boston looked like, these were the years of phenomenal growth. Conditions in England were worsening for the Puritans; letters from the Bay were eagerly read and passed from hand to hand. Every year brought new settlers by the thousands.

Plymouth people were spreading into the country, founding Marshfield, Duxbury, Kingston, in order to find richer fields for their corn and better pasturage for their cattle, there being now a profitable market for both in the multiplying communities of the Bay. Even Virginia sent its shipload of corn.

Villages were springing up all over the Bay: New Towne, as Cambridge was briefly named; Saugus, presently to be rechristened Lynn; Ipswich, which became the home of Simon and Anne Bradstreet and their eight children (for in the new world Anne became fruitful, and as she rocked the cradle her mind was busy with the composing of charming verse which would win her the title of the "tenth muse lately sprung up in America"). John

Winthrop, Jr., also built a homestead in Ipswich, but to the grief of his neighbors did not abide; he was a man of extraordinary parts, and as the Bay Colony began bursting at the seams, he too looked afield for a wider scope for his talents.

If the founders of Massachusetts had taken the precaution of avoiding interference from England by bringing their charter and hence their government with them, royal authority had taken the prior precaution of confining their patent to very narrow limits. It extended from three miles north of the Merrimack to three miles south of the Charles. It was, in contrast to the grants made Virginia and Maryland, a strip hardly thirty miles wide, and even this much was in conflict with grants already made Sir Ferdinando Gorges, who was somewhat vaguely in control of the Maine fishing villages.

By 1634 Bay Colony settlers were already poised to push beyond these limits. In that year Thomas Hooker and his congregation, founders of Cambridge, applied to General Court to move out to the Connecticut.

In spring they had "complained of straitness for want of land, especially meadow," and had obtained leave to prospect about Cape Ann and the Merrimack. It was a surprise when in September their representatives announced that their choice was "the fruitfulness and commodiousness of Connecticut." Their proposal to move out of the limits of the Massachusetts patent precipitated a debate in General Court that lasted for days.

Winthrop was by then out of office. At May court Dudley had got the governorship away from him; Winthrop wasn't even deputy. He had taken his humiliation bravely, offering the new governor and his assistants hospitality in his home when they retired from their session at Boston meetinghouse. When the Connecticut issue came to a vote in September, he had the satisfaction of seeing it defeated by the assistants, though Dudley and the majority of the lower house were for it. The objections were that the Bay Colony would be weakened by the removal and the new settlement imperiled by the Dutch, who already had a fort on the river, and by Indians who were more numerous and aggressive than in Massachusetts. "The removing of a candlestick is a great judgment to be avoided."

Two years later the candlestick was removed. In June 1636 one hundred members of Hooker's congregation with their pastor at their head, set out on Massachusetts' first westering.

Several events had prepared the way. The Connecticut Indians had been visited by smallpox with appalling consequences, a clear manifestation of God's providence. Continued immigration from England was bringing in such masses that there no longer seemed any danger of weakening the colony. "That gracious, sweet, heavenly-minded and soul-ravishing minister, Mr. Thomas Shepherd" had just arrived, and his congregation was delighted at the opportunity to buy a whole village of houses ready-made.

So Hooker's flock, many of whom had "lived in delicacy and splendor in England," set forth on foot for the west, driving their cattle before them. They broke through a tangle of virgin forest where there were only Indian paths "not above one foot broad, so that a man may travel for days and never find one." There were no landmarks that they could recognize; they navigated as if at sea by compass. When they came to a river, the Chicopee, the Connecticut itself, they had to improvise rafts.

There is no intimate account of their progress; Hooker was not a man who kept journals. But a description of the labor of getting through the woods in that same year to found Concord suggests the picture. "Sometimes passing through the thickets, where their hands are forced to make way for their bodies' passage, and their feet clambering over the crossed trees. . . . The ragged bushes scratch their legs fouly, even to wearing their stockings to their bare skin in two or three hours; if they be not otherwise well-defended with boots or buskins, their flesh will be torn. . . . In the time of summer the sun casts such a reflecting heat from the sweet fern, whose scent is very strong so that some herewith have been very near fainting."

It couldn't have been so rugged all the way, for they made the hundred miles to the Connecticut in two weeks, and began the first labor of settling what came to be known as the "Connecticut towns," Windsor, Wethersfield, Hartford. The latter was close to the little fort that the Dutch called New Hope; Windsor impinged on a trading post built by Plymouth men. They ignored the Dutch, shrugged off protests from Plymouth, and set about digging in to the richest land and fairest country that anyone had yet seen in New England.

However, the beginning was not easy. The first winter was yet another starving time, for the river froze before supplies shipped by water could be brought upstream, and many of their cattle died. Some settlers perished, some scattered to English settlements planted farther down the coast, some found their way back to Massachusetts. Yet a remnant stayed the course, and Connecticut, called into being by forces more complex than the restiveness of Mr. Hooker's parish, survived to become master of its own destiny and to call Winthrop's eldest son as governor; at long last its sons, impelled by another surge of restlessness, would march to take Manhattan Island from the Dutch.

VII EXILES IN THE WILDERNESS

1

Thomas Hooker's people left the Bay of their own will. No doctrinal dispute had been involved, at least overtly. There was a hint that Hooker chafed at the proximity of another powerfully influential minister, John Cotton, who had come on the same ship with him and became "teacher," that is, second in command, at the Boston church. But this motive was kept discreetly under cover and did not arise in the disputes before General Court as to whether a whole congregation should receive its dismission from Massachusetts.

It was otherwise with a stepchild of the Bay Colony, unsteadily founded while Hooker's congregation was trying to get through its first winter. Those who settled what was known first as Providence Plantation, then as Rhode Island, and finally (in Massachusetts) as Rogues' Island, did not depart with legislative blessing. They were kicked out. Some were "warned out" as towns would regularly warn out undesirables; the leaders, Roger Williams and later Anne Hutchinson, were expelled for doctrines deemed outright heresy.

If Massachusetts was in the decade of its most vigorous growth, it was also in the decade of its greatest peril. There was intermittent fear of attack from Indians, fear of the French, to whom King Charles had allotted Nova Scotia. Above all there was fear, and for good reason, that the charter smuggled overseas and on which the colony's whole way of life depended, would be revoked. However peaceful on the surface, the situation was close to a state of war; as in other communities caught in such circumstances, Massachusetts leaders made short work of whatever tended to disunion.

There was another element in their difficulties, a wholly unanticipated surge toward something like democratic action that began almost as soon as the *Arbella* anchored. It had both economic and political aspects.

The fleet had carried about 180 laborers who were expected to work off the price of their passage as indentured servants. Owing to the impossibility of provisioning them in the first year, their masters had to release them from their bonds to shift for themselves. When spring came, and planting and a proper building program began, the servants hired themselves out. Their late masters were scandalized at the wages demanded, especially by carpenters.

Only "freemen," that is, landowners who were church members in good standing, were elected to the first session of General Court in 1631, but in time they proved as troublesome as the ungrateful laborers. By 1634 they were arrogating to themselves the exclusive right to make laws, elect officers, levy taxes; and the lower house was bitterly embroiled with the governor's assistants for claiming the right to veto their willingness to permit the Hooker congregation to remove.

This was not yet full democracy, owing to the qualification of church membership, a privilege jealously guarded and by no means given to everyone who asked for it, but it was a movement in that direction. It was probably no accident that Winthrop lost the governorship in that year. For all his "lenity," he was firmly opposed to democracy on the grounds that it was nowhere advocated in the Pentateuch.

However the greatest problem was whether King Charles would let the charter stand. The Bay Colony had enemies in England, who were pulling wires at court and exerting powerful pressures.

One highly articulate ill-wisher was a lively gentleman named Thomas Morton. Before the Puritan migration he had a plantation at Quincy, which he called Merry Mount, a thorn in the side of Plymouth. His most scandalous act was setting up a maypole

around which he and his jolly company, including Indian mates
and friends, danced with song and pagan rituals. The Pilgrims
might have put up with his maypole; what really worried them
was that the man was selling arms to the Indians.

Winthrop promptly put an end to the fun at Merry Mount and
shipped Morton back to England. There the latter published his
own irreverent account of "The New English Canaan" (from
which one learns among other things of the stature and coloration
of "Captain Shrimp" Standish) and joined the Gorges proprietors
in attacking the pretensions of the Bay authorities.

This rival claim to the territory went back to a charter issued
Sir Ferdinando Gorges in 1620, conveying to his company all the
territory between the fortieth and forty-eighth parallel, that is,
from the head of the Delaware to the north bank of the St.
Lawrence. Actual settlement, however, had been confined to fishing stations along the Maine coast, so widely scattered, and gen-
erally so impermanent, that even little Plymouth had for a time
been able to maintain a post on the Penobscot. Sir Ferdinando
had never interfered with Plymouth itself, and had consented to
the granting of the Massachusetts charter. Since the latter was so
narrowly confined, he probably anticipated a settlement no larger
than Plymouth. It was only in 1632, when he correctly foresaw
that so massive a migration could not long be kept within its assigned boundaries, that he began to work against it.

He did not succeed. The Puritans had influence too, and at one
point Charles went so far as publicly to commend the new colony.
But the pressures and anxieties continued. It is only fair to remember that at the height of the Hutchinson controversy the king
was on the point of demanding the return of the charter and was
deterred only by events in England from enforcing his demand.

2

Roger Williams had come to Boston with his wife Mary in February 1631 on the deliverance ship *Lion*. The governor noted
him in his journal as "a godly minister," and never lost that opinion in spite of the disputes that soon divided them.

Williams was probably then in his mid-twenties; he was a recent graduate of Cambridge, and so richly endowed as a preacher that he would have been given the pulpit in Boston (John Wilson was back in England, where he was having his hands full trying to persuade his wife to join him in America) but for an obscure point of doctrine. The controversy generated such heat that when he was called to Salem, Boston interfered, and the young minister left for Plymouth Plantation.

Plymouth had been unlucky in its preachers. Its congregation could never have held with the Puritan doctrine that the child who dies unbaptized goes to hell, for they had started with no one qualified to baptize. Their beloved John Robinson had died without seeing America, and they had been unfortunate in the ministers that had later been sent to them. One became deranged and had to be sent home. Another had lied about his qualifications and caused scandal by his attentions to female members of the congregation. The town had been less shocked by his adulteries than by the fact that he had evolved a means of intercourse which precluded conception.

Now at last they had a man of genius, tireless in his zeal for the Lord, stainless in his personal life, and equipped with a gift for vivid parable that made him an incomparable preacher. And he didn't do. Unhappily for Plymouth, he was a young genius and full of young rashness. His listeners may or may not have objected to his heterodox conviction that "to punish a man for any matter of his conscience is persecution"; but they did object, and all Massachusetts with them, when he denounced the king's patent by which everyone held land taken from the Indians.

He had become a firm friend of the Indians about Plymouth; earlier than John Eliot, later Apostle to the red men, Williams studied their language, and reviewed the injustices inflicted upon them. When he attacked the patent, it was considered close to high treason, not only to the Plymouth people, always worried about the validity of their own, since they had not settled where it authorized them to settle, but the Bay authorities, who had plenty to worry them in the machinations in London. Plymouth got rid of him, and Williams went back to Salem, bought a house, and settled down.

But not for long. He was now a marked man, questionable in doctrine and subversive in action, and the fact that he captivated church members in Salem, including the fiery John Endicott, was frightening. A crisis arose when Endicott, supposedly under Williams' influence, cut the cross from the king's colors on the grounds that it was a Romish symbol. Puritans at large deplored Romish symbols, but this was *lèse-majesté*. Even some of Endicott's militia refused to train under the mutilated standard, and the scandal convulsed the whole colony. In October 1634 the seditious preacher who had inspired such conduct was called to General Court, accused of preaching "divers new and dangerous opinions," and given six weeks to "depart out of this jurisdiction."

The trial had been brief, businesslike, and attracted little attention. Williams was obscure enough to be allowed to spend some days in Boston, where he fell in the company of a youth whose friendship was to be of high importance to his future. This was Henry Vane, who had been the despair of his father because of his interest in Puritanism. Purportedly on the advice of King Charles himself, Sir Henry had sent him to Massachusetts in the hope that exposure to the sect at its most rampant would cure him.

When Williams met him, the youth, barely twenty-two, and as impetuous as the young minister, was in the first flush of his enthusiasm. Boston had fallen in love with his patrician bearing, his fair countenance framed in long curls, and his zeal for the Puritan cause, and had promptly elected him governor. It was not yet apparent that there was something in the nature of this gifted youth that would be drawn as by a magnet to the trouble-making characters that the body politic would be impelled to cast out, first Roger Williams, presently Anne Hutchinson.

Williams' friendship with Vane attracted no attention at the time, but his continued presence did when he remained in the colony so long, not holding his peace, but speaking his mind publicly and loudly, that the court ordered him seized to be deported to England. Only then did he accept exile and begin "a sorrowful winter's flight into the wilderness," taking a course southwest of the Plymouth settlements. It was January when he set out on foot, and to the end of his days he would remember the cold and hunger of that experience.

He was not alone. A young servant, Thomas Angell, went with him; he had Indian friends who probably nursed him through an illness, for he had been ailing when he left Salem; and when he stopped to stay out the rest of an unusually stormy winter on the banks of the Seekonk, he was joined by four others, two of them outcasts, and all of them poor and even less prepared than he to undertake the building of a new settlement.

When in spring they broke the ground for planting, they were interrupted by a message from Governor Winslow of Plymouth. It was a regretful message; under pressure from Massachusetts, Winslow was forced to warn them that they were within the Plymouth patent and must not stay. The exiles loaded what effects they had into a canoe, paddled it to the opposite shore, and broke ground anew in the place they called Providence.

Thus the beginning of the colony that Massachusetts would presently dub "the latrine of New England." It was only the beginning, but when a year later Massachusetts cast out a headstrong woman and her adherents, there was a place of sorts for them to go. Neither then nor after, when thanks to Vane this colony also had its patent (these things, it seemed, were after all necessary), would Williams turn away any human being exiled for his devotion to his faith.

3

Anne Hutchinson embodied both the revolutionary explosiveness that nearly tore the Bay Colony apart while it was still getting started, and the tremendous vitality of purpose that would make it endure.

She if anyone had been guided to America by no hope of material gain but by an inner voice and an inner light. In England she had gone through a prolonged travail of spirit, asking herself who was the antichrist ("Was it the Turk only?") and praying for redemption from atheism. She had turned from the covenant of works to the covenant of grace. "It was revealed unto me that the ministers of England were these antichrists. . . . The voice of my beloved I have distinguished from the voices of strangers." The voice spoke to her most clearly though her minister John Cotton, and her brother-in-law John Wheelwright. When both of them were silenced in England, and emigrated to America, "it was revealed to me that I must go thither also, and there I should be persecuted and suffer much trouble."

In spite of the delicately erotic phrasing of her statement of faith, there was nothing scandalous in all this. A nun might speak thus, and though Anne's devotion to Cotton was to embarrass his ministry in America, not the bitterest enemy of either would connect it with carnal impropriety. Anne Hutchinson was no sex-starved maiden lady, nor were her fervors the gropings of adolescence. She came to America in 1634 with the dignity of a mother in Israel. Already well along in her thirties, she had sons already grown and a womb still fruitful.

She also had, necessarily, a husband. Not much is said of William Hutchinson, and that little has contemptuous overtones. But he had good repute in England and he had means. He built in the better part of Boston, near the spring whose sweet waters had induced Winthrop to remove from Charlestown, close to the present City Hall, and served for a season in General Court. There is something remarkable in his general self-effacement. In a day when women, unless crowned, were voiceless, he in response to Anne's inner voice had undergone the drastic step of emigration, as he would later share her lot as exile. He had faith in his gifted wife.

When Anne recovered from her dismay at her first look at Boston, she threw herself into the manifold tasks facing the pioneer women and found energy to help those less robust than she. The mother of many, she had great experience in nursing and midwifery. Gladly she shared her skills with her neighbors and quickly became loved and influential.

It was natural that a woman so deeply religious should also impart spiritual instruction. This she did not do in the bleak meeting house, still roofed with combustible thatch—how different from the mellowed stones and stained glass of her native Alford. Paul himself had forbidden women to speak in meeting; but Paul had said nothing to deter a woman from gathering women about her to discuss more public discourse. This Anne did, and the women began to flock to her home to hear her explain the most recent sermon.

At times there were said to be as many as eighty gathered in the Hutchinson household to hear her "prophesy." What kind of house had William built her to accommodate so many? The chances are that as Anne's talks became popular, her followers assembled out-of-doors, as John Wilson had first preached under a great tree in Charlestown. In the open air it needed no tale-bearing to inform authority of the content of Anne's discourse. One need only linger in the neighborhood with open ear, and John Winthrop's house was just across the way.

Wilson himself at first approved this informal ministry. He had finally persuaded his wife to come to America, and now occupied his rightful place in the Boston pulpit, with the assistance of Cotton as teacher. Anne had begun by summarizing sermons for women whose household cares had detained them from Sabbath meeting. No one objected to that or to the enthusiasm she aroused, making the women doubly attentive when they next came to meeting in person. Even when Anne supplemented her summaries with glosses of her own, there was no protest until she began to speak of an "inner voice" and to distinguish between ministers who were "sealed" and those who were not.

Only then did her popularity become disturbing. Men were listening to her and attempting to win proselytes. "Come along with me," they were saying, "and I'll bring you to a woman that preaches better gospel than any of your blackcoats that have been at the Niniversity, a woman of another kind of spirit, who hath had many revelations of things to come, and for my part I should rather hear such a one that speaks from the mere motion of the spirit without any study at all, than any of your learned scholars, although they may be fuller of scripture."

Another kind of spirit? What was it? Her disciples did not take notes, not even Henry Vane, who was said sometimes to sit at

her right hand when she prophesied. The emphasis on the "motion
of the spirit" and the implied contempt of "learned scholars . . .
fuller of scripture" suggests the Quakers who were to come;
Anne's follower Mary Dyer was to join them. Like the Quakers,
Anne may have paid more attention to the New Testament than
most Puritan preachers. The latter were almost Jewish in their
preoccupation with the Pentateuch, and their references to Christ
made little of the Saviour who counseled forgiveness to the degree
of seventy times seven and much of "Christ thy King [who]
crushed with a rod of iron the pomp and pride of men."

The word for Anne's followers in their time was "opinionist."
She herself was not guiltless of "pomp and pride." For pomp she
had the presence at her meetings of the dazzling young governor;
her pride became manifest in her distinguishing between ministers who were "sealed" and those who were not. Her list of the
former was short and exclusive: John Cotton and John Wheelwright. Real trouble began when the Boston congregation, now
almost wholly on her side, began a movement to install Cotton as
minister and Wheelwright as his teacher.

She made a scandal one day in Sabbath meeting. She had expected Cotton to preach; when Wilson took the pulpit, she gathered her skirts about her and rustled out, and after a small
hesitation most of the women followed her. Honest John Wilson
deserved better than this. But his utterance was thick, his wit had
more of the bludgeon than the rapier, and he did not speak with
the "voice of the beloved." At least one church member, John
Winthrop, was wroth, and as the plot to install Wheelwright de-
veloped, preparations were made to investigate his doctrinal
purity.

4

During this time, except in Boston, the luster that had shone
on young Governor Vane had conspicuously diminished. At first
the colony had excelled itself to do him honor. When he made a
public appearance, at General Court, at Sabbath meeting, there
was a roll of drums and four sergeants walked before him carrying

their halberds. The youth rose to such ceremonies with a grave dignity that charmed every beholder. But rising to his responsibilities as chief magistrate was another matter. Wisdom had not yet ripened in him; he was new to Massachusetts, and baffled by its already intricate political convolutions. Stung by his knowledge that his popularity was on the wane, he went before General Court and asked it to accept his resignation and let him go home.

The morning that the court took to debate so unprecedented a request may have been the most trying of Vane's whole life, not excepting the occasion sixteen years later when he went to the scaffold. He was to prove himself steadfast on a wider stage and in deadlier situations; but during this morning of suspense, when one of the assistants remarked reproachfully that it was no light thing to lose such a governor in time of danger, the young man burst into tears.

He dried his eyes and stayed the course, though now everything went against him. A secret synod of the ministry held Wheelwright, whom he defended and admired, guilty of doctrinal impurities, and Boston was in an uproar. For this reason, and again contrary to Vane's will, the May session of General Court and the elections were held across the Charles in Cambridge.

It was a hot session, both meteorologically and politically. Legislators and voters gathered in an open field, in such disorder that chubby Pastor Wilson climbed a tree and exhorted them from its branches. Members of his parish had brought a petition condemning the judgment on Wheelwright, and it was Vane's will that its reading be the first order of business. He was overruled. Deputy Governor Winthrop insisted that by law the election came first, and he was supported by representatives from outlying communities who had not been exposed to Anne's teaching, and knew only what their pastors had told them of Wheelwright, and were ready to believe that Boston had gone mad. (It was not the last time that Massachusetts would overrule beleaguered Boston.)

The stormy election that followed completed Vane's humiliation. It was not only that Winthrop was chosen in his place with Dudley as deputy; Vane had had enough of that office. It was that when Boston chose him as one of their representatives, the choice was promptly overruled. It was done, to be sure, on a technicality, and Boston later got its delegates, but the reproof was obvious. Vane did not serve his term in General Court. He went home that summer, and when Anne faced her own hour of trial, he was not there to defend her. It was just as well; he could have done nothing for her and he knew it.

Boston did not take its snubbing amiably. When Winthrop looked for the four sergeants to serve as honor guard on his public appearances, he met with a rude refusal. He did not, it seemed, meet the sergeants' specifications for quality. He had got along without such ceremony before, but he wasn't going to be out-classed by a stripling; he equipped two of his own servants with halberds and walked to meeting in due dignity.

5

In his earlier terms Winthrop had often been accused of "len-ity." He acknowledged the charge but defended himself on the grounds that "a bruised reed ye shall not break." The colony was new and the settlers discouraged by illness, want, and inadequate shelter; severity would only discourage them further, as had been demonstrated often enough in early Virginia.

But now conditions had changed. People had roofs over their heads and enjoyed rough comforts under them. Their fields were yielding, their livestock multiplying. They did not want for the simpler creature comforts. At the same time the colony was in peril. To the north the French in Nova Scotia were a constant worry, and to the south the Pequot Indians, most aggressive of the Connecticut nations, were on the march. They had recently committed a multiple murder on the Sound, and Massachusetts was about to dispatch militia, with good Wilson serving as chap-lain, to take the situation in hand. Worst of all, in London the Gorges faction seemed to be on the point of success in inducing Charles to revoke the charter. The present turmoils, the divisive spirit that had all but split Boston from the rest of the colony, compounded the peril. It was no time for a governor to indulge in his natural impulses to lenity.

In the fall the subversive Wheelwright was summoned from his parish in Braintree, brought before General Court, and banished. Williams had been given six weeks to settle his affairs and get out; Wheelwright was given two. It was his turn to begin a "sorrowful winter's journey." He went into the Gorges settlements north of the Piscataqua, and eventually settled with a few followers in what became Exeter, New Hampshire.

Now it was Anne's turn. The departure of Vane and Wheelwright had not silenced her. Boston still thronged to her meetings as if she, not Wilson, were its proper pastor, and they were so vehemently with her that trying her there was impolitic. General Court again prepared to meet for the purpose in Cambridge, where her adherents could not easily pack the court. Lest they have such ideas, other precautions were taken; heavy penalties were prescribed for anyone defaming court procedure, and sixty Boston citizens were disarmed.

On a bleak November day court assembled in the bare little wooden meetinghouse, and Anne was called to stand before it. She was with child, though in so early a stage of pregnancy that even if she had not been bundled up in her voluminous skirts and cloak, her condition would not have been apparent. Everyone was necessarily bundled up, for November had come in bitter cold, and there was neither then nor long after any provision for warming a meetinghouse. However, though her judges were stern, they were not merciless; presently, one saw marks of "bodily infirmity" in Anne's haggard face and had a chair fetched.

It was a tribute to the woman that the most distinguished men of Massachusetts had come to hear her case, not only the forty members of the legislature, the governor, his deputy and assistants, but nearly all the ministers of the Bay. John Endicott, who had so recently dared mutilate the king's colors, was here as representative. So was Williams' fiery successor in Salem Church, Hugh Peters. Even Thomas Hooker was in from Connecticut.

She faced friends too, notably her idolized John Cotton, but he was in a quandary. He would do as much for her as he dared, but how much could he dare? Like Wheelwright he had received the dangerous distinction of her "seal," and other ministers, excluded from this peculiar grace, eyed him narrowly. It would take little to bring accusation upon himself, and then he would be following Wheelwright into the wilderness. A man in his fifties, Cotton had no urge for further pioneering; Boston was rugged enough. Even so, at first he summoned the courage to raise his voice in behalf of Anne; that he did not defend her to the end was partly her fault.

She began with wisdom and restraint, speaking only as questions were put to her, and answering them well. Though she protested that divine authority did not forbid her sessions with the women, she agreed to desist. "If it please you by authority to put it down, I will freely let you. For I am subject to your authority." But she would not agree that she was guilty in ascribing to Cotton the covenant of grace, and when Winthrop rather harshly pressed the point, she lost her temper. She was, according to one observer, not an "antitype of Daniel, but rather of the lions after they were let loose." And when the ministers testified against her, she outraged them by demanding that they do so under oath.

None of this, however, would have incurred worse than censure. Her suggestion that the ministers be sworn was contemptuously thrust aside as irrelevant, since this was not trial by jury. In everything else she said, Cotton was able to defend her. But it might have been better for Anne if he had not spoken. The sound of the beloved voice released the restraints with which she had for the most part guarded her tongue. Before the governor and his deputy, before General Court and the ministers of Massachusetts, Anne began to prophesy.

At first she only testified to the religious experience that most devout Puritans had shared. But she went on to the heresy of "immediate revelation," and she ended with defiance. "Take heed what ye go about to do unto me. You have power over my body, but the Lord Jesus hath power over my body and soul. . . . I fear none but the great Jehovah, which hath foretold me of these things, and I do verily believe that He will deliver me out of your hands. Therefore take heed how you proceed against me; for I know that for this . . . God will ruin you and your posterity and this whole state."

It was a chilling defiance. Winthrop for one knew better than she how close possible ruin was. But this was not the subject of this session. A vital question was raised: "How do you know that it was God that hath revealed these things to you and not Satan?"

"How did Abraham," retorted Anne, "know that it was God that bid him offer his son, being a breach of the sixth commandment?"

"By an immediate revelation," said Dudley.

"So to me, by an immediate revelation."

By these words the woman condemned herself. Puritans did not hold with immediate revelation. What had been necessary in Abraham's time was so no longer now that God had spoken to all mankind through sacred Scriptures so clearly and unmistakably that interpreting His will was only a matter of sound logic. Theology was an exact science, practiced by men carefully trained in its disciplines.

Governor Winthrop spoke thoughtfully: "These disturbances that have come among the Germans have all been grounded upon revelations; and so they that have vented them have stirred up their hearers to take up arms against their princes and cut the throats of one another." He spoke from his knowledge of the bitter religious wars that were currently tearing the German states apart; he spoke from his knowledge of what was going on in his own Boston, where good men turned rebellious had to be disarmed.

When the vote was taken as to whether Anne should be cast out of the colony as "unfit for our society," only three dared abstain, and Cotton was not one of them. But court was merciful. Winter had come early, and sending the woman into immediate exile would have been a death sentence. They let her spend the winter in the household of the Roxbury pastor Thomas Welde, while her husband went with other of her followers to make ready a home for her in Rhode Island. This time he could not offer her the fine and commodious house he had built in Boston; the best he could manage while winter lasted was to improve a cave in a bank at Aquidneck by fitting it with timbers and thatch as in the first settlements at Salem. He worked at the task lovingly; nothing that General Court could do could shake his faith in his "dear saint."

For Anne it was a grim winter. She was frequently visited not by her friends but by the ministers, coming to pray over her, exhort her, and attempt to snatch this brand from the burning.

In one moment of weakness, when Boston Church was preparing to excommunicate her, like Joan of Arc she recanted, but again like Joan she recanted her recantation.

She went in spring, worn out, and when during the summer she gave birth it was a monstrous birth. This providence was of high interest to the Bay Colony ministers, who to hear them tell it, pored over the multiple fetuses, as many according to Welde as the errors of her soul. Significantly two of her followers, Mary Dyer, young wife of a Boston milliner, and the midwife Jane Hawkins, had also given birth to monsters. Such events were often ascribed to witches as the result of carnal intercourse with the devil, and Jane Hawkins was called a witch. However, the season for witch hunting had not yet opened in Massachusetts, and just this charge was never made against Anne.

Winthrop made note in his journal when providence was visited on other of Anne's followers, like getting drowned, or lost in a storm. Much later, retribution was visited on Anne herself. Her husband died in 1642 and without him she found Rhode Island too close to Boston for comfort. The ministers wouldn't let her alone; thinking only of her soul's salvation, they came to exhort her. At last Anne gathered her daughters and servants (an elder son was in Boston) and moved into the Dutch jurisdiction, close to what Massachusetts would consider the justly named Hell Gate. And there the Indians killed her.

Thus was Anne proved a false prophet. Jehovah did not save her, nor did the ruin she had forecast come upon the Bay during the lifetime of most of the men who heard her. Perhaps God agreed with Winthrop that giving free vent to voices such as Anne's would at this stage lead only to anarchy; or perhaps He recognized that Anne was as stiff-necked as her judges, that had she stood in their place she might well have banished the likes of John Wilson. Fast-moving events in England would rescue Massachusetts for half a century from the surrender of its charter; the commonwealth would prosper and grow strong, confirmed in self-righteousness and what it called theocracy, the direct rule of God on earth.

VIII SISTER COLONIES ON
THE CHESAPEAKE

1

From afar King Charles looked on the contentions that rent his colonies and gave utterance to royal exasperation. Surely, said he, there was so much "vastness" in the land across the seas that people could manage to get along in it.

His wrath was not directed at anything so petty as the affairs of Anne Hutchinson and Roger Williams, but at an act of rebellion. The Virginians had cast out their governor, not an elected governor as in Massachusetts, where one had to rise early to know who held office today, but an appointee of the Lord's Anointed. The House of Burgesses, which a decade and a half ago had begun so diffidently, almost apologetically, like pupils looking over their shoulder to see if Teacher is pleased, had committed an act of revolution.

Its scale was petty. Virginia was defending one man's claim to one island. Its cause was inglorious; what Virginia most urgently objected to was the religion of the new claimants to the island; they were Papists.

Virginia was still a century and a half removed from any notion of adopting a statute of religious liberty. The concept of freedom of conscience was rare in an age when people cared very much about their creeds. When after prolonged searching you have found your way to the eternal verities, isn't it impiety for you to put up with people who have not? Thomas Dudley of Massachusetts was not alone in decrying religious tolerance as an evil. Virginia was as emphatic in its support of the Establishment of the

Church of England, and Virginians took it hard when Papists came in to settle the head of the Chesapeake and loose Jesuits among the Indians.

The new settlers were, to be sure, not wholly or even predominantly Papist, but the principle of toleration by which they proposed to live in amity with the Protestants who came with them was an offense. Also they were taking land which had been included in the Virginia patent. To this combination of circumstances Virginians reacted with violence.

In 1635 the colony which had had the hardest birth of any had the vigor and audacity to produce the first American revolution. It couldn't carry it through; nor did the action impede the progress of a settlement dedicated to the proposition that the lion and the lamb could lie down together, provided divergent creeds courteously respected each other's differences. In spite of the hullabaloo from down the bay, the birth of Maryland was nearly painless. For that its founders could indeed thank Virginia, whose long years of travail had instructed them in what mistakes to avoid.

2

The idea that the colony should permit freedom of conscience had something to do with the fact that its founder had recently embraced one of England's more unpopular religions. In 1625 George Calvert, Secretary of State under James, became a Catholic and prepared to retire to private life. Disturbed at losing so able a public servant, the king induced him to remain in office as a member of the Privy Council, and raised him to the peerage as Lord Baltimore. But when Charles succeeded James, the newly created peer felt himself excused from any further direct service to the state.

For years he had been fascinated by the new world. He had pored over the records of discovery like Hakluyt's *Voyages* and *Purchase His Pilgrims*, had studied the various "relations" of John Smith and the pamphlets put out by the Plymouth colony. In

1609 he had been a subscriber to the London Company of Virginia; after the founding of Plymouth he became a member of the New England Council, and presently sponsored a settlement on land granted him in 1621. It bore the romantic name of Avalon and lay "far from the sun," in Newfoundland. In 1627 he went across for a personal inspection, and pleased with what he saw, shipped thither bricks for the construction of a notable manor house. Next year he took up residence with forty new settlers, Lady Calvert, and all his sons except the eldest. It would be the fate of this son, named Cecilius for the great Earl of Salisbury, under whom Calvert had served his apprenticeship as statesman, to play a decisive role in the new world without ever laying eyes upon it.

There were, however, two things wrong with Avalon. One was the harrassment of the French, who already had pretensions in the northern territories; the other was the climate. The French could be fought off, though this was a bitter necessity for a man of peace. "I came to build and settle and sow," he wrote home, "and I am fallen to fighting Frenchmen." But the climate was incorrigible. It was well that he had had the forethought to provide himself with a mansion, for during his first winter, when, of a colony of a hundred, fifty were often sick at a time, it had to serve as a hospital. As such it must have been efficiently conducted, for only ten patients died, a remarkably low mortality rate for a new colony. What troubled Baltimore was not the sickness but the prospect. "From the middlest of October to the middlest of May there is a sad face of winter upon all this land," he wrote King Charles. "I am determined to commit this place to fishermen that are able to encounter storms and hard weather and to remove myself with some forty persons to your majesty's domain, Virginia." He asked for a "precinct of land with such privileges as the king your father, my gracious lord, was pleased to grant me here."

On his way home in October 1629 he visited Jamestown, to which he had already sent most of his family. Governor John Harvey made him warmly welcome; but Harvey was almost a minority of one. Other Virginians took violent exception to his faith, his birth, and his plan.

As a "Roman," his faith was that of the enemy Spanish, whose settlement in Florida had always been too close for comfort. As to birth, he hadn't been a lord long enough to satisfy Virginian notions of nobility; his title went back only four years and his father had been a grazier. He was no more a blue blood than was John Smith on the basis of that absurd coat of arms with the three Turks' heads. Jamestown, Virginians now recalled, had been founded by knights and nobles whose lines went back for centuries. George Percy had been the son not of the first Earl of Northumberland but the eighth. He was a younger son, and his personal claim to eminence was tenuous, but so were the memories of Virginians, who had as yet no Colonial Dames to collate their records. They knew only that their origins had been noble, as this upstart's had not been. They snubbed him.

His plan to settle land included in the sacred Virginia patent was unthinkable. One Thomas Tindall represented general sentiment when he called his lordship a liar to his face and offered to knock him down. He had to be punished, but the punishment was light: two hours in the pillory. The Governor's Council, acting with more finesse, got rid of his lordship by requiring him to take the oath of supremacy, which as a Catholic he could not do.

Baltimore went home to consult his majesty, and though he was never to see America again, he achieved for his heirs an almost royal domain; he got them a palatinate.

3

The arrangement took time. Charles himself demurred on the grounds that Calvert, having impaired his health and nearly exhausted his fortune in Newfoundland, should now remain in England. But the man would not be denied. Where to allot the land became the only problem.

Baltimore's first choice was Carolina, and it's a pity he couldn't have had it. Owing to an odd set of circumstances, the settlement of Carolina was to be blocked for many decades. In Jamestown he had already taken the measure of the Virginian objection to his moving in this direction, and when he got to England, the issue had been closed by the granting of a patent to Attorney General Sir Robert Heath. The latter was to be the most luckless of colonizers. His first shipment of settlers somehow got no farther than Virginia, and complications in England prevented his trying again. First his majesty suspected him of secret sympathy with the Puritans and deprived him of office; then the Puritans, when they came to power, impeached him for high treason and excluded him from the Act of Oblivion. Eventually he would die in exile and his patent go by default. But as of 1629 it was in force, and Baltimore had to look elsewhere. He looked to the head of the Chesapeake.

Charles had sound, statesmanlike reasons for encouraging settlement there. The Dutch, who for some years had held trading posts on the Hudson, were taking an interest in the Delaware. A strategically placed English settlement would deter them from further expansion southward. The Chesapeake had been included in the original Virginia patent, but given the "vastness" of America, Charles did not give that a thought, nor need he, since technically the original patent had been invalidated by the dissolution of the London Company in 1624. Virginians would not see it that way, but at the moment they were not being heard from. His majesty was free to consider a name. It must be a Christian name, not one of the pagan designations that the Puritans oddly went for, like Massachusetts or Connecticut, which rang strangely in English ears. He would honor Mary, his queen. His first choice was Mariana, but at Baltimore's suggestion he settled for Terra Marieae, or Mary Land.

The form of the grant was a novelty in any new-world colony south of the short-lived Avalon, though it would set a precedent for the future. Baltimore was made lord proprietor of a palatinate, an institution devised in medieval England when it was expedient to give unusual powers to the proprietors of border territories. In Maryland the Baltimores would have more autonomy than the royal colony of Virginia or the elected governors of Massachusetts, who though given to acting as if they were independent of England, were subject to their own electorates. There was a safeguard against feudal autocracy in a provision in the charter for an assembly for the expression of the will of the freemen of the province, and eventually the Baltimores would be incommoded by the energy with which the freemen would make the most of this provision. In the laying out of the boundary there was no reference to Indian rights, and Virginian claims were acknowledged only in the stipulation that the lands occupied must be those "hitherto uncultivated."

Dear to Lord Baltimore's heart and indispensable to his purpose was liberty of conscience. Unlike all other English colonies except Providence, which had not yet been founded, in Maryland there was to be separation of church and state and freedom of worship for Christians, be they Catholic or Protestant. This idealism had its practical side. Baltimore wanted a place where men of his own faith could worship freely, but he was going to have to enlist recruits, to find people willing to invest in the land, and he knew that many or most of these would be Protestants.

The charter was confirmed to George Lord Baltimore on April 15, 1632, and on that day he died. In June it was reconfirmed to the second Lord Baltimore, the twenty-six-year-old Cecilius Calvert, who began at once the arduous task of arranging to settle Maryland.

His problems were manifold, and it was two years before he began his colony. Under the charter, the settlers were to be transported at the proprietor's expense, and family resources were no longer adequate for such an enterprise. It was necessary to advertise for adventurers who would accept title to two thousand acres of good land in return for the cost of transporting five able-bodied men fully provisioned and equipped. Virginia figured in these notices as an added inducement; thanks to its proximity Marylanders could count on buying their livestock in the new world if they brought with them a surplus of wines, clothing, and fancy groceries to use in trade. The advertisements were carefully phrased and offered nothing that could not be delivered. The trouble was that friends of Virginia saw them too, and before the actual sailing late in 1633 were in full cry against the enterprise.

The passengers went aboard the capacious 360-ton *Ark* and her little companion, the 60-ton *Dove* in August, but it was November before they could sail. The knowledge that there were Catholics among them unleashed wild speculation and made for expensive delay. One report that the women were nuns en route for Spain and the men recruits for the Spanish army caused the ships to be pursued and searched.

They were off at last, separated for a time by storms, reunited in the West Indies, and together when they dropped anchor at Point Comfort. This stop had not been on the itinerary. In London, Cecilius was well aware that the Virginians "would stand but our heavy friends" and that little could be expected of them "but blows." In sending his brother Leonard Calvert as governor, he had ordered him to enter the Virginian capes by the eastern shore, giving a wide berth to Point Comfort. However, the ships not only stopped but remained under the guns for more than a week. Governor Harvey visited them and cordially promised supplies. They also met William Claiborne, who had signed a petition to England: "No Papists have been suffered to settle their abode amongst us, and continuance thereof we humbly implore." He informed them that the Indians were waiting in arms for the new settlers and six Spanish ships were on the way to attack. "This rumor," commented one of the passengers, Father Andrew White, "was most like to have begun with himself."

4

Warnings and jealousies were forgotten in the wonder of the lovely land that opened around the *Ark* and the *Dove* as they moved up the Chesapeake in early March. "This is the sweetest and greatest river I have ever seen . . . the Thames is but a little finger to it," exclaimed Father White when he saw the mouth of the Potomac. He noted the abundance of "solid firm ground" in the place of marshes, the stands of fine timber, not choked with undergrowth but "commonly so far distant from each other as a coach and four horses might travel without molestation."

They came to what they named Herne Island, from "the infinite swarms" of herons that possessed it. As it had been with the women on the *Mayflower* when they rounded Cape Cod, the Maryland women were itching to wash several months' accumulation. They had their washday, but it was a near disaster. Somehow in getting them down the side of the ships the shallop that was to set them ashore overturned and "we had almost lost our maids. . . . The linen they went to wash was much of it lost, which is no small matter in these parts."

The men went ashore to consider the island for planting. It was too small, only four hundred acres. Governor Leonard reserved it as a fort to command the river, which was narrow here, but on Lady Day, March 25, he had a cross erected and "with devotion took solemn possession of the country." Father White celebrated his first Mass in the new land.

Meanwhile Indian scouts had silently followed the ships. Claiborne had not been lying about their concern. The delay at Point Comfort had given them time to take the measure of the *Ark* and warn their emperor at Pascatoway of the approach of "a canoe as large as an island with so many men as trees in a wood." His majesty had ordered signal fires lighted throughout the country, and when the ships reached the Potomac, he was waiting with five hundred bowmen. The governor deferred plans for settlement while he detoured the *Dove* to Pascatoway for a ceremonial call.

The emperor was willing to negotiate. Nervously his warriors looked on while he went aboard with noble disregard of danger and disappeared into the great cabin for a parley. It took a long time; tensions mounted on shore and the bowmen began to murmur. The emperor had to come on deck to reassure them.

Inside the cabin the conference went amicably, though not on the emperor's part with enthusiasm. Through the services of Captain Henry Fleet, who had lived among the Indians and agreed to serve the new colony as interpreter for a share in the beaver trade, the white chief and the red came to an agreement; the latter would place no obstacles in the way of settlement.

Other Indians were meantime finding courage to come close enough to the *Ark* at St. Clement Bay to ask "where that tree should grow out of which so great a canoe should be hewn," their own acquaintance with ship's carpentry being limited to the construction of dugouts. When the pinnace returned, plans were made for the "sitting down." Captain Fleet recommended St. Marys as a proper seat and opened negotiations with the Indians there.

These people, unlike the emperor, were delighted to welcome the Englishmen. It was not alone that the newcomers paid well in bolts of cloth, axes, hoes, and knives, but their presence offered protection against an old enemy, the Susquehannas. Wigwams and longhouses were offered, so that planting need not wait on building. Seed corn was shared, and Indian women gladly instructed the Englishwomen in the cooking of that notable dish corn pone. The summer passed in industry and good fellowship, and when the harvest was in, the Indians, as had been the agreement, withdrew to other quarters. Within six short months Maryland was securely planted.

It had been done with phenomenally little difficulty, no starving time, little sickness, very few deaths. They had been blessed by providence and their own good management. The expensive delays in England had brought them here in a more healthful season than they had originally chosen. The bluff high above the river, well provided with fresh water, was not subject to the miasmas of marshy Jamestown. Many settlers had already had their "seasoning" and experience of how to take hold in a new colony, for a number of Lord Baltimore's recruits were people who had gone back to England from a first attempt at planting in Virginia. There were none of the religious dissensions that were making life in New England so lively and so difficult, though the majority, probably most of the servants and many of the gentry, were Protestant. Some might well have had misgivings about committing themselves to Catholic leadership, and must have worried about guilt by association when they were hindered so

often in leaving England. They were not, however, the more pro-
testing sort of Protestants, and the Catholics had been instructed
to avoid any egregious show of their own ritual. Masses were
privately celebrated; Father White found a wigwam for this purpose. The Protestants could have what divine services they
pleased.

The colonists fitted smoothly into their new life; both they and
the Indians kept their promises. Maryland prospered, and might
well have become one of those happy communities that have no
history, but for the furious jealousy of some Virginians.

5

The Virginian most concerned was William Claiborne. Acquainted with Smith in England, he had come to Virginia in
1621, in time to share the perils of the massacre. In the punitive
expeditions against the Indians in 1624 he had been in command.
He had played an important part in the expansion of the colony
by his work as Royal Surveyor, and since 1625 had been, as Secretary of State, an ex-officio member of the Governor's Council.
He had become a true Virginian, as much at home in the forest
as in the infant capital of Jamestown; and now that the colony
was soundly established, he looked forward to a program of virile
expansion in which he would play his part as empire builder.

Just as the fifty-year-old first Lord Baltimore was nursing his
colony through the winter at Avalon, Claiborne, ten years his
junior, had received from the Virginia governor sole authority to
explore the Chesapeake and trade with the Indians for fur and
corn. When Baltimore visited Jamestown to find land nearer the
sun, Claiborne's license had just been renewed, and he had plans
for planting Kent Island, high up in the bay.

His lordship's unconcealed intentions and the encouragement
he had from the new governor, Sir John Harvey, thoroughly
alarmed Claiborne. That the intruder had been diverted from
Carolina was no reassurance, for now he would inevitably look
north, to Claiborne's private sphere of influence. Claiborne put

his name to the letter petitioning against Catholic infiltration, and then, abandoning his plans for immediate settlement of Kent Island, left the servants and cattle he had collected at Kecoughtan, while he hurried to London to keep an eye on the Calverts. It was perhaps a mistake; his claim would have been sounder if he had effected a *fait accompli*. But Lord Baltimore, favorite of two monarchs, was too formidable an adversary to be given a free hand.

Nothing that the friends of Virginia did could prevent the grant to Lord Baltimore, but Claiborne did manage to get a royal commission licensing him not to plant but to traffic for furs and corn by land and sea in all parts of America "for which there is not already a patent granted to others for the sole trade." It was not what he wanted, but the clause in Baltimore's patent making it apply only to land hitherto uncultivated gave him a chance. He got home as fast as he could, leaving others to continue the protest and get an inconclusive decree from the Star Chamber to "leave Lord Baltimore to his patent and the other parties to the course of the law." Legal processes in England took time; before the newcomers arrived in the Chesapeake, Claiborne planned to invalidate their patent by demonstrating that they were moving in on land already occupied and planted.

His men and herd of cattle, the latter somewhat expanded by calving during his absence, still awaited him in Kecoughtan. He got them aboard the nearest pinnace, moved them up the bay to Kent Island, and worked with speed to achieve a planting. By the time the *Ark* and *Dove* were in the Chesapeake, Kent Island was a plantation of sorts. Except for the cows, the personnel was probably exclusively masculine, but that had been so with the first planting at Jamestown. The ground had been broken, shelters erected, and even fruit trees planted. All this, added to the trip to London, represented a considerable capital outlay, and any popish pretender who supposed that Claiborne would give it up without a fight would be instructed otherwise.

The Calvert family was not ignorant of this venture. The second Lord Baltimore had given it thought and charged his brother to effect a reconciliation. Claiborne was to be courteously invited to confer with the governor, promised "encouragement in his planting," and asked only to "conform to Lord Baltimore's patent." If he were recalcitrant, he should remain unmolested for a year pending further instructions from England.

Claiborne could have prospered as well under Maryland jurisdiction as under Virginia, to say nothing of the immense personal loss he would have been spared. But he was no coldly calculating businessman; he was first of all a Virginian, dedicated to the rights of the colony that he had defended, explored, and helped govern. For him, surrender to the Calverts, who were not only non-Virginian but non-Protestant, would have been an act of treason; he might as justly surrender Kent Island to the Spanish. In him was alive that concept which would make later Virginian history very stormy indeed; he was, as it were, a states' rights man. Through him Maryland and Virginia achieved the distinction of becoming the first English colonies to come into open conflict. It was not, fortunately, to be very bloody, but it would entail the first Virginian "naval engagement" and the first outbreak of an American revolution. For in this contest Governor Harvey took the wrong side.

6

The Virginia governor had a hard time keeping his promise to supply Maryland with livestock. It wasn't that there was scarcity. English cattle had long since passed through their seasoning; they battened in the Virginia meadows, and as in Massachusetts, old settlers were happy to have the profit of selling the increase to newcomers. But they would not sell to newcomers who uninvited had pre-empted good Virginia land. "I'll knock my cows on the head first!" normally law-abiding planters retorted to reminders from Harvey that the king had ordered the sale. His excellency was forced to part with some of his own herd. Very likely he brought them with him when, soon after the founding of St. Marys, he paid Governor Leonard Calvert a state visit.

It was done with colorful ceremony. Calvert was still living on the *Ark* until quarters more dignified then a wigwam could be provided ashore. In the great cabin he and Harvey sat in state to receive Indian chiefs. A Patuxent coming late was so aghast to find his chief sitting like a captive between two white men, formidable in their gold lace and wearing their swords, that he ran for it and was about to jump overboard when his chief came to reassure him. The conference finished, the colors were formally brought ashore and a volley fired.

Back in Jamestown, Harvey found almost no one willing to give a friendly ear to his account of how pleasantly settlement was proceeding in Maryland. The House of Burgesses was against him, all but one of his own Council was against him, and Samuel Mathews, Claiborne's friend, shouted, "A pox on Maryland!"

From then on the relation of the two colonies, Leah and Rachel, as a conciliator called them, was complicated by the inadequacy of communication between the new world and London. Claiborne's settlement was fortified by the commission that Charles had given him without due inspection of the charts. Anyway, the latter were full of vast open spaces; how could the license he had granted Claiborne conflict with his patent to Lord Baltimore? Moreover, Claiborne's representative, the firm of Cloberry and Company, had told his majesty that Kent Island was in Virginia.

The second Lord Baltimore meanwhile was so angered by news that Claiborne, far from accepting offers of conciliation, had been stirring up the Indians by telling them that the Marylanders were Waspains, or Spaniards, that in September he relieved his brother of any further necessity of dealing gently with the patron of Kent Island. In so ordering he was ignorant that the slander had since been traced to Captain Fleet, who confessed and apologized. When Governor Calvert moved in on them, King Charles was wroth, ignorant that Claiborne had already retaliated with the drawing of first blood.

All actions were on a petty scale. The "first naval engagement in Virginia waters" occurred in April 1635 when Maryland men seized Claiborne's pinnace the *Long Tail* and set the crew ashore to find their way home as best they could. His majesty was incensed that the commander of the pinnace carried the royal commission to trade, and Calvert's men had ignored it. It was, he said angrily, "our express pleasure that [Claiborne's men] be in no sort interrupted in their trade . . . by Lord Baltimore or any other." Then the issue was complicated by a report that Claiborne's men had attacked Marylanders within their own patent on the eastern shore and had killed one of them.

Before London could digest this intelligence, there was worse. Governor Harvey came home. He had not been sent for; he had been sent.

Harvey's quarrel with his Council was older than his championship of Maryland. A tactless man, he had already given offense, which his friendship with the Calverts intensified. Virginians claimed that he had even defended the seizure of the *Long Tail*, and that he was intercepting their own protests to London. The matter came to a head when he ordered some complainants arrested for unlawful assembly; his Council objected. This, said the governor, was treason, and he ordered the spokeman arrested. "And we the like to you, sir," retorted Captain Nathaniel Utie.

The burgesses were summoned, and acting in concert committed the first American revolution. They deposed their lawful governor and elected a successor, John West.

"Rude, ignorant, ill-conditioned people," was Harvey's epithet for the revolutionaries when he faced King Charles. "It is to be feared that they intend no less than the subjection of Maryland. . . . They intend to supplant them and send them home as they have done me."

Outraged majesty defended Claiborne no more; he ordered Harvey back to rule the rude Virginians if only for a day. It was probably pride rather than wisdom that caused him to disregard a concurrent proposal by Lord Baltimore which, had the Virginians heard of it, might have roused them to real rebellion. In London his lordship had been quietly collecting information about Virginia and had become convinced that his majesty was not receiving a just revenue from this source. Lord Baltimore now

guaranteed that if he were made its governor he could realize a
yearly profit of £8000, of which he would ask only a quarter for
his services. Tempting as the offer was to the impecunious monarch, honor demanded that Harvey be reinstated. It was done.
He went back, and was still governor when Leonard Calvert
moved in on Kent Island in 1638 and took it over, even to the
uprooting of the blameless fruit trees.

The Claiborne incident did not seriously hamper the growth
of Maryland. Virginians did not long abstain from selling supplies to the new people up the bay, and the latter profited by
their proximity to the older colony as Lord Baltimore had known
they would. From Virginians they learned the value of tobacco
as a cash crop and the method of curing it for export. They
profited by Virginian experience, and after their first "naval engagement" the colonies shared in peace that most wonderful of
waterways, the broad Chesapeake.

In only one sense was the contest a real handicap. It kept the
Lord Proprietor in London. Even when the Kent Island issue
was settled for practical purposes, he dared not come, first because of the pertinacity with which Claiborne pressed his claim
and then because of the more serious troubles that beset the monarch on whom his patent depended. The result was that in its
formative years Maryland was ruled from afar by an absentee
landlord.

IX TIMES OF COMMOTION AND COMBUSTION

1

In Italy a scholarly young Puritan named John Milton heard the call, and interrupting his conversations with Galileo, went home to England. In England Sir Henry Vane's son, still young—the problems of old age would never concern him—signified his stand in the impending conflict by cutting those curls which had so charmed the sober citizens of Massachusetts. Coiffure was now an emblem of political loyalty. Curls were for the Cavaliers, who took the field for the long-haired King Charles; the Parliament men favored the crew cut that won them the name of Roundheads.

In Massachusetts others heard the call and like Milton went home: Salem's fiery Hugh Peters, who would presently demand more of Charles than his curls; John Winthrop's sons Adam and Stephen, now grown to manhood and hot to defend Parliament. So many went that it became in New England a troubling providence. For ten years the tides of immigration had flooded Massachusetts, making it the most prosperous and populous of colonies. Now the tides ebbed, then reversed. To many young colonists the true frontier lay no longer in the new world. Adventure lay not in pioneering to the Connecticut, but in returning to the motherland to aid Parliament in its battles with King Charles.

As the crisis in England deepened—and now it was the colonists whose information was usually superficial and out of date—life was complicated by a division of loyalties. Perhaps the problem was simplest in Virginia. There had been nothing personal against his majesty in the expulsion of Governor Harvey. Virginians had not forgotten their gratitude to the monarch who had laid the foundation of their prosperity by permitting them to export tobacco. They rejoiced in their status as Crown Colony and watched nervously the efforts of the old London Company, encouraged by success in Bermuda, to regain its old charter.

Most Virginians were also nominally Church of England men. Their churching was still scanty; many plantations, far-flung again now that the Indians seemed to be under control, had little access to divine service. But the planters didn't care for Puritans. There were minor exceptions; in 1642 Richard Bennett, a member of the Governor's Council, invited three ministers from New England to take up missionary work in Nansemond County, on the south side of the James. They achieved one notable convert in Thomas Harrison, an Anglican minister, and enough followers to cause the House of Burgesses to deplore in 1648 "a schismatical party of whose intentions our native country of England hath had and yet hath too sad experience." Presently the entire group, Bennett, Harrison, and all, emigrated, leaving Virginia to rally in undivided loyalty to the defense of King Charles.

It had the leadership of a militantly loyal governor. Sir William Berkeley, then in his mid-thirties, had taken office in 1642 and at once became defender of the faith against the subversions of a Parliament of Roundheads. Under him Virginia won its Cavalier reputation. When English Royalists fled before Cromwell's victorious armies, they would be welcomed in Virginia. There were not many; most settled on the Northern Neck, where a small and aristocratic group took up a royal patent; nevertheless, in contrast to Massachusetts, where immigration had come to a standstill, Virginia did receive a small influx of new immigrants.

Berkeley's loyalty did not diminish when his king lost his head. He proclaimed a day of fasting and affirmed his allegiance to the second Charles, now in exile. When in 1651 the long arm of Oliver Cromwell reached across the seas to "reduce" such colonies as were not spontaneously obedient to the new regime, Sir William proposed that Virginia resist.

The colony was not, however, so Cavalier as all that. The commissioners, whose work had begun in Barbados and Antigua, were men of good sense and good will; in a century when the religious wars of Continental Europe were impelling conformity by measures most bloody, they worked with reason and diplomacy. England had a new government, as in the course of nature it would have had a new king; Englishmen were asked to acknowledge their lawful subjection to that government; that was all.

When the commissioners, having bloodlessly reduced the British West Indies, came to Virginia, the House of Burgesses overruled and outwitted their defiant governor. Good King Charles, God rest his soul, was dead, and drawing their swords would not restore him. There had been bloodshed enough here in a second Indian massacre in 1644, and it served no purpose to augment it by engaging in civil war. Nor was Virginia in a position to seek independence of the mother country; its welfare depended on maintaining the normal channels of trade. The commissioners' demands were modest, their terms honorable. Berkeley himself entered into the negotiations, and though he surrendered his office, he remained on his fine plantation at Greenspring until better times should come. Virginia submitted to Parliament and the Protectorate, and life went on much as before.

2

Maryland was the commissioners' next stop. Properly it should not have been, for in England Lord Baltimore had exacted a promise that his province be exempted from such attentions. In maneuvering to do so he had been sorely divided between his personal loyalty to the king and the obligation of protecting his colony. It was a predicament common to Englishmen of his time; like most of such Loyalists as did not actually follow the Stuarts into exile, he compromised. Thanks to his efforts, Maryland was struck off the commissioners' list; nevertheless they came.

Two members of the commission had a special ax to grind in Maryland. One was Richard Bennett, who had recently, on Baltimore's urging, led his Puritan group thither from Nansemond

County. The other was William Claiborne, no Puritan, but willing to temporize in a situation that offered an opportunity too good to be missed. He would repossess Kent Island and humiliate the colony that had taken it from him. In the latter purpose he was eminently successful.

Ever since the outbreak of civil war in England, Lord Baltimore had been working against heavy odds to prevent its spreading to Maryland. One measure calculated to reassure his Protestant settlers had been taken in 1641 when he curbed the activities of the Jesuit missionaries. These, among them Father White, had come with his blessing to convert the Indians. They had applied themselves with a zeal found in no other English colony. Virginia's plans for an Indian college had died with George Thorpe; John Eliot was barely getting started in his apostleship to the Indians in Massachusetts; in Providence Plantation, Roger Williams' standards were so exacting that he refused to accept converts who would willingly have followed him. Only the Jesuits, circulating among the Indians, living their lives, preaching indefatigably, had conspicuous success.

This was good. What distressed his lordship was that the fathers were not winning converts only; they were winning land. There was potential danger of their setting up a state within a state beyond his jurisdiction, and the gifts of land were stirring up the jealousies of the dangerous Susquehannas. Baltimore forbade the fathers to accept land from the Indians, and though they bitterly contested his order both in England and in Rome, he made it stick.

This step did not suffice to prevent trouble in the colony, where the Protestants complained that they were being discriminated against. Shortly after the second Indian massacre in Virginia in 1644 there was a stormy interlude when Governor Leonard Calvert was forced to take refuge in Virginia, and Claiborne briefly reoccupied Kent Island. But in 1648 Baltimore took three steps to insure peace. He appointed as governor the Protestant William Stone, proclaimed an act of religious toleration, and demonstrated his good will to Protestants by inviting the Virginia Puritans to settle in his province.

The "Act Concerning Religions," dutifully ratified by the Maryland Assembly in 1649, did not offer unrestricted liberty of conscience. It applied only to those who accepted the divinity of Christ, and was designed to enable Protestants and Catholics to live without friction. Each was confirmed in his right to worship according to his own rites, and each enjoined from disparaging the other. Catholics were not to call Protestants heretics or schismatics; Protestants were not to call Catholics "idolator, popist priest, Jesuited papist," or each other Brownist, Antinomian, Barrowist, Roundhead, or Separatist.

It was a good law, the most commonsensible yet achieved in America. But the stresses of the times militated against amity in Maryland. The commissioners were about to cause a new crisis, and in the meantime it had been a mistake to invite the Virginia Puritans. There was no real need; if they were not honored in Virginia, neither were they persecuted, not as the seventeenth century understood persecution. In Maryland, where they founded Providence on the Severn River, they became persecutors.

Claiborne himself attended to the reduction of Maryland. He ousted Governor Stone and completed the humiliation of Maryland by taking the job himself, though as he spent most of his time in Virginia, the office was nominal. But his act created an anomalous situation, with no clear point of authority. After 1654, when Lord Baltimore declared the old charter in force and ordered Stone to ignore the arrangements with Claiborne, the effect was to bring civil strife to his own colony.

It was strife on a minor scale: one skirmish on the Severn. But the newcome Puritans, aided by Claiborne, put an end to the blasphemous nonsense about religious toleration. In a new election only Protestants were allowed to vote, and the assembly not only repealed the Act Concerning Religions but denied Catholics the protection of the law.

Luckily for Maryland all this was rather late in the day. Cromwell's life had few more years to run, and after his death his son, "Tumbledown Dick," would not have the wit to hold the Protectorate together. There would be Stuarts in England again, Calverts in Maryland, and a reaffirmation of toleration.

3

The commissioners did not go on to New England, which being Puritan was by definition loyal to Parliament. However, had they looked into the situation there, especially in Massachusetts, they might have found it different from what they expected.

On the outbreak of civil war Massachusetts had by no means responded with singleness of purpose to the support of Parliament. The issues were confused even to men in England; in the new world they were doubly so. Men like Hugh Peters who had no sort of doubt of what side they were on went home; those who remained behind became chiefly interested in keeping well out of it. Massachusetts defended what it called its neutrality, on occasion with belligerence.

Winthrop was governor again at this crisis. His younger sons were posting home to fight in Cromwell's army, but the father was committing his colony to no such enterprise. When a ship commanded by Parliament pursued a Royalist ship into Boston Harbor, he had the guns of Castle Island trained on the aggressor and exacted penalties for violation of neutrality. If it seemed a curious stand for a devout Puritan, Winthrop was acting consistently with the whole tenor of the brief but vigorous history of his colony. From the moment that its founders had crossed the ocean with their charters, Massachusetts had acted like a sovereign state.

Insistence on neutrality was perhaps expediency in the first stages when no one could know which side would win. The colony would show no reluctance in recognizing a victorious Parliament. Yet when that body asked for surrender of the old royal charter in order to replace it with one conformable to the new conditions, Massachusetts ignored the request as it had ignored a similar one from King Charles. The news of the execution of his majesty was received with reserve. Regicide was an ugly thing; even the fact that Hugh Peters, late of Salem, was said to have had a hand in it, didn't make it more attractive. The elder Winthrop, whose death occurred at nearly the same time and who consequently never heard of it, would not have approved the act on the grounds that the people so willed it. Such an argument would more likely have confirmed his objection to democracy.

During these times Massachusetts went it alone so far as England was concerned. Though impulses to democracy were in operation at the town-meeting level, the power of theocracy intensified. An early phase of economic distress caused by the end of emigration was succeeded by vigorous progress in a new direction. It was then that Massachusetts turned to trade with the West Indies, which craved New England corn and salt fish, and took to building ships to carry the trade.

There was a beginning of manufacture; the younger Winthrop, a man of great learning and infinite curiosity, prospected for minerals and experimented with bog iron. Through his efforts ironworks were set up at Taunton and Saugus. Short of cash, as all colonies were, Massachusetts found a better substitute than the tobacco certificates of Virginia and the wampum of the Plymouth and Dutch colonies. It coined the pine-tree shilling. Since coinage is a prerogative of sovereignty, this would get it eventually into difficulty with the second Charles, until someone had the wit to tell him that the pine tree was really the royal Stuart oak.

This was also an era of expansion. Massachusetts leaders had an instinct for something like manifest destiny, and extended their authority far beyond the old Bay. By 1641 Massachusetts settlers were taking possession of Hampton; and the older towns in what was to become New Hampshire—Cocheco, Squamsett Falls, and Strawberry Bank (Dover, Exeter, and Portsmouth)—were inviting Massachusetts rule.

John Wheelwright, in exile ever since Anne Hutchinson had "sealed" him, had to leave his home on the Piscataqua to move farther north, into the territory of the Gorgeses, where he founded Wells. But even the Gorges grant, which had so recently threatened to engulf the Bay Colony, was no protection against the outthrusting of Massachusetts. The elder Gorges died in 1647, his colony was neglected, and though the three little settlements, Gorgeana (York), Wells, and Kittery, made a brave show of organizing themselves into a body politic, they were helpless when Massachusetts surveyors were sent to push the line farther and farther to the north until eventually the Bay included the whole of Maine.

Wheelwright was not troubled by these events. He had gone to England, where he became the intimate friend of Oliver Cromwell. With the "Connecticut towns" the Bay Colony had less success. At the time of the departure of the Hooker congregation it had been understood that they would remain under Massachusetts jurisdiction, but they were far away and communications undependable. When they formed their own government there was nothing that Boston could do about it. Connecticut was an anomaly among the colonies, settled from several directions at once: by Lord Say and Sele on the coast, by the Dutch and traders from Plymouth on the Connecticut, then by emigrations from the Bay, which resulted not only in the "Connecticut towns," but in the independent and rigidly theocratic New Haven.

But if Massachusetts authority never extended to Connecticut communities below Springfield, it seized control of a confederation set up in 1643, the United Colonies of New England. This was a mutual defense pact designed to provide the protection that war-torn England could no longer give. Defense was needed against the Indians, especially now that the settlements were so scattered, the Dutch, who also claimed the Connecticut, and the French, whose colonies in Nova Scotia and influence among the Indians were always a potential menace.

The confederacy comprised the thirty-nine towns of four colonies: Massachusetts Bay, Plymouth Plantation, the Connecticut towns, and New Haven. Each retained local autonomy, but surrendered the direction of Indian and foreign relations to a board of eight federal commissioners. For all their disparity in population, about 3000 in each of the lesser colonies against 15,000 in Massachusetts, each had equal representation on the board. But there was no doubt where the power lay; Massachusetts not only had a veto but could make it stick. In any emergency the bulk of the manpower and matériel had to come from the larger colony. There was some natural resentment against Big Brother; none the less the arrangement worked well in getting the colonies through a period of great potential danger. It might have endured to form the basis of a more perfect union but for action taken by the second Charles in 1664. New England had been too independent to meet the approval of a restored Stuart.

4

The two smallest New England colonies had special cause for anxiety during these times. Plymouth enjoyed the protection of the confederacy; Providence Plantation, though it repeatedly applied for membership, was scornfully rejected. The problems of Plymouth were less severe and arose from the decline of prosperity caused by the end of the great migration.

The settling of the Bay had several effects on its little neighbor. At first there had been a painful sense of becoming a backwater, especially as ships from England bypassed the little settlement, where they had to anchor more than a mile from shore, in favor of the better harbors and more populous ports of Salem and Boston. Then the Bay had become a source of profit and modest wealth.

Even in the first winter Massachusetts settlers had broken a path to Plymouth in search of corn or whatever provision was offered. Though the Pilgrims had long since learned to supply their own needs, they had in 1630 an insufficient surplus to meet the sudden demand. Next year, and for many years after, they enlarged their plantings, and to the affliction of Bradford, who had a sentimental regard for the humble *status quo*, they moved out of the narrow lands of their first settling to the fatter, broader fields of Marshfield and Duxbury, to plant beyond their own needs and find richer pasturage for the fattening of their cattle.

The latter became particularly important in the new prosperity. One of the most difficult problems of migration had been the transportation of livestock. Jamestown had not attempted it in its first years, and though the Massachusetts founders seem to have reserved some of their ships for this purpose, the expense was prohibitive and the results disappointing. Cattle, goats, sheep and hogs customarily rode on deck, where they got knocked about in heavy weather. Some broke their legs, others got washed overboard, and all were as subject to distempers as the human passengers. This Plymouth well knew; its people had finally accumulated a modest stock, and now that the country up the Bay was overrun with people insufficiently supplied but with plenty of money to buy, they diligently looked to its increase.

Every year for a decade new settlers poured into the Bay Colony in numbers hitherto inconceivable to poor little Plymouth, and all eager to buy what the older colonists had to sell. Soon the latter included the firstcomers to the Bay, who also husbanded the livestock they had from Plymouth and sold the increase. But there was always a market for what Plymouth had to sell; it grew into a cluster of towns and knew real prosperity. The land put food into the mouths of the farmer's family; the surplus livestock put clothes on their backs and little luxuries into their homes. The farmer's wife could have a silk bodice and bright ribbons from England to relieve the drabness of homespun; there was a mirror on the wall and pewter on the table.

When immigration abruptly ceased, this happy expanding economy came to a dead standstill and then went into depression. It wasn't a matter of famine; farmers could still subsist on their soil, but for their surplus there was no longer a market. The cattle bred and raised with such high expectations could be sold if at all at prices that hardly covered their keep. Times became hard and seemed harder because they had lately been so good.

New outlets were found as Massachusetts turned to export and building the bottoms to carry it. There was some shipbuilding on the South Shore. But this took time and capital; the small farmer was ill-equipped to build ships to carry his produce to Antigua and the Bahamas. He could only adapt himself as best he could to the law of diminishing returns, and in the meantime he lived through a decline very depressing to the human spirit.

Except for supplying the Bay, Plymouth had often been baffled in its attempts to enter the larger fields of trade. The French had balked them after a promising start in the beaver trade in Maine;

the Dutch had let them keep a post on the Connecticut but the English pioneers had been less generous. By 1642 all ways seemed blocked, and Plymouth experienced one of the results of despondency. It had been hitherto immune to the fierce doctrinal disputes and heretic-hunting that had marked Massachusetts' first years; now it had a touch of hysteria and a *cause célèbre*.

One would have thought the occasion hardly worth the while of the Plymouth authorities to draw on legal opinion in Massachusetts to help them judge the case of a hapless lad in his teens caught in unsavory misconduct. The charge was bestiality, an offense harshly spoken of in the Pentateuch. The Plymouth elders, humbly aware that their church seldom had an ordained minister —in contrast to the Bay with its abundance of men of the cloth educated at Oxford and Cambridge—did not trust their own judgment. They sought counsel from Massachusetts, whose clergy addressed themselves with zeal to debating the theological, moral, and clinical aspects of the case. They had had nothing comparable since their ghoulish inquest into Anne Hutchinson's "monstrous birth."

The boy gave no trouble. He confessed freely and repented truly, though not without an expression of bewilderment that what he had seen practiced so often on back-country farms in England should merit such extraordinary attention in America. When the ponderous evidence, including the advice of the clergy, had been digested, Plymouth hanged him. First before his face they slaughtered and threw into a pit his passive partners in crime: one cow, two goats, two calves, one turkey. That none was permitted to eat of the flesh of these victims was proof how far Plymouth had come past its own starving time, and perhaps also an indication of the low value of livestock.

Odd that the town should do to death a miserable lad who had corrupted only soulless livestock when it had merely expelled a grown man, the self-styled minister who had endangered the souls of females in his congregation. Bradford brooded over the matter in his journal and asked how such vileness could come among men dedicated to an enterprise so godly. "As it is with waters when their streams are stopped or dammed up, when they get passage they flow with more violence and make more noise and disturbance than when they are suffered to run quietly in their own channels. So wickedness being here more stopped by strict laws, and the same more nearly looked into, so as it cannot run in a common road of liberty as it would and is inclined, it searches everywhere and at last breaks out where it gets vent."

It was an insight that more sophisticated men in Massachusetts would share before the century was out.

5

One might have supposed that both gratitude and expediency would have impelled the admission of Providence Plantation into the New England Confederation. No one was so skilled in dealing with the Indians as Roger Williams. His Indian acquaintance was wide and included a warm personal friendship with the venerable Narragansett chief Canonicus. At Providence his farm often more resembled an Indian village than the homestead of a white man because of the quantity of tepees and campfires set about it while his friends settled in for a visit. In the crisis of 1636 he had at great personal risk carried out negotiations that deterred the Narragansetts from joining the dangerous Pequots in an effort to annihilate the English.

Gratitude there was. John Winthrop felt it and so far as political and doctrinal differences permitted remained a friend. Had it occurred to Williams to set a price on his services he might conceivably have got his tiny commonwealth into the confederacy. But he was no politician, and bargaining where human lives were concerned was not his way. When other communities needed his help, he gave it ungrudgingly.

It was in any case difficult for outsiders to view as a real colony the maverick settlements about Providence, especially as for a long time there was little unity among them. No royal grant, no London Company of joint stockholders, no Mayflower Compact had preceded their founding. The land had been obtained by negotiation with the Narragansetts, the only funds then available

were what Williams had realized from the sale of his house in
Salem, government was improvised as needed; and all that the
first settlers had in common was their inability to get along with
Massachusetts.

Most peaceable of their number was William Blackstone, who
having repented his inviting the Puritan lord brethren to his own
private Boston Neck, moved out at nearly the same time as Roger
Williams, built a shelter for his library, and planted an orchard of
yellow sweetings at what he called Study Hill. His whole bent
being for solitary meditation, his contribution to community life
was limited to the rare occasions when he rode his bull to preach
at meeting. His real friends were his Indian neighbors.

Some other early settlers were of a different breed. Williams,
who assumed that the handful of refugees who gathered around
him were as high-minded as himself, soon found out different.
Anne Hutchinson and her followers were driven out by religious
bigotry, but others would have been unwanted in any orderly
community. Enough of the improvident and ill-behaved whom
Massachusetts towns "warned out" rather than go to the expense
of keeping them in jail resorted to Williams' settlement as to earn
it the title of "Rogues' Island."

Williams once pondered the feasibility of raising barriers, requiring standards for admission. He never did so; it was difficult to
arrange, and for him not in character. "Give me your tired, your
poor," he might have said, "your huddled masses yearning to
breathe free, and wretched refuse of your teeming shore." He
would prefer that the really shiftless, the constitutionally malcon-
tent, and certainly the criminally inclined stay where they were.
But these were on first arrival hard to distinguish from men and
women expelled from theocracy for their conscience's sake as he
himself had been.

His one political principle, if one can call it that, was what he
termed "soul liberty." No one here should be persecuted for his
creed, and so his colony became the natural first refuge for anyone deemed doctrinally impure elsewhere, from the Hutchinson
"opinionists" through an assortment of familists, Arminians, and

eventually the Quakers. The latter were currently tolerated nowhere else, not even in Maryland.

The principle gave character to Rhode Island, especially since these sects by no means accorded each other the large tolerance that Williams accorded them. In leaving for the Dutch jurisdiction, Anne Hutchinson was motivated as much by the petty bickering of rival sects as by pressures from Massachusetts. Viewing the turmoils in Rhode Island, Winthrop and Dudley could justify their conviction that the only way to civil peace lay in the stern suppression of dissident belief.

Part of the colony's troubles derived from Williams' innocence of any notion of political organization. He had not come to America with the purpose of founding a colony, and when he found himself willy-nilly in that position, a fugitive surrounded by other fugitives, his plans were limited to the immediate necessity of finding good soil outside of any white man's jurisdiction and treating with the Indians for its purchase. Since only he then had the means, he retained a vaguely proprietary control over the lots he assigned to his fellow settlers, and the instinct for private ownership being firm throughout the new world, this curious harking back to a kind of feudalism involved him in furious controversy. A contested piece of land, he would say, was as much his "as the coat on my back." It was not that he was greedy. "It was not price or money that could have purchased Rhode Island. Rhode Island was purchased by love," he wrote. In the meantime the colony had a difficult birth, evolving in storm and stress the beginnings of town and provincial government, and its founder, whose genius was not political, was frequently a prophet without honor in his own country.

His greatest problems, however, arose from the invasion of the adjacent colonies on the good lands of Narragansett Bay. There was an infiltration of land-hungry settlers who were not refugees and preferred the jurisdiction of their own governments to the still inchoate regime they found here. The Bay, Plymouth, and even Connecticut considered extending their bounds into a territory which lay in a legal vacuum, whose self-styled government lacked the authority of a royal grant or charter, and whose settlers

accordingly held their ground by nothing better than squatters'
rights.

In Williams' eyes the land was held by a better right than any
in New England. But grown sophisticated in political necessities
he had not even suspected in his younger, brasher days, he saw
that another sort of right must be obtained if his colony was to
survive. Letters addressed to his friend Sir Henry Vane in England had no reply. It was time that the man who had negotiated
so skillfully with the Indians go home to try his diplomacy on his
own people.

6

He dared not risk the direct route from Massachusetts. He had
no legal right to go there, and if he had, there was danger that if
he sought passage from Boston his errand would be suspected.
Even so good a friend as Winthrop might then be morally obliged
to detain him, or at least alert friends at court to work against
him. He went by New Amsterdam.

In London, which he reached by midsummer, he quickly
learned why Vane had not replied to appeals from Rhode Island.
All England had become a place of "commotions and combus-
tion," and Vane, now one of the most powerful men in Parliament,
second only to Oliver Cromwell, was up to his neck in them.

The battle had been joined between Parliament and king for
close to a year, but even after Edgehill the issue was still in doubt.
The position of the Presbyterian Scots was uncertain, and though
Vane welcomed his old friend warmly and gave him invaluable
help, he could not see much of him, his presence being required
in Scotland to negotiate the Solemn League and Covenant.

Williams himself had to undertake the delicate task of persuading a majority of the eighteen commissioners Parliament had appointed to regulate colonial affairs to grant him a charter. He had
friends on the commission, but he also had enemies, one of them
Hugh Peters.

His cause was aided in a way he could not have foreseen, by the publication of a little book he had written while he crossed what he called "the dreadful Atlantic." This was his *Key into the Language of America,* composed for the practical purpose of enabling those who had contact with the Indians of southern New England to speak to them in their own language. That so simple a phrase book would interest Englishmen living in a time of civil war would never have occurred to its author, but it did. There had been nothing like it. John Eliot was still decades away from completing his translation of the Bible into "American," and John Smith, the only man who had tried to commit Indian terms to writing, had contented himself with a few capricious phrases presented more as curiosities than as an aid to serious study.

Williams had written no formal grammar, but he had laid the groundwork. Moreover, he had prefaced each chapter with narrative and description which threw a more revealing light on Indian ways than the orotund rhetoric of Smith. Londoners bought the book and were fascinated; and Williams, approaching one commissioner after another on his mission, was surprised to find the cordiality with which he was welcomed as author of the *Key.* By March 14, 1644, he had his charter, the Narragansett Patent, as it was called. Hugh Peters and his coterie had opposed it to the last, but in vain. By September 17 Williams was back in America with it, taking advantage of a safe conduct in Massachusetts to land in Boston.

His welcome there was less than warm. Boston could not be expected to congratulate him on the charter, and was incensed at some of the activities in which Williams had engaged after securing it. He had been in England long enough to indulge in what was impossible to him in pioneer Rhode Island: putting his convictions on paper and publishing them. He was now the author of several pamphlets inspired by his doctrinal differences with John Cotton of Boston. Like Anne Hutchinson he had been pursued by denunciation, particularly from Cotton, to which he had no means of reply. In England at last he had his chance; he replied at length in his masterpiece, *The Bloody Tenent of Persecution.* It appeared at the same time as Milton's *Divorce Treatise* and suffered the same fate, public burning by the executioner. But a book-burning is seldom complete, and some copies reached America. Bostonians were annoyed, and the Cotton family would never forgive him.

This one time the prophet was honored in his own country. When Williams, plodding on foot through woods blazing with the honey gold and scarlet of the New England fall, came to the Seekonk River, he found a reception committee. His friends and neighbors, crowded into fourteen canoes, awaited him, and when he came in sight shouted their welcome. At home his wife, plain Mary, never sound in doctrine, but loving and loyal, waited with the little son whose birth he had not been able to tarry to see. Life was good.

Life was also far from easy. The colony now boasted four towns, Providence Plantation, Portsmouth, Newport, and Warwick, and in all were men from Massachusetts and Connecticut who clung to their former allegiance and saw no benefit in accepting a new one. There was danger that the precious patent would go by default while Williams went his rounds negotiating and persuading, as he had done with the Indians during the Pequot troubles of 1636, as he had done in London. It was May 1647 before he prevailed and all four towns accepted the charter and united.

When the Restoration came it had to be done all over again, a new visit to England, a new charter confirmed, but it was done. In spite of pressures without, in spite of dissensions within, little Rhode Island was never to lose its charter. That was more than could be said of its most implacable enemy, the proud Bay Colony.

X THE HUDSON: A DEED OF
ROMAN VALOR

1

E N ROUTE to England in 1643 Roger Williams had been
the guest of the Dutch governor, William Kieft. Though New
Amsterdam was already a sightly town, it lacked an inn, and the
governor, called William the Testy in Washington Irving's historical fantasy the *Knickerbocker History*, and worse things by his
countrymen, had already expressed to the Nineteen in Holland
his exasperation at the number of sea captains he must perforce
entertain when they broke their voyages between New England
and Virginia with a stop in the fine harbor off Manhattan Island.

Williams was a welcome guest. Any man who had got into trouble with the fiercely righteous founders of New England had a
natural claim on the governor's sympathy. He too was hard
pressed, particularly by settlers along the Connecticut who were
now invading Long Island. Besides, Williams, like the Director
General, that being the title Holland gave its new-world governors, was a man of parts. While the Rhode Islander waited for a
ship to give him passage to England, they found a common interest in Indian linguistics. Williams, already full of plans for the
Key, which he may well have started composing here, was fascinated by his host's theory that there was kinship between the local
Indians and the Iceland Eskimos, and the analogies in speech he
cited to prove it.

Probably Kieft showed his visitor some of his water colors.
These have been lost to posterity, for the new-world Dutch were
careless, or in this case unlucky, with their early records. All one

knows is that the most hated of New Netherland administrators
did sometimes find time to paint.

Ironic that Kieft and Williams found a common interest in the
Indians, for if there was one thing that Kieft did not understand,
this was it. Williams had had to find his way across Long Island
through deathly disorders for which Kieft was personally and out-
rageously responsible, and for which his own people, let alone
the Indians, would never forgive him. It was a time of senseless
massacre on both sides, during which Anne Hutchinson had been
slaughtered with most of her family. It was also the beginning of
the end of Dutch rule of the lovely lands about the Hudson, and
that this should be was partly due to Kieft's recent indulgence in
what he called "a deed of Roman valor."

2

The Hudson had been explored under Dutch auspices in 1609,
when it was still touch and go in Jamestown and the New England coast was visited only by fishermen. The Englishman Henry
Hudson, navigating the *Half Moon* under the flag of Orange, had
explored the vast, island-girt bay, and taken his ship past the ba-
saltic palisades, the rich bottom lands, and the mountains for 150
miles, until he reached soundings too shallow for his ship.

Like most discoverers of his time he was looking for a passage
to the Pacific and a short route to the East Indies. A year later he
pressed his investigations far to the north, and this time he was
on the right track. However, it would take centuries to achieve
circumnavigation of the ice-locked northern continent, and Hudson's crew would not wait so long. They mutinied against their
master's heroic pertinacity, set him adrift in a boat in the great
bay that bears his name, and went home to Holland.

The great river, variously called the Montagne, the Mauritius,
the North River, and at last the Hudson, was not forgotten. At
least as early as 1614 the Dutch set up a trading post on Castle
Island, near present Albany, at the end of the Iroquois Trail, and
probably another in the lower Hudson, at Esopus. The English

would claim that in 1613 a Virginian, Samuel Argall, found them building a fort on Manhattan Island and warned them off. But that story, probably apocryphal, was recorded late in the day when the English were looking for proof of their right to this area. The immediate interest of the Dutch was upstream, where the fur trade was better. Their posts were semipermanent in that a factor was in year-round residence, but they were not true colonies. No land patents were awarded, supplies came from Holland or by barter with the Indians instead of by planting, and there were probably no women.

In 1619 the Hudson just missed receiving a real colony, when John Robinson's congregation in Leyden negotiated with the States General for removal to New Netherland. Had the project gone through it would have been much to the material advantage of the Pilgrims; they might have come expenses paid, well supplied, and received the broad lands along the river instead of the sandy strip at Plymouth. As it turned out, Plymouth was already a year old when the Dutch West India Company was founded, and it was not until 1623 that serious colonizing began.

The Dutch even more than the English had found their sense of national destiny in counterpoise to the decaying grandeur of Spain. Two decades before the English defeated the Spanish Armada, the Dutch had thrown off the Spanish yoke from their northern provinces, and had since been contesting the power of Spain and its satellite Portugal through the seven seas. On the West African coast they had seized the fort El Mina that the Portuguese had built to guard their trade in gold and slaves; soon they would take Portuguese provinces in Brazil. Their ships had wrought havoc on the Spanish "plate fleet," diverting treasure to Holland. Seven years before Hudson came to Manhattan Island the Dutch East India Company had been organized, and its ships were driving an immensely profitable trade with the spice islands in the East, and even penetrating the mystery of Japan.

The Dutch West India Company was founded as an adjunct to this profitable venture, and unfortunately for Dutch history in the new world never attracted the same interest. Colonizing is in the nature of things slower, less immediately rewarding than raiding ships loaded with treasure or bringing spices home from Java.

Even after planting began, many colonists felt as the factors at
the trading posts had. As Company servants they would serve
their term, take what profit they could, and go home to spend it.
The Dutch had less reason than the English for emigration. Narrow as their lands were, they were not overpopulated; deviant
religious sects were not persecuted among them, for the Dutch,
having had enough of the Inquisition under the Spanish, were the
first Europeans to accept freedom of conscience. Their land, no
less than America, was an asylum for the persecuted.

However, it did happen that the passengers on the first immigration ship, the *New Netherland,* were mostly Protestant Walloons,
who had been driven into Holland by Spanish and French persecution. There were about thirty families, and this time they included women and children.

This ship and many of those that followed came to the Hudson
by a roundabout route, the Canaries, the African Gold Coast,
Dutch Curaçao in the West Indies, before reaching the American
mainland. By virtue of an offshore breeze, landfall was often made
by the nostrils. "And the air it bore was sweet, because the
savages at this time of the year burned the underbrush for hunting. The land is full of sweet-scented herbs such as sassafras.
. . . The fragrance drifts seaward, permitting the land to be
smelled before it is seen."

This was a late report by David de Vries, the nearest the Dutch
had to a Bradford; he was describing the scent of autumn. But
he too would know strawberry time, the fine patches by the great
river of the Dutch, where a man could lie on the ground and eat
his fill without moving. He knew the June woods, so full of birds
that the shrilling, caroling, and roundelaying of their hymns to
the sun were deafening. Among them a rarity, "whether bird or
bee, which sucks flowers." The hummingbirds were too delicate
to be kept alive, so people dried them and pressed them like flowers to send home as curiosities. In the fall the waterfowl, especially the swans, swooped down upon the Hudson with a mighty
clamor and in such numbers that bay and shore appeared "as if
covered with white drapery."

Sea creatures came too. Whales venturing into the shallows and stranded by the tide, died and rotted, making the air rank for miles around. On flat beaches were crabs, "their claws displaying the same colors as the flag of our Prince, orange, white and blue, thus showing plainly enough that it is our destiny to people and hold the country."

The Dutch were on the whole a rational, matter-of-fact people, little given to searching for signs of a wonder-working providence. Nevertheless the crabs were a good augury, and the Dutch needed one, what with the English denying their right to settle at all, and even little Plymouth asserting English rights to the Connecticut.

The first emigrants were widely scattered, some in the Albany area at what the Dutch called Fort Orange, a few at Manhattan, some at the Fresh, or Connecticut, River and even some on the Delaware. Only amicable relations with the Indians and careful attention by the Company to problems of supply could have enabled the little settlements to survive. There had been foresight in Holland. The settlers had been directed to maintain just and friendly relations with the Indians. The Company, at great cost, was apparently a better provider than the London Company had ever been. Livestock accompanied even the first shipload, and eventually a cattle ship was dispatched, fitted with stables and manned with an extraordinary number of attendants to see that each animal made the trip safely.

In 1626 the then governor, Peter Minuit, transacted the famous land deal whereby Manhattan Island was bought for twenty-four dollars; two years later that settlement almost rivaled Plymouth in size, with 270 inhabitants. It had yet to achieve the architectural charm of later New Amsterdam. Like most newcomers, the Dutch dug in, raising a thatched roof over a square pit lined and shored with timber and bark. But there was already a stone counting house, a star-shaped fort, and a promise of better things in a wind-driven sawmill, a device unknown to the English. There was also a building whose upper story was commodious enough to house a congregation. The lower part was a barn or "horse mill." As yet New Amsterdam, like Plymouth, had no ordained clergy; two laymen, S. J. Crol and Jan Huych, acted as "comforters of the sick" and on Sabbath read Scripture to the congregation. But plans were afoot to build a tower to house the bells taken in the sack of San Juan in Puerto Rico in 1625.

If the colony's growth was slow, its people were for a long time in the happy position of being almost without history. The English jostled them, especially on the Connecticut, but English and Dutch were more often friends than not, and first and last would settle their disputes without bloodshed. They were pressed by a counterclaim from yet another nation, on the South, or Delaware, River. Minuit, annoyed at having been dismissed as governor, had revenged himself by planting there a colony for Sweden. But contests with the Swedes would also be bloodless.

With the Indians no English colony had managed more wisely. The one serious incident, a massacre at Swanendael on the Delaware, had its origin in an almost ludicrous misunderstanding rather than bloodthirstiness. But in 1638 Wouter van Twiller, incompetent, but a trusted friend of the Indians, was replaced by William Kieft, and in less than five years the good record would be ruined.

3

Holland sent only its best men to administer such American possessions as lay south of the Hudson, the Baía province of Brazil, taken in 1624, the Dutch West Indies. With New Amsterdam it was a different story. Partly because of the protests from England, partly because in a decade and a half the colony had not begun to compare with what Massachusetts had accomplished in half that time, many members of the States General favored abandoning this attempt at colonization. Friends of New Netherland prevailed, but they defeated their own design in their choice of the successor to Van Twiller.

Nothing in the past of William Kieft suggested administrative competence. He had failed as a merchant in New Rochelle, and was said to have practiced outright chicanery when he was sent to Turkey to ransom Christian captives. He was supposed to have struck a bargain with the Turks: he kept some of the ransom money and they kept some of the Christians. A man so talked about was a strange choice as administrator sent to take a firm hand in a young colony. However, Kieft really did, according to his lights, take a firm hand.

The local government centered in the Director General, his Council, which he appointed, a secretary directly responsible to the Company, and the Schout-Fiscal, who had the duties of sheriff and public prosecutor. The nearest the settlers had to a voice in their own affairs was the right to appeal to the States General. It was at least a right they exercised, but given the breadth of the Atlantic, it was difficult to put into effect.

Nominally the five members of Council had some influence over the governor, but Kieft appointed only one, the Huguenot physician Johannes La Montagne, and nullified his position by giving himself two votes to the other man's one. In practice he took counsel more often with Cornelis van Tienhoven, who had been bookkeeper under Van Twiller and was now secretary. This was unfortunate, for though Van Tienhoven had *expertise* in playing both ends against the middle in his relations with the Company and the States General, he was a man of no moral scruples whatsoever.

In 1641 the governor took an unprecedented step. For a moment it looked as if he were about to give the settlers a hand in self-government. He summoned the heads of household of New Amsterdam to elect twelve representatives "to aid me in the direction of the affairs of the country." The Twelve lost no time; they asked that the people have the share in government that was given burghers in the smallest villages in Holland; they demanded that the Council be expanded to the specified five members, four chosen from their own number. They demanded other things and they did not get them.

It was not for this that Kieft had called them together. Popular government was the least of his interests. What he wanted was support for what he was about to do to the Indians. Perhaps at the moment he did not wholly trust Van Tienhoven; or perhaps when he reported to the Nineteen of the governing board of the

Company (the Dutch were fond of numbers; the board was always thus known, as this group would hereafter be the Twelve), he wanted to deflect personal responsibility by saying that he acted from popular demand.

There had lately been Indian trouble. David de Vries, who headed the Twelve as president, had in 1641 lost his bowery on Staten Island when the Raritans killed his servants. More recently a harmless old wheelwright, Claes Smits, had been brutally tomahawked on upper Manhattan while he bent over a chest to find the duffle cloth that an Indian had asked to purchase. The local sachem had refused to give what Kieft asked, the head of the murderer; indeed, he was reported to have expressed regret that twenty Christians hadn't been slaughtered. It was because of this second outrage that Kieft had summoned the Twelve; he wanted to declare war.

De Vries, who had suffered the most, was the most vehement for peace. Like the retired Van Twiller he understood the Indians. Even the loss of his patroonship on Staten Island (he had since planted a new one at Tappan) did not inspire him with revenge, for he knew the cause. The Raritans had been reacting from an attack by Van Tienhoven, who had wrongfully accused them of depredations committed by white men. The murder of Claes Smits was an act of Indian justice. In 1626 the murderer, then a boy, had seen his uncle robbed and killed by three of Minuit's servants, and had brooded ever since over the fact that the Dutch had done nothing to punish the murderers. To him and his people the killing of poor innocent Claes was the retribution that honor demanded.

De Vries led the Twelve in reminding the governor that war would profit no one and would endanger the scattered Dutch settlements; that the Company enjoined peace. The Twelve would agree to war only if at least three missions were first sent to the sachem. But the governor would not wait, and dispatched eighty men on the warpath.

This time no harm was done. The expedition got lost in the woods and never did engage the forces of the Wickquaasgeeks, northeast of Manhattan. They did make contact with the sachem, who this time agreed to surrender the assassin. This promise, though never kept, pacified Kieft. The rest of the year was peaceful.

In the winter of 1643 it was a different story.

4

It was on the night of February 25, 1643, a month or so before Roger Williams was to enjoy Kieft's hospitality, that another guest sat before the dying fire in the governor's kitchen. It was David de Vries, and he was sunk in helpless dejection. In spite of all he could do the governor was on the warpath again.

On the previous day he had stood before the governor in his newly completed great hall and had dared pull rank. He was, he reminded the governor, still president of the Twelve, and without his consent the governor had no right to carry out his plan "to wipe the mouths of the Indians."

His statement was a desperate bluff. The Twelve had no official standing except as Kieft chose. But De Vries had already exhausted more rational arguments. He had appealed on the grounds of Dutch safety. No precautions had been taken to warn the widely dispersed farmers of the governor's intention. Once the Indians were aroused—and Kieft could not hope to kill them all —they would fall upon the farms. "Let each one take care of himself," retorted the governor. "You will murder your own nation!" cried De Vries.

Kieft was not listening. He now placed his whole reliance on Van Tienhoven, who had been in the colony for a decade and knew Indian customs intimately. "He has run about the same as an Indian, with a little covering and a small patch in front of him," his detractors said, and though the secretary was a family man with not only a wife but a doughty mother-in-law with him, he had a reputation for interracial wenching. Recently, Kieft, relying on his sharp-witted intelligence, had sent him across the Hudson to reconnoiter an Indian encampment in Pavonia. According to Dutch citizens, who claimed that Van Tienhoven "bites when asleep," he had brought lying reports. He was said to have convinced Kieft that the Indians were employing their acquaintance with black magic to cast spells on him.

Other incidents had inspired the governor's decision. Indians had taken to killing some of the unfenced Dutch cattle which trampled their plots of maize, or "Turkish wheat," as it was called here. Mohawks had invaded the middle reaches of the Hudson, driving other tribes before them; among those encamped at Pavonia were such refugees. Most important, a white man had been senselessly killed by a drunken Indian while thatching his roof.

This time the Indians had deplored the deed and tried to make amends by offering several hundred fathoms of wampum. Their chiefs had also pleaded with the Dutch to avoid such mischances by selling no more brandy to their people. The plea fell on deaf ears with a folk who were virtually weaned on "the good creature," and found it their most valuable commodity in the Indian trade. The Indians had also made difficulties about surrendering the murderer, who was a chief's son.

Kieft had been collecting coats of mail for his men and perfecting his plans for some time. In the dark of the night between February 25 and 26 he dispatched two expeditions across the Hudson, one to Pavonia (Jersey City), the other upstream a few miles to Corlaer's Hook. And De Vries sat alone by the fire and waited.

The night was clear and still; whatever wind blew must have come across the broad Hudson. So it was that at midnight, even at that distance, the sounds of "a great shrieking" came to the ears of the man waiting by the hearth. He ran out to the ramparts of the fort. The shrieks came louder there, and in the darkness he could make out the flash of musket fire.

His excellency had had his way then, and there was nothing he could do. Yet there was. When he sat by the fire and shut his eyes he presently opened them on an apparition: two Indians whom he knew well, a man and wife who lived within an hour's walk of his former home on Staten Island. He stared at them aghast. The woman crouched dumbly by the fire while the man told how they had fled across the Hudson in a little skiff; the Mohawks had fallen upon them in Pavonia.

"You can't come here!" exclaimed De Vries.

They looked at him blankly. The invasion of the Mohawks had taken place only two weeks ago, and the refugees flying to New Amsterdam for protection had never been refused food and shelter until they could make a more permanent camp at Pavonia.

In the face of their trust De Vries found it unthinkable to tell them what he nevertheless did tell them, that this attack came not from the Mohawks but the Swannekens, that being the Indian name for the Dutch, and that the fort was no sanctuary. The woman stretched out her hands while she could to the fire; the man looked at De Vries and then asked how they should leave. Again De Vries went to the fort, to find a passage where there was no sentry. Man and wife went mutely into the frozen woods.

At both Pavonia and Corlaer's Hook the Indians, caught in the dark, had supposed it was the Mohawks who slaughtered children with their parents, hacking to pieces even infants strapped to their cradle boards. Even at daybreak, when some who had hidden all night in the sedges saw the Dutch encamped where their own fires had been, they knew no better than to go to them to ask for bread and a place by the fire. When the Dutch turned on them they were better informed, but they were also dead. Some were heard to give a strange cry, an invocation of Governor van Twiller, who had befriended them. "Wouter! Wouter!" they cried.

Unfortunately for the Dutch there were some who after daybreak saw who killed their friends, and crept away to spread the alarm.

The expedition came home triumphant, "considering that they had done a deed of Roman valor in murdering so many in their sleep," eighty at Pavonia, thirty at Corlaer's Hook. They bore heads as trophies; and the lady mother-in-law of Van Tienhoven, or so his enemies said, took sport in kicking them about the lanes of New Amsterdam. Did she think she recognized the faces of some with whom the secretary had gone wenching?

But her notions of sport were not usual. Most Dutch had lived in amity with their Indian neighbors; their children had played with Indian children and learned their language. They heard of the slaughter of the children with horror, and even in the moment of glory looked to the future with dread.

Indians could kill too. As De Vries had warned Kieft, his deed had murdered his own nation. In Pavonia and later on Long Island the Indians hunted down the Dutch on their isolated farms and killed "all the men they could surprise, but we have never heard that they have ever permitted women or children to be killed."

In this De Vries was misinformed. One day Indians came to the farm on Pelham Bay which was Anne Hutchinson's latest refuge and asked that the dog be tied. The servants refused, but Anne, scorning cowardice, obliged. Then they killed her, dragged her elder daughter to a chopping block, and a younger into captivity. Only some of the servants escaped. Massachusetts authorities rejoiced at this definitive revelation of God's providence in regard to the froward, schismatic woman, but members of the family in Boston were allowed to reimburse the Dutch who had ransomed the daughter.

Another of Anne's ilk, though she never achieved such notoriety, took precautions and defended herself successfully. This was Lady Deborah Moody, according to Winthrop "a wise and anciently religious woman" until she got herself expelled from Salem Church for denying infant baptism. She and some forty followers, including her young son Sir Henry, set up guards about their homes at Gravesend and so survived.

The massacres by the Dutch and of the Dutch did not end with that bitter February or for years after, though in spring, when the Dutch wanted to put their cattle out to pasture and the Indians wanted to plant their maize, a peace of sorts was patched up. A time came when Kieft was so hard pressed as to offer New Haven a mortgage on New Amsterdam in return for aid against the Indians. Not that he got it. In their own good time the English would help themselves to what they wanted; but that was after Kieft's day. In 1647, four years after his "Roman valor" nearly destroyed his colony, the vehemence of public outcry caused him to be sent home. His ship went down off the Welsh coast, and all his folio of water colors was lost with him. One regrets the water colors.

5

It was mid-May 1647 and New Amsterdam was ready to receive the new Director General, sent at last to replace Kieft. At the mansion the women were giving a last scrub and polish to the tiles of the great hall, which Kieft had added just before the Indian troubles began. In the fort most men of military age stood under arms, their officers hoping by the smartness of their bearing to distract attention from the condition of the fort itself. Those who had armor had been polishing it for weeks, or their women and their servants had; the glitter of their breastplates would draw the directorial eye from the crumbling ramparts that men and cattle trampled at will.

Others crowded at the waterside to watch the fleet, the *Great Gerrit, Princess, Zwoll,* and the *Raet,* come splendidly past the Narrows, sails rippling in the breeze, before they dropped anchor and prepared to launch their longboats. The ships had been coming since Christmas, and the journey had included the Canaries, Curaçao, and St. Christopher. The detour had been necessitated by storms, and besides, this new man, Peter Stuyvesant, was not only governor of the little village on the Hudson but of all the islands in the Dutch West Indies.

He was coming ashore. The descent from the flagship must have been difficult for a crippled man in his mid-fifties, but he stepped up the road to the fort as briskly erect as if he had been born with one wooden leg. He had not been; he had lost the leg of bone and muscle tissue only three years ago in an assault of Port St. Martin when he was governor of Curaçao. He bore his wound proudly, like the mark of valor it was, and it was the first thing anyone noted about him. "Wooden leg" the rude and simple would call him, "silver leg," the Indians, some of whom, barring special restrictions, were always about. The leg was wooden, but it had been richly chased with silver which caught the sun.

The new director no doubt wore his armor, for surely he did not dress less formally for this occasion than for the limner to whom he would presently sit for his portrait. Long hair, sparse in front, flowed from under his black skullcap to a starched white collar fitted above the breastplate. He had a hawklike nose over lips tightly compressed, and his narrow eyes narrowly scrutinized whatever came in their range, the small boys hovering at the waterfront, the stray cow nimbly leaping a ruined rampart, the men, armed miscellaneously, who having dressed their ranks for the last time, stood at attention, eyes front, within the fort.

But his mouth, when looked at closely not so tightly set as it had first seemed, opened to utter words of conciliation. When Kieft formally presented his resignation, Stuyvesant replied, "I shall be in my government as a father over his children, for the advantage of the privileged West India Company, the burghers, and the country."

It was what the people wanted to hear. They were in the mood for a father image and did not quibble with the naming of the Company's welfare before their own. Joyously they applauded, and they were not deceived. This time the Nineteen had made a worthy choice. The director was honest, experienced, and able; it was not his fault that he was also unfortunate.

A patron of the arts, as most intelligent Netherlanders were in his day, Stuyvesant had perhaps seen a charming drawing by the elder Brueghel, "Big Fish Eats Little Fish." The moral of the fable would become all too pertinent as time went on. No effort on his part could prevent his colony from being swallowed by the big fish to the north already nibbling at the bait. But before it happened he would have one consolation, one deed of Roman valor, this time bloodless. It would be given him to swallow the smallest fish on the seaboard, New Sweden on the Delaware.

XI LOG CABINS ON THE DELAWARE

1

New Sweden, like the lost colony of Roanoke Island, had the romantic distinction of owing fealty to a virgin queen. Nor was there in this case any of the doubt sometimes cast by the malicious on England's Queen Bess, at least at the time of the founding. Queen Christina was far too young. She was the daughter of the great Gustavus Adolphus, whose courage and military genius had turned the tide for the Protestants in the Thirty Years' War. His majesty had craved a male heir, and did his best to raise what he got as a prince rather than as a princess. He was less than wise. Fortunately for England no one had taken such a line with the hapless Anne Boleyn's little girl, and as queen, Elizabeth had known better than to impress her subjects by assuming a false masculinity. The child of Gustavus Adolphus would at no time of life know exactly what she was.

But it had been a royal childhood. At three she had sat beside her father when he reviewed those troops that were the terror of northern Europe, and like a small war horse she had shouted ha ha at the sound of trumpets and the roar of cannon. She was only six when her father fell gloriously at Lützen, and thereafter, though she sat her throne every chance she got, to impress embassies from Muscovy and the like, she was perforce until her majority in the hands of her tutors, while her father's brilliant chancellor, Axel Oxenstierna, did the work of government.

In 1638 when New Sweden was settled, she was just turned

twelve, barely older than Pocahontas when she first met John
Smith. Her personal contribution to New Sweden was considerably less than that of Pocahontas to Virginia. She did not, like the
Indian princess, hover protectively over her colony; as a woman
grown she had sophisticated tastes, required pet philosophers to
dance attendance at her court, and would never have dreamed
of amusing herself by visiting the roughhewn, mosquito-infested
posts along the Delaware.

Her positive contribution was to provide a touch of color in the
distance and lend her name to Fort Christina. Lend is the word,
for when one fish had swallowed the other, it would become Wilmington. Otherwise her contribution was negative. Once she attained her majority she got rid of the chancellor who had ruled
during her interminable minority. The departure of Oxenstierna
from public office was the beginning of the end for New Sweden,
just as Kieft's martial ways with the Indians were for New Netherland; New Sweden had been his baby.

2

In the spring of 1638 one Van der Nederhorst, Dutch agent in
what they called the South River, was surprised to come upon a
ship and yacht tied up at a kind of natural dock on the south
shore. The place was at the mouth of Minquas Kill, where the
junction of two creeks with the Delaware created a promontory
at a channel so deep that a ship could safely rope itself to the
rocks, rather as a ship could tie up to a tree in Jamestown. This
was no news to Van der Nederhorst, but the ships were. They
were the *Vogel Grip* and the *Kalmar Nyckel*, and they flew the
flag of Sweden.

Stopping to investigate, the agent had another surprise. The
master of the ships was none other than Peter Minuit, once Director General of New Netherland, the same who had purchased
Manhattan from the Indians. Minuit turned the protest with a
soft answer. He was, he explained, only breaking a voyage to

the West Indies to take on wood and water; the agent could not deny him this courtesy.

Later, however, the Swedes were found hard at work breaking the ground for planting, and still later building what was unmistakably a fort. It was time to notify New Amsterdam, and Kieft responded promptly. "The whole South River, both above and below, has already for many years been our property, occupied by our efforts and sealed with our blood," he wrote Minuit. Caustically he added, "which was also done when you were a servant in the New Netherland and you are therefore well aware of this."

Minuit had been telling a half truth in the classic equivocation of anyone caught trespassing in the new world from John Smith on. He personally was not planning to stay, not at the time; he did continue his voyage to the West Indies, and, since there he was lost in a hurricane, Kieft was troubled with him no more. But he had left behind him little Fort Christina, and that was not so easily disposed of.

Minuit had taken ill his recall in 1631, and when his efforts to pull wires with the Nineteen and their High Mightinesses of the States General availed him nothing, he went to Sweden, where two other disgruntled Dutch had already aroused an interest in Swedish colonization. William Usselinx, a founder of the Dutch West India Company, and Klas Fleming, a stockholder, had persuaded Gustavus Adolphus of the wisdom of claiming a corner of the new world for Sweden. An expedition might have set out at the time of the abortive founding of Swanendael but for lack of funds. Gustavus Adolphus was almost the most puissant monarch of Europe, but he was also nearly its poorest.

The chancellor's interest remained even after the untimely death of his king. When in 1638, through the efforts of the expatriated Dutch, capital had been raised and he had time to assess the qualifications of Minuit, who had the merit of having already governed an American settlement, the chancellor gave the enterprise his blessing, and the *Vogel Grip* and its little companion the *Kalmar Nyckel* set out for the Delaware.

Even so, the chancellor had his sights set on the wrong thing, the profit motive, which had made the early history of Virginia so disastrous and the Dutch venture so much less substantial than that of New England. However, he knew better than to expect quick returns; the founding of a colony was not to be equated with freebooting on the Spanish Main. Settlers had to be shipped and supplies sent after them.

Settlers were something of a problem, for Sweden, the least land-hungry of nations, had a population of three to a square mile. It would eventually seem like a good idea, as it once had to the London Company, to send criminals to redeem themselves by working out their sentences for the glory of the fatherland, and to get rid of some Finns. This subject people, originally from beyond the Urals, were a trouble to the Swedes not only because of their repute as practitioners in the black arts but because of their wasteful methods of agriculture. When they settled new ground, they first cleared the way by setting a forest fire. Even in heavily forested Sweden this was a dangerous trait, and it was good to have a place to resettle some of them. Thus among all shiploads of "Swedes" bound for the new colony there was always a number, often a majority, of Finns. And they made good settlers, among the best.

If on the Delaware the Finns prepared the land for planting by burning it over, no one objected. The woods seemed inexhaustible, and the Indians themselves regularly burned the underbrush in fall to clear the way for hunting. The Finns supplemented this practice by Herculean work with the ax; the celerity with which a "Swede" could fell and cut up a massive tree would be the wonder of this area long after Christina's time. The results of this prowess were put to a novel and invaluable use; they were apparently the first American settlers to construct that which was to become the very symbol of pioneering, the log cabins.

All settlers built as best they could according to the customs of the homeland. Though the English used logs placed upright to the ground to "palisade" their stockades, the building of a proper house meant laborious work at the pit saw to fashion clapboarding. At first they could not wait to season the boards, and green wood rotted quickly. That was probably one reason why Boston in its first decade gave so mean an appearance; some buildings were always falling to pieces. The Finns wasted no time with pit saws or the windmills of the Dutch; they laid the logs horizontal to the ground, notched them to overlap each other, and built the same kind of log cabins, snug against all weathers, that they had had at home.

They furnished them with trestle tables and stools and in them enjoyed their old-world customs. Christmas, merely another working day in New England, was a time of gaiety here. They cut pine twigs to strew their earthen floors, erected a cross of straw outside the entry, and unless it was a starving time (1643 was their year for that), they gave their cattle extra rations and put out sheaves of rye and corn for the birds, and then sat down to the Christmas bread and Christmas beer.

Their towheaded children ran about the forest with their swarthy Indian playmates and became linguists in no time. In fact, without benefit of formal grammar, piecing the words together as fitted the occasion, the younger Finns and Swedes were probably the most accomplished linguists in the new world. Swedish and Finnish they spoke perforce; they added the dialects of whatever Indians were in the neighborhood or came to trade; there were always Dutch about, so they learned Dutch; as necessity arose, they learned English.

The practice of the black arts that had made the Finns unpopular with their Swedish overlords survived here. "Lasse the Finn" and "Karin the Finnish woman" ran afoul of the law for sorceries otherwise unspecified and were locked up. Karin had to be locked up twice, for the bars of Fort Elfsborg were not proof against her magic. Next time they put her in Fort Christina, where she settled down and served her term.

Finnish emigration was to continue after the Dutch took the colony, and even for a while after the English got it. Letters had gone home from the Delaware urging friends to come to this place so much "nearer the sun" than old Finland, with a gentler climate and more abundant and richer land. Christina didn't like it; while she still had her say in Sweden she reproved prospective colonists with the reminder that there was plenty of unoccupied land at home. Swedish authority would later protest to the Dutch for enticing their citizens across the sea. They still came, and if their numbers were small, they were sufficient to print their own character on the land.

This love of the Delaware had not existed from the first. The year of the real planting, 1643, was a hungry time, and supplies came slowly from a country that had little to spare. The settlers were as restless and homesick as the men of Jamestown. Convicts hectored the governor with claims that they had now served their sentences and were entitled to go home, driving him to ask Swedish authorities for proper records so that he could judge the truth of such claims. Finns were clamoring for wives left behind; until they had their families with them, they took small pleasure in their snug cabins.

3

The Swedish claim to the river had by no means gone undisputed. Its shores were fertile, and though the river had shallows requiring careful navigation, the bayhead had a potential as a port second only to New Amsterdam. The English claimed it under the Virginia patent, the Dutch claimed it by virtue of prior occupation; everyone could claim it by grants from the local Indians. Their chiefs, one by the name of Matterhorn, gave land titles to anyone who came bearing gifts, with affable disregard of previous arrangements. In this there was no willful duplicity; the likes of Chief Matterhorn, ignorant of European possessiveness in regard to real estate, knew nothing of the legal sanctity of land titles.

The English might have firmly possessed this land had the Pilgrims been able to get the *Mayflower* past Cape Cod. When others came later they found the Dutch and Swedes in occupation, and as fast as the English were found they were cast out. The expulsions were bloodless; once some Connecticut Yankees from New Haven were given two hours to pack up and get back on their ship. The Dutch and the Swedes did not expel each other. They protested, contented national pride by raising appropriate flags; when they finally came to the point of hauling down each other's flags, they still managed the feat without bloodshed.

The Dutch had a just claim to priority, though it was a claim dubiously based on settlement. Some of their first immigrants had been sent to the South River, but they had established only trading posts. In 1632 there had been a serious attempt at colonizing. They then planted Swanendael just above Cape Henlopen on the south bank of the river.

But the Valley of the Swans became a lost colony. David de Vries, visiting it a year later to find its houses and stores ruined and its settlers dead, got the story out of the Indians. The massacre, rare for these peaceful parts, had its cause in a sheet of tin which the Dutch had nailed to a pole and a chief had appropriated for the making of tobacco pipes.

The Dutch had taken their loss hard; their coat of arms, complete with lion rampant, had been painted on that tin. Other Indians, gathering that a great sacrilege had been committed, pacified them by bringing them the head of the guilty chief. Ignorant of Indian ways, too inexperienced to distinguish one tribe from another, the Dutch assumed that this friendly gesture settled the matter. They saw no reason to be on their guard some time later when Indians came for a social call, mingling with the Dutch in their stockade and in the fields. These, however, were friends of the dead chief. When they had deployed their forces they fell upon the white men and slaughtered twenty-nine of them; only one man took alarm in time to escape. And that was the end of Swanendael.

Its brief existence was not without utility. There had been a colony planted with intentions of permanence. It was what Kieft referred to when he used the phrase "sealed with our blood" to Minuit, under whose administration the settlement had been made. A greater colonist, at this time still unborn, William Penn, would invoke the history of Swanendael in contesting Maryland claims.

The Dutch never recognized the rights of the Swedes in the

Delaware, but for two decades no attempt was made to eject them by force. When in 1643 the Swedes began more extensive colonization, Kieft's attention was absorbed by his Indian wars. Nor would the Dutch States General risk war. As a Protestant country Sweden was nominally a friend, and so long as Oxenstierna remained chancellor, the might it had achieved under Gustavus Adolphus was not forgotten in Europe.

Besides, a formidable governor had come in 1643, and during his ten years in office even Stuyvesant dealt with him warily. Quite apart from his character, Johan Prinz was America's biggest governor; the ubiquitous De Vries, who stopped in at the Delaware soon after his arrival, estimated his weight at four hundred pounds.

Under Prinz the colony expanded far beyond anything the Dutch had there achieved. When Dutch ships cruised up the river to the intermittent little post that they called Fort Nassau, on the Jersey side at present Gloucester, they suffered the annoyance of having to dip their colors before they could pass Fort Elfsborg, which Prinz had built to command the approach to the river. The Dutch took malicious pleasure in hearing that the Swedish garrison didn't relish the post. The Jersey mosquitoes abounded there. They "almost ate up our people . . . sucked the blood. . . . They were so swollen that they appeared as if they had been affected with some horrible disease." The garrison privately called the place Myggenborgh, which means Mosquitoburgh. But they stayed where they were told. Prinz took no nonsense, and among his retinue there was an executioner.

He made his capital at New Gothenburg on Tinicum Island, just below the Philadelphia that was to be. Here he built a fort of hemlock logs and his own Prinzhof, two stories high, with a brick fireplace and glass in its windows. It was reported to be the finest governor's mansion in America. Prinz settled here with his wife and five daughters, the latter including that self-willed Amazon (rather like her queen) Armegot, who later became Madame Papegoya, but still clung to the name of Prinz, and remained to rule over her lowborn neighbors long after her father left the country. Prinz took pride in his mansion, and when Indians destroyed it, promptly had it rebuilt, though other colonial matters were more urgent.

Other hamlets were scattered along the river, and there was a blockhouse at Upland, which the English would call Chester. But for all the extent of Prinz's domain, the country was thinly settled. Supply ships came seldom, immigrants even more rarely. One shipload of settlers, on the *Katt*, detoured to the Caribbean, where the ship was captured and its passengers lost to New Sweden.

Christina reached her eighteenth birthday in 1644; for five years thereafter she ruled ably, but then eccentricity set in. In deference to her father's desire for a male heir, she had herself crowned not queen but king. She had got rid of Oxenstierna, whose long regency she had resented, and with his departure the glory of Gustavus Adolphus was extinguished. The "king's" extravagance and frivolity drove her subjects to rebellion; in 1654 she abdicated, and henceforth roamed Europe as an anomalous count.

Even in her days of wisdom she had shown scant interest in her colony. However, in 1653, in one of her last acts as monarch, she had permitted three hundred colonists to sail on the *Orne*. The voyage was unblessed; pestilence was picked up in the Canaries, and only two hundred passengers survived. When the *Orne* sailed back to Sweden, the fat governor heaved himself aboard and went home.

Prinz had his reasons for leaving. Until the arrival of the *Orne* he had not had so much as an answer to a letter, let alone a supply ship, in three years. His people, like Christina's, were mutinous; even the Finns were tired of his highhanded ways. Possibly Lasse and Karin were being encouraged to work their spells against him.

Prinz feared no mutineer; he had his executioner. But he was tired of the country, tired of neglect, and he wanted to go home to spend his money. In his ten years of administration he had yet to see a rix-dollar of his salary, but he was a rich man. He had driven a shrewd bargain in the beaver trade, and had profited hugely by sending the pelts not to Sweden, but to England and Holland. So said his enemies, to whom Prinz did not condescend to reply. They sent their accusations after him, but Charles XII was too preoccupied by the problems left him by his royal cousin to take an interest. Even if he had, the subject of New Sweden became speedily academic. Prinz's successor, Johan Classen Risling, made one mistake that Prinz had never made, of arousing a governor even more headstrong. He raised the flag of Sweden over Dutch Fort Casimir, and Peter Stuyvesant, as the Swedes put it, came "stilting" to the Delaware.

4

Casimir had been Stuyvesant's answer to Fort Elfsborg. He had had it built in 1651 at what was to become New Castle, and thereby seized control of the river. Its position made Elfsborg obsolete; to the probable joy of its garrison it was given back to the mosquitoes. Since then, it was Casimir that challenged ships approaching Fort Christina and made them dip their colors. Little as he liked the arrangement, Prinz had to accept it.

Governor Risling took over with a vigor and an intelligence deserving of a better fate. His administration began in 1654 when his commission came to replace Prinz's son-in-law Johan Papegoya, whom he had left as deputy. The country was still restless. "The mutiny here is now fully suppressed, but there is still some smoke after fire," he reported, and asked that "an executioner with a sword" be added to his staff. He listened unsympathetically to complaints against his predecessor, but he did listen, had the grievances put into writing, and sent them home for judgment while he worked at more pressing matters.

He negotiated with the Indians, gratified his subjects by permitting them to enter freely into the fur trade, dealt with delegations from Maryland and New Haven, both of whom claimed the Delaware. And he won that victory which was his fatal error. He sent a detachment to Fort Casimir and captured it from the Dutch. The feat was childishly simple. "What can I do?" Commander Gerrit Bicker said when one of his officers urged resistance. "There is no powder." So Christina's colors flew over Casimir,

and this being Trinity Sunday, the Swedes named it Trefaldighet.
Stuyvesant was in the West Indies at the time, and apparently
Holland heard of the affront before he did. He made a leisurely
trip home with a stop at Barbados, and reached New Amsterdam
to find the warship *Waegh* awaiting him, armed with thirty-six
guns and carrying two hundred soldiers. There were also instructions. The Nineteen and the States General had been thoroughly
aroused by the Swedish violation of the symbiosis that until then
had prevailed on the South River, and there was now no reason
to fear Sweden. The Company had written Stuyvesant specific
orders in November 1653: he was to avenge the outrage and expel the Swedes. To his credit Stuyvesant heeded only the first of
these instructions.

Owing to the delay caused by his absence, it was late summer
in 1655 before he got into action. He called a day of fasting and
prayer, recruited volunteers, found new ships. On September 6
he entered the Delaware with the *Waegh,* a French privateer
called *L'Espérance,* and five lesser craft. The Indians warned
Risling, who reinforced Trefaldighet and made ready to fight.

But the tradition of peaceful coexistence was too strong. Officers
at Trefaldighet prepared to open fire when the fleet came within
range, but their men threatened to mutiny if they did so, and the
commander, Captain Sven Skude, demurred. Instead, the fort
made honorable surrender "with burning fuses, loaded guns, beating drums, and pipes, and bullet in mouth and such things."

Stuyvesant then sent to Risling a demand that he surrender
the whole river, landed his troops before Fort Christina, and laid
it under siege. To the unhappiness of the colonists, Risling held
out until October. His people cared little what colors flew over
the little log fort where the governor sat holding councils of war,
but they cared very much about their houses and livestock, and
the Dutch were looting the one and slaughtering the other. Before they were done they burned the hamlet of Christianham.

Yet Risling won substantial concessions by the delay. While
Stuyvesant camped outside the fort in "a large and beautiful
tent," he was distracted by bad news from home. When on
October 10 Risling finally surrendered, he got from Stuyvesant

terms far more favorable than the Nineteen's curt order for expulsion. Settlers who accepted Dutch rule could remain and enjoy "the privilege of the Augsburg Confession." Those who wanted to go home could have eighteen months to dispose of their property, and free transportation to Sweden.

Having made these concessions, Stuyvesant struck his handsome tent and hurried home to deal with the Esopus Indians. They had risen during his absence and were threatening Manhattan. He left the Swedes to pick up and go, or rebuild and settle in again. Most, especially such Swedes as were really Finns, remained. In less than a decade they would be called upon for a new surrender and a new transfer of loyalty, and this time the circumstances were more cruel than in the bloodless conquest by the Dutch. The English were coming to carve out Delaware, New Jersey, and finally Pennsylvania from what had been New Sweden. But before the remnants of New Sweden had to cope with the English, they had the satisfaction of hearing that Stuyvesant himself had been through the humiliation of surrender. New Sweden's days were over in 1655; New Netherland's were narrowly numbered.

XII BATTLE OF MANHATTAN

1

NEW AMSTERDAM had become the most interesting little metropolis in North America. It was not the largest town; only Virginia, where the scattering of plantations on the tidewater inlets hampered the growth of towns, would consider it metropolitan at all. Boston, with a population of two thousand in 1650, was twice its size, the Connecticut towns were growing vigorously.

But it was New Amsterdam that had style, and even so early an unmistakable skyline. The newer, better houses of Dutch brick were placed gable end to the street and had the stepped roofs of red and the brick tile of old Holland. They were a far cry from the sod huts and dugouts with which the settlement had begun, and made a far gayer appearance than Boston.

Stuyvesant had been improving and cleaning up the place. The tile roofs had come in because thatch had been found too combustible for town life. By his order the "little houses" or "necessaries" were no longer placed close to the street, and neither were the hog pens. The fort had been repaired, and the church, which Kieft had started, was finally completed. Most dwellings stood in their own orchards and had gardens of formal beds and borders.

Under their gabled roofs the women kept house with such a passion for cleanliness that a Frenchman said a man didn't know where to spit. In their ruder beginnings they had only earthen floors to sweep and cover with fresh reeds. Now that they had wooden floors they scrubbed them insatiably, scoured them with sand, and kept them shining. They gave the same care to their treasures from the old country: fine china and earthenware, little porcelain dogs and swans, and the pictures on the walls, not only portraits, but seascapes, still-lifes, battle scenes, Biblical studies like "Abraham and Hagar."

They came from a land where the arts were a part of daily living. It was no accident that one governor painted water colors in his leisure and that his successor found a good limner to do his portrait. Stuyvesant also arranged a sitting for his son, the seventeen-year-old Nicholas, and in this instance the painter had to abandon realism. The boy insisted on posing in the saddle, and there wasn't a canvas in the colony that would accommodate the horse on the scale that the limner had begun the head. He had to improvise: a realistic head with the Stuyvesant hawk-beak, placed on a diminished body mounted on a curvetting doll-horse.

Between wars and rumors of wars, life was good in town. The folk were churched on the Sabbath, and grogshops had to close at the hour of worship, but the people did not take their religion grimly. They ate well, drank companionably—their young were said to be allowed their grog as soon as they could lick a spoon—and enjoyed diversions like bowling and market day. There was a guardhouse for malefactors—rather a wild lot came in from the ships and sometimes from the woods—a whipping post, and a gallows, but the latter was seldom used. The Dutch were not fond of capital punishment. When they, like Plymouth, got a case of sodomy, this one involving a man and a boy he had seduced, they put only the man to death; the lad they exiled.

It was the most cosmopolitan town on the Atlantic coast. One visitor said that eighteen languages were spoken. He did not specify. Obviously they included the three tongues of the Netherlands, Dutch, Walloon, French. English must have come fourth, for many Englishmen lived as subjects of the colony, and Stuyvesant even had an English secretary, one George Baxter, who helped him negotiate with New England until he fell to conspiring with Long Islanders against Dutch rule.

Perhaps Latin counted as a fifth language, this being the lingua franca used by some of the earlier governors in correspondence with New England. After 1654 when the Portuguese reconquered the last Dutch posts in Brazil and many refugees came to New Amsterdam, Portuguese was heard, and Portuguese Jews from Brazil brought Yiddish and liturgical Hebrew. That makes eight languages. What were the ten others? Was the observer counting Indian dialects? Indians were not allowed in residence on Manhattan, but they visited often, and Dutch parents were awed at the fluency with which their children jabbered with Indian visitors while they dickered for keepsakes. Add an X quantity of Indian tongues, and another X for the dialects spoken by the Africans, Domingo Angola and Anthony Congo.

The Dutch trading posts in Guinea were little more remote than Holland, nearer than Brazil, and the Dutch, who had introduced the first Negroes to Virginia, brought them also to New Amsterdam. Some, having served their time like the Dutch laborers, became free, were given their own morgens of land, and built boweries. Half a dozen were listed as receiving land in 1646, and there were others later. Their status as freedmen was not lowly. Some served in the militia, and one Dutch woman, Martie Hendrick, bound herself out during the absence of her husband to serve in the household of a freedman of color for a hundred florins in wampum, "a white apron and a pair of black."

The troubles in Brazil that preceded the expulsion of the Dutch had added an exotic element to the population. In 1644 in the midst of the Indian wars Kieft had been delighted to accept soldiers from Brazil who had been transferred to Curaçao, where no one knew what to do with them. Two hundred came in all, arriving on the *Blue Cock* in July. Then there were problems. War-torn New Amsterdam could not easily feed so many, and worse was the problem of clothing them. Their service had been in the tropics. They would not only have to be "seasoned," a term not often used in these robust latitudes, but clothed for fall and winter. Thanks to their arrival, Kieft had been able to dismiss English soldiers hired to defend the colony, but he had to continue and even increase taxes imposed as a temporary emergency measure.

A decade later twenty-three Jews arrived on the bark *St. Catherine*. They also had been ousted from Brazil, and what few possessions they had were seized by the shipmaster to pay for their passage. Then they were destitute, and the only Jewish merchant in town, a Dutchman to whom these Portuguese-speaking Jews must have been as alien as any Indians, refused to take responsibility for them. "He would not lend them a single stiver," indignantly reported the Reverend Mr. Johan Megapolensis, annoyed at having to give several hundred good Dutch guilders from the alms box to these paupers.

There were by this time in the pastor's opinion too many strange creeds in New Amsterdam: Papists, Puritans, Lutherans, Quakers, atheists, and "servants of Baal." Megapolensis especially objected to the Lutherans; their local pastor was "a snake in our bosom," and he knew of one at Fort Casimir who "would prefer drinking brandy two hours to preaching one." He was plagued by the Quakers, and now he pleaded for the expulsion of the Jews, "these godless rascals . . . who have no other God than the Mammon of unrighteousness and no other aim than to get possession of Christian property." The good pastor had an ally in Stuyvesant, who had already forbidden Lutheran services and wanted to oust the Jews.

But the Nineteen in Holland were liberal men, and knew that the colonial venture owed much to Jewish investment. They pronounced the suggestion "unreasonable and unfair" and ordered Stuyvesant not to interfere with the peaceful transaction of business.

It was a polyglot city that soon after witnessed Stuyvesant's last stand against the English.

2

It was unfortunate that Kieft had remained in New Amsterdam for several months after Stuyvesant took over. The deposed Director General obviously had some personal charm and persuasiveness. The Nineteen had given him the job in spite of his already questionable reputation; Roger Williams apparently liked him; so did Stuyvesant. The latter, primarily a soldier who expected instant, unquestioning obedience from his subordinates, was shocked to learn that while the burghers had waited on an answer to their remonstrance to Holland, there had been talk of ousting Kieft bodily, as they heard had been done with an unpopular governor in Virginia.

To the old soldier such an intention was mutiny, and it confirmed him in sympathy with Kieft. Stuyvesant was a good man, brave, resolute, and tireless in the multiple campaigns that fell to his lot. But he would take no nonsense about pretensions to self-government, and his unwillingness to examine the justice of the complaints against Kieft served him ill in coping with the problems the man had left behind him.

Thanks to the Indian wars, the colony was for the first time faced with want. The Company, though sympathetic as the London Company had not been with the plight of the settlers after the massacre, was bankrupt and unable to help. Kieft had been raising money to pay recruits from Connecticut by imposing import and export duties, and an excise on beer and wine, thereby compounding his unpopularity. Since no one in New Amsterdam willingly drank water—and indeed the local water supply was hardly better than that of Jamestown, even the wells were brackish—the excise was an abomination earnestly evaded to the best of everyone's ingenuity. Stuyvesant's attempts to collect it and put a stop to smuggling endeared him to nobody.

He too had to summon councils, if only in the interest of public relations: the Twelve, the Nine. But just as it had been under Kieft, such bodies, having given respectful consideration to the current emergency, bore down with demands for administrative reforms which were in Stuyvesant's eyes none of their business. Sometimes he had to comply; New Amsterdam got a measure of municipal government in 1653, but he complied grudgingly, and when possible his left hand took back what his right hand gave.

Such demands came also from the settlements on Long Island, both Dutch and English, and Stuyvesant had to give the latter some local government to insure their loyalty. Far up the Hudson, Rensselaerswyck, the most successful of the estates established under the patroon system, which at one time threatened to fasten a kind of neofeudalism on the colony, had a disposition not only to consider itself independent of the Director General, his taxes, and his requisitions for arms, but to encroach on nearby Fort Orange. Stuyvesant had to take a firm hand.

He did not repeat Kieft's mistake of making unnecessary war upon the Indians, and could he have preceded Kieft the history of the colony might have taken a different turn. One mistake he did repeat. The first trouble with the Esopus Indians, who lived some score of miles upstream from Manhattan, had started in a drunken brawl among Indians employed in harvesting Dutch crops. The chief had begged Stuyvesant to cut off the supply of brandy; intoxicants had been unknown among their people, and once the young men got the taste they were uncontrollable. Stuyvesant's response was prim to the point of idiocy; let the Indians stop asking for it, said he, and it would not be sold.

It would perhaps have been impossible to return to the policy of live and let live which Kieft had blindly destroyed. The Dutch had not been sentimental about their Indian neighbors, had shown small zeal for saving their souls. They took them as they found them, and the Indians had responded in kind. But there was no restoring that mutual trust after what Kieft had done. Stuyvesant had to spend much of his time putting down one uprising after another.

The worst coincided with his triumph on the Delaware, when he was called home to deal with one of several attacks by the Esopus. The Dutch settlers had done well, were even exporting wheat to the West Indies. Now, thanks to the raids, they were eating their seed corn and so late in the day coming to a starving time. At his best in military crises, Stuyvesant managed to hunt down and destroy the Indian strongholds.

For this deed of valor it was the English who should have thanked him. For a year later, smarting at the injustice of it, humiliated by the cowardice of his own people, Stuyvesant handed over his colony to a representative of the Duke of York.

3

Until then he had kept the English out of the Hudson. He had had no luck at all at keeping them out of the Connecticut Valley or Long Island.

The trouble on the Connecticut had begun long before. Plymouth had protested in 1633 when the Dutch built the fort that they called the House of Hope. Not that Plymouth was belligerent. Its people had reason of old for friendship with the Dutch, and in 1627 a Dutch mission to them, headed by Isaack de Rasières, had done them a good turn. The emissary had sold Bradford some wampum, an invaluable medium of exchange in a country that had little other currency. The Pilgrims had become skilled at making it from the abundance of shells on their coast. Far from considering it counterfeit, the local Indians valued it more highly than their own mintings. When the Dutch refused to keep off the Connecticut, relations remained friendly. There was room for both.

But there was small room for either when three years after the building of the House of Hope, Thomas Hooker's congregation came in. The Plymouth men, deeply hurt at the disregard of their prior claim, soon withdrew; the Dutch doggedly held their ground and became an enclave swamped by the robust village of Hartford, whose citizens not only denied the Dutch right to the fort but objected to their leaving the palisades to plant. Dutch husbandmen who went out to plow got their heads broken. Their farm tools were seized and thrown into the river, their livestock commandeered. Once a clergyman—surely not the upright Hooker—ordered their cattle driven to his own barn and would not give them back. Later the English walled in the fort, cutting off the Dutch from their own spring.

The English justified such action on the grounds that the Dutch sold guns to the Indians, gave sanctuary to runaway servants, and had no rights here anyway.

Soon the Connecticut towns, Hartford, Wethersfield, Windsor, had a rival on the Quinnipiac, New Haven, which jealously maintained itself as an independent colony as long as it could. Other settlers moved south to found Stamford and Greenwich, and in no time were all over Long Island, which they also claimed for the English as having been bequeathed to the Duke of Stirling. Refugees from New England like the Mennonites who settled Gravesend with Lady Deborah Moody were, however, willing to accept Dutch jurisdiction.

There was no question of Stuyvesant's fighting Connecticut. He was no fool and would not like Kieft go headlong into action to satisfy a notion of "Roman valor." He negotiated with the Connecticut towns and New Haven. His first attempt with the latter nearly collapsed when he made the semantic error of speaking of their "pretended settlement." He had to apologize for his bad English before the New Haven authorities would talk to him at all. He had some success. Greenwich was recognized as Dutch and some Long Island towns professed allegiance after promises of local autonomy.

Stuyvesant had in the Bay Colony an unexpected ally against the encroachments of Connecticut. There was in Massachusetts some deploring of the celerity with which the Connecticut towns had escaped the jurisdiction of the mother colony and an inclination to see them contained. When in the mid-fifties other members of the New England Confederacy wanted to take advantage of hostilities between England and Holland to march on New Amsterdam, it was the Massachusetts veto that barred the way.

The proximity of New England was a hazard in a way that Stuyvesant never understood. New England town meetings, New England elections were having a subversive effect on his own people. In Kieft's time they had been inspired by the example of Virginia in casting out their governor. In New England they saw more than this. New England cast out unpopular governors as regularly as elections recurred. No governor was imposed on them from afar by directors interested chiefly in their profits; they chose their own, as they chose lesser officials, from hogreeve to selectman; each town elected its own representatives and debated its own problems in town meeting.

This looked very good to burghers who had enjoyed privileges something like these at home but could not here. If the encroachments of the Englishmen were a constant irritation, their ways were a source of envious admiration. The time was fast approaching when Stuyvesant, all Roman valor, was inspired to fight against overwhelming odds. But it was not in him to rally his people to his standard; they were too soft, and a part of the softening process had been this secret admiration of the enemy.

4

In July 1664, when in England the second Charles had had four years to get the feel of his throne, Stuyvesant got word of a fleet dispatched from England with predatory intentions. He heard it from a friendly English captain, Thomas Willett, who had the news from Boston. Stuyvesant looked to the defenses of the city, set up guards on the approaches to the Sound, and ordered a shipload of grain intended for Curaçao held in case the city was placed under siege.

Then he was reassured by his own government. Some English frigates were indeed about to sail, but their business was only with Boston, which had too long acted like the capital of a sovereign state. Willett, confronted with this news, nervously retracted his own story. The Director ceased his preparations, let the cargo sail for the West Indies, and went to Fort Orange to attend to upcountry Indian affairs.

Thus he nearly missed his own surrender. Willett had told him nothing but the truth; by a stroke of British diplomacy the States General had been sadly misled. War between England and Holland had inspired his majesty to bestow New Netherland on his brother James. The fleet did have business with Boston, but its most important mission was to take New Amsterdam.

Four frigates were already in Long Island Sound when an express reached the Director at Fort Orange, and he barely made it back in time. When he reached Manhattan on August 25, the flagship *Guinea,* armed with thirty-six guns, was only a day's sail

away. Three days later, during which Stuyvesant worked fever-
ishly to get the fort repaired and his twenty-four guns in position,
the frigates seized the blockhouse on Staten Island, cut communications with Long Island, and anchored in the bay. On August 30
he was presented a formal demand for surrender.

Stuyvesant consulted the burghers and the officers of the new
municipal government. This again was a matter of public relations; he needed no authority to perform his manifest duty. Their
attitude stunned him; they reported that it was the overwhelming
will of the people that he comply. The outraged governor ignored
them.

On September 2 he had a visit from the younger John Winthrop
and another commissioner from Connecticut. Under a flag of
truce they brought him a message from Commander Richard
Nicholls of the fleet. In the presence of the burghers Stuyvesant
read the paper silently, tore it across, and flung it to the floor.

The burghers looked on cold-eyed. "Dilacerating that paper,"
as one of them put it, was irresponsible conduct; they had a right
to know what was written on it. They picked up the scraps, pieced
them together, and learned that Nicholls was offering concilia-
tory terms. Then they forced Stuyvesant to reply.

The old man took his time about it. The letter had been brief
and businesslike; his reply was long, for he took to official correspondence as Kieft had taken to water colors, and on this occasion composed a lecture on the history of New Netherland. But
surrender he would not, and Nicholls readied for action. Two
ships disembarked their troops below what was still spelled
Breuckelen, and two others were laid broadside, with their guns
trained on the town.

From the ramparts Stuyvesant watched the frigates take their
positions. He was, for the moment, free of the pusillanimous
burghers; his gunner, who stood at the ready with his match, was
no debater but a soldier trained to instant obedience. At a word
he would apply the match and open fire. Yet Stuyvesant, for reasons that he was never able to explain to the Nineteen, hesitated,
and while he hesitated he was lost. Two ministers got to him,
Johannes Megapolensis, father and son.

"Let us not begin it," they implored him. "Let not the blood be on our heads."

Negotiation is not forbidden to the military. Stuyvesant left the fort to compose yet another letter to Nicholls. Was there, he asked, no means of coming to an understanding. "Hoist the white flag of peace," replied Nicholls, and there was tact in the phrase, "peace," not surrender, "and then something may be considered." But he warned the governor that there would be no parleying once the fighting began.

And now the dogs of peace were loosed on Stuyvesant. There was not a trace of Roman valor in all the town. The burghers thought only of their china, their graceful stepped gables, their peach trees and tulip beds, all so placed in relation to the fort, which had been designed only as a refuge from the Indians, that the first broadside from the *Guinea* would destroy everything they had. Wives and children joined the men in the tearful plea for surrender.

The old man stared at them incredulous. Were these the people whose fathers had so recently won the Netherlands from the terrible Duke of Alva? There had been no talk of tulip beds and stepped gables then.

"I'd rather be carried a corpse to my grave!" he shouted, and stumped away from them on his wooden leg.

The people got together on a composition of their own, a Remonstrance, and the ministers wrote it for them. They pointed out the impossibility of defense. Not only the four frigates but hundreds of volunteers from Connecticut stood ready to begin the assault, and all the troops had been promised leave to plunder if the city did not surrender peaceably. No help could be expected. Long Island would not and could not send aid; Rensselaerswyck had already refused on the excuse that it needed its manpower against the Indians. There was not powder enough in the fort to strike a telling blow, food supplies were inadequate for a siege, and if the people had to take refuge in the fort they would be waterless, for there was no well there.

Nicholls had offered generous and honorable terms. No looting would be permitted if the surrender were voluntary; the people could come and go as they pleased and rule themselves under their municipal officers. Nor would the surrender be absolute; the fate of New Netherland would depend on the outcome of negotiation.

What unmanned Stuyvesant was not the passion of the plea but the names signed to it. Ninety-three of them, apparently every householder in New Amsterdam. High among the signatures was that of his own son, not the young gallant who had insisted on being painted astride his horse, but Balthasar.

On Monday, September 8, he surrendered. The terms had been negotiated on the 6th and ratified at once by the British. On Sunday the Dutch rested from their labors and Stuyvesant grimly listened to a sermon. On Monday he summoned his Council and signed the paper.

With all the honors of war the aged Director placed himself at the head of his garrison, marched down Beaver Street, and embarked on the *Gideon* to begin his journey to Holland. But Holland was no longer home to the old man. If he had been unable to impress on New Amsterdam the scruples that had deterred him from surrender, he found it as impossible to explain to the Nineteen the scruples that had prevented his drawing first blood. He came back to his bowery on Manhattan in 1667, and died there in 1672, just one year too early to enjoy revenge when the Dutch recaptured what the British now called New York.

It would have been a brief revenge. The colony was fated to be British until such time as it became American. But its roots remained Dutch, and coming under the rule of the Duke of York made small difference. The Dutch were still free to emigrate to their former colony. Dutch customs still gave character to the place, and Dutch names would persist and take high place on the honor rolls of the new world.

XIII BROTHERLY LOVE: PENN'S HOLY EXPERIMENT

1

CHARLES II had come to the throne in 1660 with a quantity of old scores to settle. His father's enemies must be punished, his friends rewarded. The first task was simpler than the second.

The merry monarch was not by nature a revengeful man. Milton, though technically in hiding, was not hunted down; he was let alone to dictate to his resentful daughters his masterpiece *Paradise Lost*, a subject suitable to a Puritan under these circumstances. Two regicides who escaped to Massachusetts were not pursued so implacably as to be caught. Other former New Englanders were less fortunate, including two who had taken opposite sides in the Hutchinson affair. The younger Sir Henry Vane went to the scaffold, and so did Hugh Peters, though his end was less edifying. He did not conduct himself with the firmness with which Anne had faced her judges, though in fairness to Peters, he had not caused Anne to be dragged through the streets on a hurdle.

Rewards were more difficult, for during his exile, mostly on the Isle of Jersey, Charles had accumulated no fortune; in fact, he was heavily in debt to many of his friends. Some details could be simply arranged. Maryland could be restored to the Calverts; Virginia could be returned to the governorship of the loyal Berkeley. The latter was aging, approaching senility, and his conduct would not always please his majesty, but at the moment there was no problem. He could also bestow baronetcies with a lavish hand and raise those who had them already to earldoms. But some debts of honor required more substantial reward. Cash payment was not to be thought of, but in America there were lordly parcels of real estate still undisposed of. Charles looked to his charts; no more than any other Stuart did he examine them with full attention, but he looked at them long enough to find what he wanted. Then he distributed largesse. He gave New Netherland to his brother James, leaving Commander Nicholls to attend to the detail of taking it from the Dutch. He bestowed Carolina on a group of illustrious noblemen. Finally he repaid the sum of £16,000 that he owed to a loyal admiral, Sir William Penn, by a grant of rich lands at the head of the Delaware. The admiral did not receive this grant in person, being dead; it went to his son as his heir.

2

In youth this son had been a sore affliction to his father. He was no ordinary prodigal bent on sowing his wild oats; it would have been simpler if he had. When he was expelled from Oxford, it was not for wining and wenching but for reasons beyond his father's comprehension. He was too devout to attend chapel; its Anglican service offended his conscience.

The father had packed him off to France, hoping that there the youth would acquire a proper appreciation of the gay vanities of the world. He returned so fine feathered a young gentleman as to merit mention in the diary of Sir William's subordinate in the Admiralty Office, one Samuel Pepys, who suffered from professional jealousy and took malicious pleasure in reporting his superior's anxieties for his son. When the boy settled down to read law at the Temple, the father was emboldened to send him to Ireland to learn to administer the paternal estate. It was a fatal misjudgment.

Until now the boy had been nothing worse than a sort of Puritan. In Ireland there were Quakers, a group so radical as to make the Puritans look like conformists. Young Penn attended one of their meetings, and thus ended forever his father's peace of mind. The youth was so moved that when he rose to give testimony he could find no utterance but tears. A few days later the constables descended on another meeting and caught him there. They would have let him go, for in his Cavalier finery, complete with a finely curled French wig (aside from fashion Penn had the excuse of being nearly bald since an infantile attack of smallpox), he did not look as if he belonged. Penn insisted that he did, proclaimed himself a Quaker, and went to jail with the rest.

From then on the father had no need to send to ask the whereabouts of his heir; he was in jail—in Ireland, in the Tower of London, in Newgate Prison. The Restoration was not a time when any nonconformist sect was suffered gladly, and they who were derisively called the Quakers because they said that even a monarch must tremble before the Lord, were the most extreme nonconformists. They gave offense socially because in their belief that all men were equally humble before the great God they would not uncover before their betters, and addressed high and low with the thee and thou suitable only for inferiors. They gave offense politically because they would swear no oaths, and were for this reason incongruously confused with the Papists, whose consciences forbade their taking the oath of supremacy. They ignored ordinances forbidding dissenters to meet in groups larger than five, and instead of giving often sympathetic authority a chance to ignore them by observing a decent privacy, they invited arrest by making their assemblies scrupulously public.

They offended the Puritans by the implicit levelism of their faith and by their reliance on the "inner light" in interpreting Scripture. Thus, unlike the Puritans, members of the Society of Friends required no university-trained ministry to expound doctrine, but would give as earnest heed to the simplest illiterate if they believed that he was instructed by the light within him. The arrests had begun during the Commonwealth, for all that Cromwell had been deeply impressed by George Fox, their first leader. Suffering arrest came to be a kind of mission to be performed for the glory of God. They were perhaps akin to young Latter Day Saints who give the first years of their maturity to

expounding the gospel to skeptical Gentiles, or to young Negroes
who quietly sit at lunch counters until the police remove them.
English jails were noisome places, destructive of health, and sometimes the hardy offered their bodies to undergo the punishment of
the weak.

Whatever physical suffering the younger Penn endured in his
jailings, it was nothing to the moral suffering of his father, honored
confidant of kings, to know that his son had come to this. He tried
to reform him with gentle persuasion, he tried the "bitter usage"
of whippings, once he disowned the pious prodigal, but couldn't
keep it up because of the tears of Lady Penn. In the end he surrendered.

In 1670 Sir William fell mortally ill. His son was at the moment
in Newgate, in the company of a jury which had defied a judge
by refusing to convict him and his fellows of anything more felo-
nious than "speaking in Gracious Street." The father sent money
to pay the fine and summoned him to his deathbed. "Let nothing
in the world tempt you to wrong your conscience," said the dying
man. "I charge you, do nothing against your conscience, so will
you keep peace at home, which will be a feast to you in a day of
trouble."

It was a touching surrender; it was also in the Stuart tradition.
It was almost in these words that the first James had charged his
son, the unlucky Charles.

The older man did more, and this would be of profound importance to the dwellers by the Delaware, present and future; he
sent to his friends the Stuarts, Charles II, and the Duke of York
who was to be the second James, and got their promise that they
would continue their favor to him through his son.

It was more than a decade later before the younger William
Penn asked and received Stuart bounty. During this time conditions had first improved for his people, and then worsened. The
Act of Indulgence in 1672 had released thousands of Quakers
and another dissenter named John Bunyan from prison, but then
the persecutions were resumed, and this time authority bit at the
Quakers by imposing heavy fines. It was a more vicious blow than

jailings, because repeated fines would end by reducing the most provident to beggars.

By 1680 William Penn was in his mid-thirties. Maturity had not diminished his faith or his youthful élan, but it had brought him to the understanding that if the Friends were to fulfill their mission in the world, they must find a place where they could build on a surer foundation. Already, like the Separatists and Puritans before him, he had been looking to the new world which God had miraculously provided.

Yet where in America was there a place for this most despised of sects? Even Maryland wouldn't have them; the Dutch could no longer defend their rights on Manhattan; and Massachusetts had hanged four of them. Mary Dyer, once a follower of Anne Hutchinson, had been a victim. Rhode Island was a haven, but Quakers were tolerated, not welcomed, there. The aging Roger Williams had published a tract attacking their doctrines with one of the punning titles so dear to his age, *George Fox Dig'd out of His Burrows*. Penn wanted something better for his people than mere toleration; above all he wanted land better, greener, broader than that found along the crabbed shore line of little Rhode Island. He looked abroad and saw the Delaware.

The English had to date done little for the area beyond conquering it. Even the restless Connecticut Yankees had lost interest now that the Hudson Valley was open to them. The settlements were still small and scattered.

That Quakers might get permission to colonize somewhere thereabouts had been suggested in 1660 by George Fox, who visited America in 1671. He then recommended the upper reaches of the Susquehanna, partly because he knew that Maryland had a technical claim to part of the Delaware, and partly because he had no hope that the despised Quakers would be granted richer lands. Penn's attention had been riveted on the Delaware itself in 1676 when a group of Quakers succeeded in buying patents for a settlement in West New Jersey.

What was now New Jersey had had a confused history since the English conquest, the Duke of York having disposed of the whole area to Lord Berkeley and Sir George Carteret in disregard of the fact that settlers from Long Island had already been given land in the east. Colonists had also come from New Haven, distressed by their recent annexation to Connecticut, and had founded Newark. But West New Jersey had been neglected until the Quakers were allowed to found Burlington in 1677.

As trustee of the new plantation, Penn had settled a quarrel between two of the founders (even Quakers bickered sometimes) and cooperated in working out a frame of government. The exercise fired his imagination. The notion of a Quaker colony had been with him ever since Fox made the suggestion, but here was action, if only on a petty scale. What had begun small could with God's blessing become magnificent.

Room must be found for a Quaker commonwealth, founded on the proposition that all men are brothers, tawny as well as white, Anabaptists, Anglicans, Catholics, as well as Quakers. There must be space to grow, land capable of providing "all foison, all abundance to feed my innocent people." The little community of Burlington was not enough; given the squabbles about jurisdiction, the rest of New Jersey might claim it, as in fact presently it did. What was needed was unquestioned proprietorship, and Penn went forth to get it.

Not for nothing had the elder Penn sent from his deathbed to ask the Stuarts to continue their favor to his son. Only in fulfillment of a promise would they have granted such bounty to one of the most despised of sects. Not that they despised it; as members, secret and acknowledged, of another unpopular faith, Catholicism, they could have a fellow feeling for the hounded Quakers.

Even so, they might not have been able to make the grant on favor alone. The unallotted portions of the new world had shrunk fast during the reigns of the Stuarts; what Penn asked for was nearly the last. And though by now no informed Englishman looked to America for gold mines, the value of the lands was known, and they could not be lightly bestowed. Penn might have asked in vain had not a debt to his father given Charles the necessary pretext. He extinguished the debt (the sum was about £16,-000) by awarding a proprietorship like that of Maryland, and exercised his royal prerogative by naming it. Penn demurred at the show of vanity implied by the name Pennsylvania, but his majesty laughed at him. "It is not you but your father I honor," he said.

This was in 1681. At once Penn was the busiest man in England. There was a prospectus to write and distribute among possible settlers; there were terms to be arranged, ships to be chartered, lands to be surveyed, another frame of government to be drawn up.

More adept at map-reading than any Stuart, Penn chose the right, the inevitable, site for his metropolis, the junction of the Schuylkill with the Delaware at the approach to the rich alluvial valleys that would make the best farmland in the world. He sent his cousin, William Markham, to act as his deputy until he could follow, to make a specific selection of the grounds and supervise the surveying.

The town was to be the first full-fledged example of city planning in America. Penn had lived through the plague and fire of London, and would not permit in the city of his dreams the crowded, tortuous ways that facilitated such disasters. The streets were to be given a width generous for their time and laid out like a checkerboard. Lots were to be ample enough to allow not only building but the planting of gardens and orchards; the best trees were to be spared. Its name would symbolize his holy experiment, Philadelphia, or Brotherly Love, "named before thou wast born," as he apostrophized it.

His instructions to settlers were both inspirational and realistic; he had studied the experience of earlier colonies as carefully as he had read his maps. He devised a Frame of Government; he did not in it foresee all contingencies, and he was to be hampered by being seldom on the spot to deal with them as they arose; nevertheless, abdicating the absolute control to which his position as proprietor entitled him, he provided the self government for which Virginia had waited so long, New Netherland in vain, and which had been so successful in New England. There would be complete liberty of conscience. The Indians would be accepted as men, not savages, and treated with justice.

His prospectus won immediate response. He had great hope of the Welsh Quakers, of the sturdy yeoman class that made the best pioneers. (He had planned to name his colony Welsh Sylvania.) They did not disappoint him. He had hopes of German Quakers along the Rhine where he had made proselytizing missions. Most of the people who responded and founded Germantown were actually Dutch and Swiss. The real German emigrants (perversely called Pennsylvania Dutch) would not arrive in number until after his time.

The response was eager and continuous. In less than a decade Philadelphia's population of four thousand slightly exceeded New York's, and if it could not match Boston's seven thousand, it was a more sightly town. Its streets followed an orderly pattern, not the cow paths of Boston legend, and brick houses stood on them, some three stories high and balconied. Many people both here and in the lovely countryside already had wealth. Penn had no inkling of how rich the lowly Quakers could become. The colony had taken root with nothing like a general starving time, without serious illness. It was America's most notable success story.

But not for its founder. The tremendous cost of establishing even so promptly productive a colony exhausted Penn's fortune; he was to see prison again, a debtor's prison. His colonists would with apparent ingratitude default on the quitrents on which he depended. Granting freedom of conscience did not eliminate bickering on doctrinal matters. His eldest son would prove unworthy. "I am a man of sorrows," said Penn.

He was perhaps the only Pennsylvanian who suffered chronic homesickness. With him the nostalgia was for Pennsylvania itself; it was given him to see the land of his prayers only twice, in visits nearly a generation apart.

3

He first visited his colony in late October 1682, and the two years he spent there were the happiest of his life.

The voyage out on the *Welcome* had been unlucky. Though

once in a while favorable winds brought a ship to America in little more than three weeks, the *Welcome* was more than two months on the way; smallpox broke out and thirty died of it. Immune himself, Penn helped nurse and comfort the stricken, and profited by the experience. It gave him the idea for one of his first civic projects for Philadelphia, a hospital, and enabled him to give future immigrants practical advice. He directed that in passage they were to be in the open air as much as possible, to "scrape often the cabins under the beds, and either carry store of rue and wormwood and some rosemary, or often sprinkle vinegar about the cabins. Pitch burnt is not amiss sometimes against faintness and infectious scents." He recommended arrival in early spring or fall, preferably the latter, for "it is more healthy to be followed with winter than summer."

He landed October 28 at old Fort Casimir, now New Castle, and there took formal possession of his proprietorship by receiving the symbols of turf, twig, and water. His next stop was Upland (Chester) and then he saw Philadelphia.

It was still a-building. Many people were cave dwellers, having dug shelters into the high river banks. But the men were hard at work laying foundations for more stable quarters, and in the meantime they were gay. Later they would spin yarns of these days, for the children born in good houses of bonded brick. A Mrs. Morris would say that once she didn't know where her next meal was coming from until her cat came in with a fine rabbit.

Francis Daniel Pastorius, a Pietist from Frankfort, arrived with his followers shortly after Penn, whom he had known in the days of his Rhenish missions, and proudly invited the proprietor to the little house he built in Philadelphia while awaiting an allotment for his "German colony." The house was fifteen by thirty with oiled paper over the windows, but it bore a motto in sonorous Latin over the door: "A little house, but a friend to the good; remain at a distance, ye profane." Penn studied the inscription, roared with laughter, and then walked in.

He himself lived in Chester, where the first Pennsylvania Assembly was held in March 1683, until a house could be built for him in Philadelphia. His own homestead was to be Pennsbury,

twenty miles up the Delaware on a site commanding a magnificent
view. The rest of his life, homesick in England, Penn would be
sending gardeners and carpenters to Pennsbury, instructions for
planting, for the laying out of his great hall, the placing of a
Dutch door, the dimensions of his stables, the upkeep of the little
wharf at which were moored the barges on which he depended
for transportation to Philadelphia. On his second visit his son
John would be born there and nicknamed "the American."

He was much afield, rejoicing in his woods, his "sylvania," like
Adam in Eden. He found tall, rough-barked chestnuts, fruitful
after a century of growing; their nuts were roasted against the
winter, or stored as they were in the lofts. There were cedars,
oaks, groves of great beech, their flanks silver smooth, their
branches forking into the sky like white lightning. The country
abounded in what Penn called peaches, possibly the American
wild plum, or, as he suspected, the offshoots of peach orchards
planted by the Scandinavians and Dutch. Whichever they were,
they had a rosy radiance in the spring; in the summer they bore
so heavily that the boughs sometimes broke under the weight.
The fruit lay on the ground and hogs ate it; it was gathered,
sun-dried, and then stored in the lofts to be stewed with the
meat in winter. Or it was crushed into a pleasant drink and spirits
were distilled from it. Penn tasted the punches and brandies
(Quakers no more than other Englishmen were yet teetotalers)
and found them good.

There were the dwellers of these forests, the Indians. Penn's
greatest personal triumph, and one that brought no aftertaste of
bitterness, was that the Indian troubles that beset other colonies
would be unknown in his for more than three generations. Partly
he was lucky. The Indians here were less warlike than tribes farther west and had already had fair treatment from the Dutch
and Scandinavians. But more than luck, it was foresight and
philosophy. Under Penn's direction the colony not only treated for
the land and paid for it (most colonies did that), and kept promises with a fidelity less commonly practiced; but they were prepared to respect the Indians as fellow human beings.

Penn had given thought to this matter from the moment that

he had his charter. In the thick of the business of recruiting and provisioning his colonists, he had in 1681 found time to write a letter to the Indians. God, he told them, had given him his province, "but I desire to enjoy it with your love and consent that we may always live together as neighbors and friends, else what would the great God say to us?"

In America he lost no time in visiting the chiefs (one in Bucks County was named Tammany) to win their friendship and their consent to selling land. Where and when he made his celebrated Treaty, he did not report; actually there were many treaties, there being many chiefs. His account of a negotiation in 1683 is representative.

The king sat in the center of a half moon, with his Council, the old and wise men, ranged at either side, and what Penn called "the younger fry" settled behind him. All sat on their haunches, legs upright, with grave dignity, and when one man spoke the others listened in complete silence.

Penn was absorbing the local tongues fast, especially the place names, which seemed to him wonderfully melodious, but he had to convey his message through an interpreter. The best interpreters were such Scandinavians as had also learned English. But if John Smith could give Powhatan lectures on astronomy by means of signs, Penn was no less ingenious, and unlike Smith he was under no compulsion to lie. The English were not here for a visit but to stay; they wanted land. Would the chief let them buy it?

It was not for the chief to decide so important a matter. He must discuss both willingness to sell and the price with his people. Penn observed that during successive negotiations the price rose rapidly; "that which would [formerly] have bought twenty might now buy two." But agreement was reached; land was awarded and paid for in kettles and bolts of cloth. (Pennsbury had been paid for partly in rum, but Penn quickly learned the inadvisability of that.) The chief expressed his appreciation that Penn had come in person. "Many governors had been in the river . . . but no governor had come to live and stay here before, and having now such a one that had treated them well, they should never do him or his any wrong." After each sentence the people shouted "and said Amen in their way."

One thing impressed Penn about such transactions. When the price was paid, the chiefs kept the least part. All the rest was distributed among their people. "They are not disquieted with bills of lading and exchange, nor perplexed with chancery suits."

Penn made a point of attending festivals, such as the one when the corn came in. He sat "on a green seat by a spring under some shady trees," and ate venison and hot cakes, and once took part in the games. The younger men were exhibiting their prowess in leaping when the governor left his "green seat" and leaped as high as the best of them. He was still only in his thirties, and in the full vigor of life, though his baldness may have made him look older. Or was his baldness revealed to the Indians? Later generations of Quakers would renounce such worldly vanities as wigs, but it is difficult to picture Penn without one, since his only portrait, painted in Ireland when he was fresh from France, shows him curled and powdered.

Friendship was established on so firm a foundation that when a farmer had to leave for a few days, it was to his Indian neighbors that he turned for protection of his family. Not uncommonly a white couple left their children with the Indians when they made a journey together. Raids were unthought of; and not even the devoutest Quaker, not even the Pietist Pastorius would hear of deriding these good friends by calling them savage.

But the arrangement was not altogether to the advantage of the Indians. As the white colony grew the red men diminished perceptibly. As the Europeans poured in, they grew more and more willing to sell out and retreat to the headwaters of the Susquehanna. Pastorius noted an odd superstition among them, that one Indian would die for every white man who came. It was no superstition. There is no record of such epidemics as nearly depopulated the nations of eastern Massachusetts, but from the arrival of the Swedes the Indians had inevitably been exposed to unfamiliar infections. The white men, however kind and honest, brought the red men death. Quietly, with no fuss about it, the Indians moved up-country.

4

Penn left for England in 1684, hoping to return at once with his dedicated wife. But his beautiful Gulielma died without ever seeing America; one complication after another detained the proprietor until nearly the turn of the century.

The most pressing reason for his stay was a boundary dispute with Maryland. The current Lord Baltimore insisted on the fortieth parallel, and Penn's surveyors had made the dismaying discovery that this would run the line just north of Philadelphia, to say nothing of the lower Delaware. Penn now based his hopes on that clause in the Maryland charter which applied it only to lands "hitherto unsettled." Poor martyred Swanendael had been founded just before the *Ark* and the *Dove* entered the Chesapeake, and Penn had been sedulously collecting evidence of that brief settlement. But the dispute dragged on for years; eventually Penn kept Philadelphia at the cost of Delaware.

Another complication was the turn of political events in England that culminated in the Glorious Revolution of 1688. The second James, who had succeeded the second Charles, was deposed for his Catholic proclivities, and Penn suffered guilt by association; he was even accused of being a Jesuit. Again he saw the inside of the Tower, and he lost his proprietorship. But there was no evidence against him aside from his favor with the Stuarts. His prison term was brief, his colony was restored, and these events were the least of his real troubles.

Money was the problem. He had invested nearly everything he possessed, had often provisioned settlers who lacked means, and had entrusted management of his affairs in England to an agent who cheated him and made preposterous claims that eventually would land Penn in debtors' prison, again briefly. He had asked no salary for his services to the colony, but he did count on quitrents, payable yearly at the rate of one shilling for every hundred acres. It was a modest return for the benefits received, but it was rarely paid, and this to the harried Penn seemed like base ingratitude.

The colonists didn't see it or mean it that way. In their eyes they had already paid for their land twice over: first by buying it at the rate of £100 for every thousand acres, second by the Herculean labor of clearing it and planting it. When their Assembly voted a tax, they paid it, usually. What then were these quitrents, which harked back to feudal custom already obsolescent in England and anachronistic in the new world?

Even settlers who appreciated what Penn had done for them, who realized his need and had no prejudice against archaic tradition, often defaulted because they lacked the means to pay. A mint was one institution that Penn had neglected to set up in Philadelphia, and if he had, its coin, like the pine-tree shilling of Massachusetts and the Indian wampum most colonies found useful, would have had only local value and would have been of no use to Penn in coping with his creditors in England. The colonists used whatever currency came to hand: English shillings and crowns, Spanish pieces of eight, Dutch rix-dollars. But there were never nearly enough to go around, let alone send to England to pay an obscure, uncomprehended obligation to an absentee proprietor. Later, when conditions were more stable, the rents would be paid and become the basis of the Penn fortune. But by that time the founder would be in his grave.

Worse than such anxieties was news which seemed to spell utter ruin for his colony. He heard of the infamous use to which the caves were put, once the settlers moved into proper homes; they became grogshops and a trysting place for prostitutes. He heard of religious dissension set off by one George Keith, who was leading some Quakers, including eventually his scapegrace son the third William Penn, back into the Church of England. The Church was welcome in his colony, free to proselytize, but the hostilities Keith was unleashing in a place consecrated to brotherly love were gall and wormwood to the man of peace. Was his Holy Experiment after all to be only another Massachusetts?

The dissensions carried over into Assembly, where the Anglicans hoped to wrest the balance of power from the Quakers, and without him the legislature was taking the bit in its teeth. It was rendering all but superfluous the Council which he had placed over it to restrain it, and the transition was not taking place in sweet amity. On the spot Penn might have coped with the situation, or at least have seen it in proportion; during his short residence he had already made changes in his Frame of Government. Now, an absentee landlord, he was like a hen frantically clucking from the shore to a brood of ducklings that have taken to the water. In his anxiety he appointed one deputy governor after another (his oddest and most unpopular choice a Puritan from Boston), and once considered putting an end to the representative government which he had created, by abrogating every law passed since his departure. Luckily he did not.

5

Actually, in spite of discords, the colony was progressing famously without him. The politico-religious garboils were not cataclysmic. They were the subsiding wake of a century given to such turmoils; Philadelphia was on the way to providing a suitable sphere of activity for that very secular child of Puritanism, Benjamin Franklin. Probably the bulk of the settlers were oblivious to the disputes. The rapid growth of Philadelphia as a seaport had brought in a floating population, some of whom put the caves to questionable uses; but the city fathers had them filled in, and it is hard to believe that there were many prostitutes.

The position of women was high. As in most colonies, they were in a minority. As seamstresses, knitters, spinners, they could command high wages, and there were none so ill-favored as to lack opportunity to marry. A spinster of twenty was rare, "and seldom any young married woman but hath a child in her belly or one in her lap."

Orderly villages were springing up through the magnificent farmland. The picture more resembled New England than Virginia, for Penn had taken a stand against the creation of large, isolated estates. He wanted the settlers to congregate in villages, not as a protection against the Indians, there being no need, but that each might live near a meetinghouse and his children near a school. These had been provided. Not even Philadelphia had as yet a Latin School such as existed in Boston, and there was no thought of a university. Quaker philosophy supported education, but only in its plain, pragmatic fundamentals. Everyone should read his Bible for himself without interference from one trained in the finespun theorizing that went on at universities.

The English communities were widely distributed; the non-English concentrated in settlements where they could be among their own kind, speaking their own language, following their own customs. Penn was not one to worry about assimilation. The Scandinavians and the Dutch occupied some of the best land along the Delaware, in narrow strips running back from the shore. The Welsh were giving old-world names like Radnor and Bryn Mawr to their communities. The "Germans," under the lead of Pastorius, had founded Germantown.

Each settler had his story. It is time to take a sampling.

The first Welshman in the country was young Thomas John Evans. Early in June 1681 he heard of Pennsylvania, and was so stirred that three weeks later he was off to London, stopping first at St. Peter's fair in Bala to say good-by to his friends. He was single and unencumbered.

These were early days for prompt service to Philadelphia, where Markham had just begun surveying, and Evans had to wait three months for passage. Then the ship, beset by storms and a broken rudder, was months on the way, and when the youth was set ashore at Philadelphia his means were exhausted. He was told that this was Philadelphia; what met the eye was "only the wild woods nor anyone to welcome." At random and alone he set off to find a means of livelihood. This was his personal starving time; later he remembered that "he longed very much at this time for milk."

So wandering he met an old man who had been taking something stronger than milk, for he was very drunk. He was a strange old man; drunk or sober he understood neither Welsh nor the

English that Evans had learned on his travels. But he was also cordial and by signs induced the youth to follow him home. There at last he had his welcome. He had fallen in with some of the Old Settlers, Swedish or Finnish, an aging couple with several hearty sons. Evans could even tell the saga of his voyage, for the sons understood English.

He was still working and living with this family in August 1682 when forty of his countrymen arrived, many from Bala. There was still little to Philadelphia but the stakes driven by Markham's surveyors. Until Penn came and they could negotiate with him for their own tract, they took to the caves, where Evans visited them. They had little to do with and no livestock, "yet no one was in want and all were much attached to each other; indeed much more so perhaps than many who have every outward comfort this world can afford."

Evans remained with the Old Settlers, and for three years, discouraged about his prospects, planned to take the next ship home. There was no want of shipping now. Almost daily, ships beat up the Delaware and into the Schuylkill; Philadelphia was rising from the woods and had docks. Carpenter's Wharf could receive a ship of two hundred tons broadside. Yet somehow Evans missed one passage after another.

The matter was settled in 1686 when he got land of his own and married a wife. She was Lowery, widow of Thomas Llwyd, or Lloyd as the English spelled it, who had been a bard before he abandoned such frivolity to become a Friend. The land was three hundred acres in the new Welsh community of Radnor Township, not far from Bryn Mawr. It was still woodland; "it was a rare and pleasant thing to hear a neighbor's cock crow."

Evans started with only one horse, and his wife fell victim to a recurrent "tertian ague." But the man had learned to swing an ax from his hosts; he had fellow countrymen about, and they were pious, friendly; "everything was agreeable to these innocent people." The Lord blessed him with more horses, twelve good milch cows, and in due time eight children.

Yet the old world was never forgotten. John, the oldest boy, liked to listen in winter when his parents sat by the fire to remi-

nisce of places like Bala, Llanagen, Llyn Tregid. Sometimes, in
spite of their frugal habits, they spun their yarns until midnight,
and even after they had settled in bed they would "fondly recall
to each others' recollection some man or hill, house or rock."
What they so cherished must not be lost, and after the father died
in 1707, but with the mother still there to refresh his memory, the
eldest son made pious record of these things and sent them to a
kinsman in Wales.

From Bucks County a little girl wrote home to tell her English
grandmother about Pennsylvania. It was the "28th of the 11th
Mo., 1685." Penn had had time to visit his province and go home.
Sally Brindley was writing of her home newly completed.

"I wish thee could see our big kitchen. It has a fireplace entirely
across one end of the room. Papa brings the back log in with the
horse, and when the boys pile up wood against it, such a fire as
it does make. . . . The new house is built of logs and all nicely
plastered. We'll be good and warm this winter. There is room in
the fireplace for Papa's big chair and Mama's rocker. There is a
bench on the other side . . . for us children. There is a little
window near the chimney where the spinning wheel stands."

Children were busy in the new world. Sally gathered chips,
roasted chestnuts ("I have four quarts dried"), and was learning
to bake johnny cake Indian fashion on the coals. Another little
girl nearby had the job of driving home the cows. Since during
the day the animals ranged at will in the wild wood, this could
be a perilous task, and once the child got lost. "Dark came on
and she heard the wolves howling. It was very late when she found
the cows all huddled together. Her father found her next morning fast asleep alongside of the bell cow. She was safe and sound.
I'm glad I wasn't that little girl."

Sally went to "school" to her mother. "She is the teacher and I
am the scholars. I am the head of my class. Papa says if I keep
on doing that well he will send me to England when I get big."
Quakers had their family jokes. But Sally's letter would entitle
her to stand at the head of larger classes.

Her brothers, being older, were often afield. There was a
meadow to be ditched; their father was ranger, and they helped

him pick up stray cows and horses in the woods and inspect
their earmarks to identify the owners. In the spring there were
shad to be taken from the river and salted. Now in November
there was hunting; they had just brought in two wild turkeys.
"We'll have one for dinner on sixth day, which is monthly meeting, and the other on first day."

Sally described the herb garden, planted with sage, camomile,
thyme, comfrey, rue, yarrow, and onions. There was room for a
bushy, fruit-laden plant cultivated only as an aesthetic curiosity.
"We have great big love apples. . . . Uncle Henry found them
last summer among the Indians and brought some of the seeds
home. Mama says they are poison if we eat them. They are just
pretty to look at."

As of 1685 the Brindleys could not have been long in the country, and the child remembered affectionately but without a trace
of homesickness "the dear old place I love so well." In sending "lots
of kisses" to her grandmother she did not forget to add "two pats
for dear old Rover."

The "German" Quakers, most of them Dutch and known as
Mennonites, settled Germantown under the leadership of one real
German. This was Pastorius, who had come in 1683 as agent for
the projected Frankfort Company, whose colonists never came.
A man as learned as he was devout, he had pursued his studies,
mostly in law, at four universities, Altborg, Strasbourg, Basel,
and Jena.

He had come on the *America*, which he called a Noah's ark.
Its eighty passengers ranged in age from twelve weeks to sixty
years, and represented a diversity of the Protestant sects of Europe. They included the Welsh doctor Thomas Lloyd, a future
governor of Pennsylvania, with his wife and eight children; he
and Pastorius talked in Latin, which to Pastorius' satisfaction
the Welshman "did pronounce right in our German way." There
were a French captain, a Dutch baker, one Cornelius Bom, who
would set up his bakeshop at the edge of Philadelphia and ride
out to peddle his cakes to the Indians. There were the German
weaver Isaac Dilbrick and his wife and two sons, the English

glass blower Joshua Tittery, and an assortment of servants, husbandmen, and mechanics.

Pastorius tarried in Philadelphia, which already boasted a tavern, the Blue Anchor, until he could settle the matter of the allotment for the Frankfort Company. He was disappointed; Penn would not make grants to emigrants not yet on the way. Pastorius had to join forces with the Crefeld "low Germans," whom he seems not to have liked. "Send only Germans," he wrote to Frankfort, "for the Hollanders, as troublesome experience teaches me, are not so pleasant, which in this land is a highly necessary quality."

Pleasant or not, it was to the Dutch that Pastorius owed the privilege of laying out a city in which he would be the leading citizen, Germanopolis, which soon became Germantown. This ceremony took place on October 24, 1683. The site was a two-hour walk from Philadelphia, on "good black fertile soil," watered with "many fresh wholesome springs." There was good pasture, and an abundance of oak, walnut, and chestnut. He laid out his tiny metropolis on the square-set plan of Philadelphia. Its main street was sixty feet wide, its side streets forty; each plot was three acres, except his own, which was double.

Germantown started with forty-one settlers in a dozen families. The people were poor, having "laid out all their substance on the journey, so that if William Penn had not advanced provision to them, they must have become servants to others." They were rather deficient in agriculture, being mostly linen weavers. But they learned to raise flax, and linen was in demand; within a year "by frequent going to and fro" they had trodden out the path to Philadelphia "into good shape." By 1686 they had a little church, and two years later could boast of fifty houses.

In June 1691 Pastorius opened the first Council meeting with divers "holy admonitions," drawn from New Testament and Old, and the Council adopted its seal, a trefoil, each leaf representing an industry of the place: a grape leaf, a flax blossom, and a weaver's stool, "to signify that one may in this place maintain himself by cultivating the vine, by growing flax, or by manufacture, to the satisfaction of God and his own." Pastorius was the first burgomaster and justice of the peace. He also became schoolmaster, composed a kind of encyclopedia for his students, the *Beehive*, and had the distinction of contributing to the first American protest against slavery, drawn up by his fellow Mennonites in Germantown.

6

In 1699 Penn made his second and last visit to his colony. His arrival coincided with a more sinister visitation, Philadelphia's first experience with yellow fever; for all his careful planning he could not preserve his city from pestilence. This time it was not severe—Charleston, already planted far to the south, was the real sufferer—and it did not mar the happiness of his visit. He had been absent so long that he had something of the quality of a legend, a figure recalled from a heroic age, and he was so received. He looked on his work and it was good; in his presence the bickering that had so distressed him from a distance became manageable.

In Europe, Pennsylvania was the most famous of American colonies, quite apart from its attraction to prospective emigrants. Of its predecessors, only Massachusetts had achieved such rapid progress. But the philosophy of the Bay Colony founders, with their stern emphasis on religious ideology, represented a past that Europe was finally glad to be rid of. It was a product of the bitter sectarian wars that had made the waning days of the Renaissance so bloody. The colony achieved greatly, and during this century was already beginning the painful evolution of a more liberal outlook; but while theocracy endured, its appeal in Europe would be to the like-minded.

Penn's philosophy, on the other hand, anticipated what was to be called the Enlightenment. It was not that he had more virtue and genius than Massachusetts men like the two John Winthrops, both of whom would have been happy in a more liberal age. It was a matter of timing; he had been born late enough to sense the shape of things to come.

So his colony quickly became a suitable nurturing ground for that child of theocracy who was to become America's most distinctive contribution to the Enlightenment, Benjamin Franklin. Europe looked on Penn's achievement and admired it. Voltaire remarked of his treaty with the Indians that it was the only one "that had not been ratified by an oath and that was never broken." Penn's acceptance of the Indians as brothers found a reflection in Jean Jacques Rousseau's concept of the noble red man. And even Muscovy had heard of Pennsylvania. The interest of Peter the Great is a picturesque footnote to Pennsylvania history.

Young Peter was in England in 1698 to study shipbuilding, and Penn met him. The Russian giant, whose engaging quality was his eagerness to learn, was fascinated by the encounter. Penn's plans for Philadelphia were of extraordinary interest to one who, exasperated by the hold of tradition on Moscow, was about to design a metropolis according to his heart's desire. But when Penn told him that his colony had no militia, Peter stared. How, he asked, could any state survive without training in the arts of war?

Penn could not win him to what the Quakers called a "convincement," but he made a lasting impression. Years later, when Peter was engaging in one of his perennial campaigns against the Swedes, he came upon a town where there was a Friends' meetinghouse, at the moment occupied as a barrack. Peter evacuated the troops so that he could see for himself what Quaker meeting was like. What if the testimony there had moved this willing listener as Penn had once been moved in Dublin? But that is only an if of history. Peter was not moved, not convinced; the kingdom of heaven cannot be taken by storm, and the Inner Voice does not respond to a command performance.

1

Just before Philadelphia was founded, just as Carolina (whose story is to come) was taking root after a series of false starts, the two oldest and most populous colonies were threatened with extinction. In Virginia and in New England the original landholders united in an effort to push the white trespassers back into the sea. Given a more perfect union they might have succeeded.

Both attempts were begun in the same year, almost the same month, June and July 1675. Was there a direct connection? Before hostilities began in New England, the Wampanoag sachem whom the white men called King Philip was known to have made secret missions to the west to secure alliances. Did he also find the means to send emissaries to Indians as far south as the Chesapeake? The Virginia governor, for one, suspected that he had done so.

But it is also true that conditions were ripe in both sections for such an outbreak. Since the massacre of 1644 the Virginia Indians had been relegated to something like reservations, and even these were menaced. The whites were beginning to press westerly from the tidewater regions, and in the early 1670s Governor Berkeley caused alarm by sending discoverers to find a path through the Alleghenies, finally with success. In New England, between the villages in the Plymouth and Providence Plantations, settlers were disregarding old treaties in order to take land of their choice, and King Philip, son of old, friendly Massasoit, was brooding over an unforgivable insult. If there was ever to be a stand against the whites, the time was now, in the summer of 1675.

What could have saved the Indians, who deserved so much better than they got? Virginia's brief impulse to Christianize and assimilate had died with George Thorpe in the massacre of 1622; the College Lands that Thorpe had managed were still available, but they were not to be put to use until the 1690s, when William and Mary was founded, and it was no "Indian College." Penn may have had something of the anthropological viewpoint in respecting the red men as they were, but in 1675 he hadn't come, and even when he did he gave no thought to protecting his Indian friends against white man's infections. The Indians also had to be "seasoned" to the new conditions. But though the white settlers early learned to set up quarantine at their ports, these were for their own protection; no one thought of quarantining the Indians against them.

There were portents in 1675 to warn the colonists of impending disaster, and perhaps to nerve the Indians to attack. For a week a comet spread its tail across the sky. In Virginia there came an extraordinary invasion of wild pigeons; while they passed they darkened the sky like thunderheads, and when they alighted they broke the boughs of trees under their weight. Such a sign had preceded the massacre of 1644. And when the raids and captures and tortures began, and survivors fled the frontiers, and even the great plantations in Tidewater Virginia and the inhabitants of Boston were afraid, people searched their consciences to find cause for this manifestation of God's providence. The Virginia House of Burgesses no less than the General Assemblies of Puritan New England multiplied their laws against profane speaking, improper carriage, Sabbath-breaking. Their consciences thus instructed them in their offenses against God; they seem to have been silent on offenses against such fellow men as were red.

In neither section did the Indians win; the white men stayed. In Virginia there would be intermittent troubles for decades to come as the westering continued, but the established plantations were no longer troubled. In New England, King Philip and his allies fought for more than a year on widely flung fronts; but in August 1676 the king fell at last, and Plymouth and Boston were each awarded a trophy to put on display: Plymouth the head, Boston the right hand.

Aside from the demonstration that safety could not be taken for granted, but must be vigilantly guarded, the importance of the Indian wars lay chiefly in their aftereffects on the white man. In New England it was the beginning of a long train of events that would effect radical transformation, especially in Massachusetts. In Virginia it was the immediate cause of a second American revolution, this one of a far deadlier nature than the bloodless expulsion of Governor Harvey.

2

One of King Charles's first acts after his Restoration was to reinstate as governor of Virginia Sir William Berkeley, who had with such spirit tried to hold Virginia for the Cavaliers against Cromwell. Berkeley had been waiting for this day ever since, in his many-gabled mansion, Greenspring, about seven miles from Jamestown.

The governor's early administration had been able and honest, and so was the start of his second. But well before the Indian outbreaks, his popularity had conspicuously waned. His rule had become autocratic; instead of holding annual elections for the House of Burgesses, he had kept one set of representatives for fourteen years. Though the phrase "taxation without representation is tyranny" had yet to be coined, many freeholders already felt the force of its sentiment. They were oppressed by a poll tax levied without reference to ability to pay at closed court sessions from which the "commons" were excluded. In England the price of tobacco had fallen, and the Navigation Act, imposed by Cromwell and continued by Charles, prevented their finding a market in Europe. For this last detail Berkeley was not to blame, but he had no patience with protests.

He had begun life in Virginia as a youngish man; in 1675 he was approaching his allotted three score and ten. He had grown deaf; it was a complaint that no one could confer with him without raising his voice to such a degree that it sounded like a brawl. It is possible that in the crisis now approaching, Berkeley sometimes did not understand what he was told. Always aware that he was missing something, and not acknowledging the cause, a habit of suspiciousness had been growing on him.

He was still a fine figure of a man, if one can judge from a portrait by Sir Peter Lely. He stands in dignity, his face looking out with imperious authority from under a fluffy wig. Only the disposition of the arms and of the rather feminine white hands is curious. Was it the sitter's idea or was it the painter's (he had to finish the portrait after the death of the governor) that his excellency pose them with an incongruous affectation, rather like the stance of a not very graceful dancer?

Old as he was, he had a young wife. Or at least the former Dame Frances Culpeper was only half his age. It was her distinction to become first lady to three governors. When Berkeley married her she was already the widow of Governor Samuel Stephens of Carolina; after Sir William's death she would marry the secretary of Virginia, Colonel Philip Ludwell, and go with him when he was sent to govern Carolina. She was apparently a loyal helpmeet, though, being of aristocratic connections, of no help in enabling Berkeley to grasp what "the commons" wanted. And taking a youngish wife does not necessarily rejuvenate an old man. Unfortunately for the reputation of Sir William, the supreme crisis of his career came when he was already showing symptoms of senility.

It came a year after the start of the Indian troubles when outside the House of Burgesses a young man addressed him with strange oaths: "God damn my blood, I came for a commission, and a commission I will have before I go."

The speaker was Nathaniel Bacon, Jr., not yet thirty, kinsman of the great Sir Francis of Elizabethan England. He was demanding a commission as general of the colonial forces in order to legalize the defiant acts that he and his followers had been performing for some months.

3

When the Indian troubles began, Berkeley did not play the dotard. He assigned the militia of the Northern Neck under the able leadership of Colonel John Washington to investigate three killings and obtain satisfaction. Consistently he showed an anxiety to deal justly with the Indians, at least to the extent that white men hold their fire until friend could be distinguished from foe. An early vigilante party had killed friendly Susquehannas; Washington's attempts at investigation were balked by the killing of several chiefs who had come in good faith to negotiate; Marylanders said the Virginians did it, Virginians said it was the Marylanders. It was this act more than any putative instigation from King Philip that accounted for the ravaging of the upper Rappahannock Valley.

What aroused Virginians was Berkeley's apparent willingness to accept the word of Indians against theirs. In January 1676, hearing that the chiefs were ready for peace, he canceled a second expedition in order to wait on action by the House of Burgesses, which would not meet until March. He ascribed public hysteria to the ignorant and worthless, and when William Byrd, not of this category, reported the killing of three of his men near present-day Richmond, the governor said that the men "were really shut up in a chamber to make the world believe that they were dead."

Such a response did not soothe people thrown into panic by killing raids. Hysterically they took issue with the governor's sane behest that they distinguish friend from foe. How could it be done, they asked, when both wore red skins?

Nor did the burgesses appease them. This was still the "long assembly," its members mostly pro-Berkeley. The only attention they gave the crisis was to order the building of ten forts to contain the Indians. Protest was angry. The Indians would easily avoid such "mousetraps." Forts were less effective than a mobile striking force and much more expensive. To people long exasperated by high taxes and inability to learn where their money went, this measure was the last straw.

In April residents of Charles City County on the south side of the James, hearing that Indians were on the march, acted on their own. An appeal to Berkeley had got them denounced as "fools and blockheads." "A pox take you!" he concluded. They turned for leadership to a young man not long in the colony, who had recently lost in the raids his good friend and overseer.

Young Bacon had the advantage of a Cambridge education, a Grand Tour of Europe, and a devoted young wife who had forfeited a legacy to elope with him. "Nothing in the whole fair garden of Eden would serve her but this forbidden fruit," remarked the judge in settling her father's estate. Bacon had somehow lost his own fortune, and his father, inspired by the fact that a cousin known as Nathaniel Bacon, Sr., had made out well in Virginia after a debt-ridden start in England, had sent his son to the colony in 1673.

Apparently the young man was doing well. As of 1675 he already had two plantations, one near William Byrd's. His wife had joined him, and the governor, a cousin by marriage, had shown him favor; he had made the youth a member of his Council. But when the Charles City men surrounded him shouting "Bacon! Bacon!" and promised "damnation to their souls to be true to him," Bacon responded. Stopping only to collect some forces from New Kent County, he led his men to an Occaneeshee village on the Roanoke River and slaughtered some one hundred Indians.

Justification for such an act against a people who claimed friendship with the English remains a moot point. Berkeley had no sort of doubt that it was treachery. He had tried to head off Bacon, had threatened him and his men with hanging. But he was now sufficiently impressed by the popular uproar to call for the first election in fourteen years. Bacon was the unanimous choice of Henrico County.

Heavily guarded, he moved warily upon Jamestown, but the old governor was warier. He managed to capture "the greatest rebel that ever was in Virginia," and took the occasion to enact a theatrical reconciliation before the burgesses.

"If there be joy in the presence of the angels over one sinner that repenteth, there is joy now, for we have a penitent sinner come before us. Call Mr. Bacon."

Bacon entered on cue to kneel before the governor, confess his guilt, and pray forgiveness. His cousin, the senior Bacon, had been working on him, and apparently he was thunderstruck by the governor's clemency.

"God forgive you, I forgive you," said the governor, and to a question added, "Yea, and all that were with him." He even restored Bacon to his seat on the Council.

For all the drama and dignity of this scene, Berkeley, now thoroughly aware of popular discontent, and exhausted from his days in the saddle when he had tried to head off the rebels, was acting from desperation. Four days before he had sent King Charles a cry for help. "On my knees I beg his sacred majesty would send a more vigorous governor." Could he have had modern communication and modern transportation the course of events might have been far different. But Berkeley was faced by the implacable time lag of communicating across the Atlantic, and Virginia was in for some of its unhappiest days since the garboils and starving times of early Jamestown.

Uneasily Bacon marked time on the Council, and then got away, just in time, on the pretext that his sick wife needed him. When he returned on June 23 it was at the head of a clamorous little army. He too had a sense of the theatrical. When he got the governor to come out of the House, he threw open his coat. "Shoot me, Forgod. Fair mark. Shoot."

Berkeley knew better. Instead he granted Bacon his commission as general of the Virginia forces, which had been promised him, and which he now demanded with many strange oaths. As soon as he marched away, the governor denounced the commission as obtained under duress, and the civil war was on.

For a time Berkeley was the captive of his own people. The newly elected House, which until then like Berkeley had marked time, went into action and passed what were known as Bacon's Laws. They provided for a more vigorous conducting of the Indian war and attended to old abuses: they required rotation of office among sheriffs, prohibited the engrossing of power in one man by multiple office-holding, penalized excessive court fees, opened the closed corporation of the church vestrymen to freeholders.

Meanwhile it was a long hot summer in Virginia with many things happening. Berkeley escaped to Arlington on the Potomac until such time as he could muster shipping to recapture Virginia. Faced with this prospect, Bacon exacted of his followers that they would fight for him even against the British Navy. His officers were aghast; it was still a century to Patrick Henry, and in taking up arms against Berkeley they had no thought of going this far; but they swore.

They captured Berkeley's Greenspring; they seized Jamestown and burned the sorry little capital to the ground. But most of the summer went to an exhausting campaign in Dragon Swamp, where the Pamunkeys had gone into hiding. Nominally these were friends; their queen had appeared before the burgesses and under pressure had promised aid. But killings along the York had been laid to them, and it was Berkeley not Bacon who insisted on distinguishing friend from foe.

The Pamunkeys had their revenge. They did not kill Bacon; their swamp did it for him. He came out of it haggard, stricken with dysentery, and in October died at the home of a friend in Gloucester County. God, remarked Berkeley, had responded to his impious oath "God damn my blood," by so infecting his blood "that it bred lice in incredible numbers."

And he quoted a clergyman:

> Bacon's dead. I am sorry at my heart
> That lice and flux should act the hangman's part.

It was Berkeley who acted the hangman's part. Without Bacon, the rebellion was soon quelled. Charles had heard of it at last, news being brought by Lady Berkeley. Three commissioners were dispatched to investigate and see that order was restored. They bore a royal proclamation offering pardon to those rebels who surrendered voluntarily. In reading the proclamation Berkeley suppressed the reference to pardon.

What had happened to the man who so recently had made a morality play of Christian forgiveness? Until now his part had not been discreditable; he had been dilatory, but his attitude toward the Indians had more justice in it than Bacon's. Had the crisis come in his earlier maturity there might have been no need of a Bacon.

But he was old. During the rebellion he had had a stroke of some sort. It happened publicly, in Gloucester County, where he had hoped to command loyalty and had been greeted with the cry of "Bacon! Bacon!" At the sound the old man had fallen from his horse in a faint. Some said it was sunstroke, but it may have been the more ominous sort, the kind that impairs personality and character.

He had been humiliated. The queen of the Pamunkeys, ordered to withdraw her people from Dragon Swamp to his protection, asked how he could protect her when he couldn't protect himself. And Bacon had begun the hangings; he had put to death at least two men loyal to the governor. Now Berkeley was infected with the old Indian notion of retribution that makes the Biblical precept "an eye for an eye" a concept of enlightened justice; for every death among his followers, for every humiliation he had suffered, he wanted multiple hangings.

The commissioners from England couldn't stop him. They couldn't even conduct a real investigation, for the people, in a greater panic than the Indians had caused, dared not talk. The cowed burgesses industriously repealed Bacon's Laws.

"The old fool!" cried Charles when he heard what was going on. "That old fool has hanged more men in that naked country than I did for the murther of my father."

The old fool was sent for; Berkeley interrupted the dancer's pose for the portrait that Lely was painting and went to England. Fate was kind to him there; he died without having his audience with outraged majesty.

Virginia was left in sorry plight. It took the efforts of several governors and most of the rest of the century to restore it to prosperity. If a term may be set to the beginning of the greater Virginia, future mother of presidents and in the meantime a place of gentle manners on the great estates, one might pick the year 1699. It was then that the capital was moved to the Middle Plantation, or Williamsburg, and battered old Jamestown, whose scant dozen buildings served as inns when the House was in session, peacefully disintegrated. Williamsburg benefited from some of the civic planning that distinguished Philadelphia. A new House of Burgesses was built, with some of its woodwork painted to simulate marble. There was a college nearby, for a charter had at last been secured to take advantage of the income from the College Lands. In time William and Mary would have a distinctive alumnus; when the likes of George Wythe and Thomas Jefferson attended classes they could look across to the little mock-marble House as the natural sphere of their talents.

4

In Massachusetts, Harvard, founded long before, did admit an occasional Indian. John Sassamon, one of John Eliot's "praying Indians," attended for a time and learned enough to serve King Philip as secretary at the time when the latter was plotting against the whites. Philip did not find him trustworthy; the secretary was found dead one day at the bottom of a pond, and the Plymouth authorities hanged three Indians they believed responsible. It was this incident that caused the terrifying intercolonial convulsion known as King Philip's War to break out when it did, on June 24, 1675.

Philip's resentment against the whites went back a long way. A younger son of old Massasoit, he had seen the office of sachem decline from that of a ruler whom the Plymouth authorities held in awe to that of a man who could be picked up like a vagrant, hustled before white magistrates, and rudely called to account. In 1662 this humiliation had been visited on Philip's elder brother Alexander, who had succeeded their father, and Alexander had died of the fever brought on by his anger. After Philip (whose Indian name was Metacomet) became sachem, it happened to him, in 1670, when Plymouth sent for him, disarmed his men, and demanded the surrender of every English gun held by his Wampanoags.

Philip was no man to fold up and die because of insult. He was bold, farseeing, and devious. He put his mark, a capital P, to the papers the magistrates presented him to sign, and then ignored their contents. One was a promise to surrender such arms as the whites had not already taken; when he failed to do so, Plymouth appealed to Boston for backing in a punitive expedition. But Boston had small experience of Indian troubles, and Philip, choosing this moment to make a personal visit, made a great and favorable impression on Bostonians. The Plymouth appeal was dismissed as alarmist, and Philip gained time to work out his grand strategy.

His people were scattered through the Rhode Island and Plymouth jurisdictions. He had one home at Mount Hope in the former, and another near Taunton in the latter. His personal animus was directed at Plymouth rather than Rhode Island, where Roger Williams, very old now, and getting about with a staff, still commanded the affection of his Indian friends; but his plan envisioned far more than the destruction of Plymouth. If his people were to be free, if they were not to be hounded off their lands altogether, the white men at large must be pushed back into that sea whence, on no man's invitation, they had come.

It was to this end that King Philip addressed himself. Strange chiefs came to him at Mount Hope; he went on long journeys. Some said that he went as far west as the Mohawk territory in search of alliances, but that this nation rejected him. He had better success with the Nipmucs, scattered through central and western Massachusetts.

The defection of Sassamon had put him in a quandary that the man's execution did not solve. Details of the campaign were still incomplete (the theory is that it was scheduled for 1676), but his people were aroused by the execution of the executioners, and uncertainty as to what Sassamon might have already divulged made it dangerous to wait. There was a brief period of aimless disorder when Philip's men roamed the country, sniping at cattle, and indulging in petty plundering. It was not until after June 24, when an Indian was wounded by a white, that the killings began.

At once the white men were on the march. Militia came in from Massachusetts, Connecticut, and Plymouth, all under the direction of Josiah Winslow. Rhode Island, though closest to the scene, sent none. Roger Williams was exerting his aging powers to protect his friends, the local Narragansetts. He did not succeed. Though these swore that they had made no pact with Philip, they aroused suspicion by harboring women and children sent to them for protection and by their refusal to surrender "so much as the paring of a Wampanoag's nail" to the whites. The militia, arriving at Swansea to be greeted by the heads of eight white men placed on poles, were disinclined to draw fine distinctions.

King Philip's War nearly ended in mid-July when the militia drove his men into Pocasset swamp, near his Taunton village. The sachem was by then in deep distress, but so were his pursuers, lost on unfamiliar terrain, firing on each other through the thickets. However, the Indians seemed so securely cornered that the militia from Connecticut and Massachusetts withdrew, leaving the mopping-up operation to Plymouth. It was a mistake; Philip escaped to his allies to the west.

Until now these allies had been bewildered by the premature explosion in the east; without a signal, they hardly knew their part, though one Nipmuc group had ventured a raid on the town of Mendon. But with the arrival of Philip, the tribes went into action on so many fronts that it was as if there were a malignancy running through the bloodstream of New England. Captain Edward Hutchinson, eldest son of Anne and William, died in an attempt to restrain the Nipmucs; by September the western part of the colony was in terror, after raids on Deerfield, Hadley, Springfield.

Winter brought a lull in the west, and Philip was believed to be hiding among the Narragansetts. Again militia from three colonies invaded Rhode Island. At South Kingston they lost two hundred men in the Great Swamp Fight, in which they slaughtered three hundred, mostly Narragansetts. But they didn't get Philip. In February he was west of Boston, leading an attack on Lancaster; then he and his allies were in the east, attacking Medfield, Weymouth, destroying Groton and Warwick in Rhode Island, burning much of Providence, including the house of Roger Williams. Then they were despoiling one town after another in Plymouth Plantation; on May 11 they burned sixteen houses in Plymouth town.

Then came another lull. Philip had not been able to wait on the harvest, as he had probably hoped, before starting this war. Some of his famished men stopped at the Great Falls of the Connecticut to fish, and there in mid-May they were surprised and about three hundred were slaughtered. But when the whites heard that Philip was coming with one thousand, they fled.

When summer came Philip retired to his own swampland, this time to die. For him the end came on August 12, and there was little resistance after. The cost to the English had been six hundred killed, thirteen towns razed, and about a thousand dwellings burned. The cost to the Indians? They had no census; there was no accounting the total loss, not even of the women and children shipped to slavery in the West Indies and Bermuda. Philip had failed to push the white men back into the sea, and after him there was no force sufficient to make the attempt.

As evil as the destruction, was the hatred engendered. The Narragansetts' protestation of friendship had been bloodily disregarded. A party of Indians who came to Dover, New Hampshire, to treat for peace were summarily seized and sent to Boston. Women of Marblehead lynched prisoners brought to their town. And one group of Indians who had accepted white man's ways and white man's faith, the "praying Indians" of Natick, were rudely wrested from their homes and relocated in miserable quarters on Boston's Deer Island.

These were followers of John Eliot, who for thirty years had conducted the Puritans' most notable effort to Christianize the Indians. Land had been set aside that his people might live withdrawn from the corruption of rum, and his people governed themselves by rules adapted by Eliot from the Pentateuch. He lived among them studying their language, preaching, patiently answering their questions. "Why does not God kill the devil that made all men so bad, God having all power?" "What is the effect of your religion? We have no contentions about property and no

man envies his neighbor." During earlier disputes in Massachusetts some Indians had asked, "How is it . . . that Mr. Williams is
hunted from his home among Christian men, and Mrs. Hutchinson's body is shut up in prison and her character blackened? Why
is this? Do not all appeal to the Bible and stand fast upon it?"
    During these years Eliot was at work on the Indian Bible. Aside
from the sheer labor of the project, he had difficulty in finding the
exact Indian equivalent for Old Testament concepts, nor dared
he risk misconception by adopting the heathen term for God.
"Weske kutchinik ayam God kesuk kah Ohke" read his translation of the first lines in Genesis. Aided by benefactions from both
Boston and London, in 1661 he published the Indian New Testament, and two years later the Old. At the time of King Philip's
War he was at work on a revised edition.
    The war brought misery for both the Apostle to the Indians and
his bewildered disciples. How explain to them the Christian necessity of their starving time as prisoners on Deer Island? Or that
when Eliot appeared in public godly men reviled and attacked
him?

5

    The losses to New England during King Philip's War were se-
verer than those of Virginia during their concurrent Indian troubles. But New England was spared the bitterness of civil war.
Here there was unanimity of opinion that the Indians must be conquered. Williams had somewhat resembled Berkeley in pleading
that friend be distinguished from foe, but he had valiantly tried to
protect Providence, and he incurred no resentment. On the contrary, when the war was over, the Bay Colony, in compassion on
his "uncomfortable and disabled state," revoked the old edict of
banishment and invited him back for a visit. But Williams was
old and tired and did not long survive his neighbor King Philip.
    If the war did not produce rebellion in Massachusetts, there
was rebellion in the making. The colony had fallen on evil times;
King Philip was only one incident in a chain of disasters that

seemed to betoken that God had withdrawn His grace from a people who had come to the wilderness for His greater glory.

The decline began with the Restoration. When Charles took his place on his father's throne, Massachusetts did not hasten to flatter him with oaths of allegiance. It waited a year to recognize the new regime. There was always the chance that the news was inaccurate, or that Charles would not last. Boston observed the Restoration by hanging four Quakers; the timing was purely coincidental, but it was also unfortunate.

When the Dutch States General had heard in 1664 that the fleet commanded by Sir Richard Nicholls had the purpose of reducing the Bay Colony, it was not wholly misinformed. That was one purpose of the fleet. It did put in at Boston in July, and three commissioners, headed by Nicholls, did remind the Bay of the king's demands, which included an oath of allegiance and liberty to use the Book of Common Prayer, and it did not achieve these ends. Massachusetts officials were old hands at protecting their way of life. Three decades before, when Gorges was threatening their patent and the first Charles explicitly demanded the surrender of their charter, they had successfully practiced evasion. They were no less successful now.

In anticipation of the fleet they set up a watch at Castle Island, and when it came, prevented most of the sailors from going ashore on the grounds that their presence would corrupt the morals of the town. They went aboard and received the commissioners with all courtesy, except that they questioned the authenticity of the letter the commissioners bore from the king. They parried all demands with an expression of satisfaction with the *status quo*. Nicholls, having other things on his mind, had to go to New Amsterdam leaving the issue unresolved. Nor did he have better success when he returned, though he had found Connecticut and Rhode Island cooperative.

His majesty was not amused. This colony's determination to conduct itself like a sovereign state was more obvious than ever, and he had now heard of the hanging of the Quakers. It was not his policy to encourage this sect; imprisonment of Quaker preachers had his approval, but hanging them had not been counte-

nanced in England, and Massachusetts, whatever its delusions to
the contrary, was still English.

The hangings were of importance in attracting royal attention
to the rigidity of Massachusetts intolerance. Before London
heard of the hangings, the colony had on its own volition put an
end to them. It was not that the Quakers had endeared themselves; one young woman dramatized the nakedness of the human soul before the Lord by walking unclothed into Sabbath
meeting, an exploit that would have aroused a more permissive
community. Mary Dyer, nearly the last Quaker hanged, had insisted on it. On her first sentencing she had been pardoned at the
foot of the gallows and sent home to her family in Providence
with the charge that she stay there. But her family couldn't hold
her; she came back and she was hanged.

There was only one after her. The law pronouncing a death
penalty on Quakers who persisted in preaching their subversive
doctrine had been passed by the margin of only one vote. When
an eleven-year-old, Patience Scott, pronounced herself a Quaker,
the magistrates were in a quandary. They packed her off to
Providence, and fortunately for their peace of mind she stayed
there. When William Christison came in the wake of the martyrs,
the magistrates suffered a revulsion and refused to sentence him.
"Thank God I am not afraid to pass judgment!" shouted the outraged Governor Endicott, and did so. But the sentence was never
carried out.

A change in public opinion could not restore lives, and Quakers
were still flogged and marched through town at the tail of a cart.
Even worse, as proof of defiance of royal authority in its attribute
of defender of the faith, was the fact that members of the Church
of England were permitted no house of worship of their own.

Nor had it escaped royal attention that Boston merchants were
ignoring the Navigation Act.

While New England was fighting King Philip, the case of
Massachusetts was being reviewed in England; in 1676 a judgment was obtained against its charter. The *quo warranto* was
brought over in 1683, and two years later the charter was abro-
gated. By this time Charles was dead, and England and New

England were at the mercy of a Catholic king, James II. He sent Sir Edmund Andros to govern not only the Bay but all New England.

Connecticut resisted him with ingenuity. When in October 1687 he descended on Hartford with sixty troops and demanded the charter, it was laid before him. This document was little more than twenty years old; John Winthrop, Jr., who had a gracious way with the Stuarts, had secured it in 1662. It had confirmed Connecticut in its liberties and extended its jurisdiction over New Haven. Only the latter, whose founders were even stricter theocrats than those of the Bay and considered the Connecticut towns peopled by "Christless men," had any quarrel with it. Some of them had set off on their pilgrimages again, to New Jersey among other places.

The charter was obediently placed before Andros, but he never possessed it. Suddenly the house went dark, and when the candles were relighted, the document was no longer there. Legend is that it had been spirited away and hidden in the hollow of the Charter Oak. Fume as he might, Andros had to leave without it. The conduct of the Connecticut legislators had been impeccably correct; they had complied with his demand, and it was only his excellency's fault that he did not pick up the charter in time.

Massachusetts could not be saved by a sleight of hand. It was not a matter of preserving a magic bit of paper; they were victims of a judgment in London. And a proud people who for more than half a century had chosen their own governors, were now subject to an appointee of a Papist monarch, who was a Papist himself, and had no patience with ways to which he was a stranger. They would as happily have accepted Lucifer.

He imposed taxes by decree and questioned the very land titles on the ground that they had been granted under a government that no longer existed. "The calf died in the cow's belly," was one way of putting this theory. But he lacked time to work much mischief; in April 1689 the people of Boston arose and locked him up. They had just had word from England of the Glorious Revolution, of the ousting of the hated James by William and Mary.

It was Boston's first revolution, but it was only a halfway revolution. The shock of the vacating of the charter had been severe, and without authority from England, Massachusetts dared not return to it. Simon Bradstreet—who was very old now, and his poetic Anne had died—was set up as provisional governor. The people waited on a new charter, and it came in 1692, and with it the new governor, Sir William Phipps. At least he was no stranger, being a New Englander born and bred; but he, like all his successors until Massachusetts nerved itself to rebel again, was a royal appointee. Election Day was still a solemn occasion in Massachusetts, but now only for selectmen, representatives; the people must make do with what governors were sent them. Theocracy was at an end, and in Boston the stones had been laid for King's Chapel, which was Church of England.

Connecticut and Rhode Island were luckier; their charters were confirmed, and life went on much as before. Plymouth was not lucky at all, for under the new charter it was merged with Massachusetts, and so were the little villages of Maine.

Theocracy was dead, but its spirit was not. It was no coincidence that the year that destroyed the hope of the theocrats brought to Massachusetts such a social convulsion as made the Anne Hutchinson controversy pale in contrast. The ministers and magistrates joined battle with the devil himself; they fought him in the person of his servants the witches, who, it was now revealed, had in these dark days overrun much of eastern Massachusetts.

While they were secure in their power, the Puritans had taken little account of reports from the invisible world. When a follower of Anne Hutchinson was said to have practiced witchcraft, the charge was not pressed. But now sober, intelligent, Harvard-bred ministers, magistrates, judges caught hysteria from a pack of disorderly teen-age girls in Salem Village, and on the basis of preposterous charges based on no rational proof, tried scores of "witches" and hanged twenty. A few were vagrants. At least one, though not so accused, was probably a Quaker, Susanna Martin, who for thirty years had been a figure of Amesbury folklore. But most were solid citizens, good church members, who demonstrated the toughness of the Puritan fiber by the courage with which they fought what they called the "delusion."

The panic was mercifully brief. In six months it had run its course, and tragic as it had been, the ultimate consequences were wholesome. Not only New but old England, where there had been far deadlier and more prolonged witch hunts, profited by what Massachusetts judges learned about rules of evidence. And theocracy acquired something of that saving grace that it had lacked before, a sense of humility. The witch jury and Judge Samuel Sewall made public confession of error. Later the public revulsion was so powerful that the legislature revoked the convictions of such witches as had survivors to plead for them (not all witches were so blessed, and this movement has continued into very recent times) and made restitution to their families.

Puritanism was by no means at an end in Massachusetts, nor given its sterling qualities should it have been. Hot sermons were still heard in Sabbath meeting; but the Book of Common Prayer was being read in other houses, and such Quakers as heard the inner voice were no longer persecuted for giving it utterance. Massachusetts did not otherwise greatly resemble Maryland, Rhode Island, or Pennsylvania, but in this respect it was following the same road.

XV LAND OF THE PALMETTO: CAROLINA

1

SOUTH of Virginia lay the land long known as Carolina, whose history was a series of paradoxes. It contained the first bit of Atlantic coastline to attract settlers and the last to keep them. When the first enduring English colony was planted, it was peopled more from the Sugar Islands than from England, and had little rapport with the northern colonies; the islands, and even England, were easier of access.

In the part that became Carolina, and presently the Carolinas, there was from the outset what Virginia was still evolving, a mature slave economy. The colony also started with a local aristocracy dignified with exotic titles unknown to *Burke's Peerage,* and a constitution designed by a philosopher.

The greatest paradox was that part which became Georgia. Not only was it founded on principles that ran counterclockwise to the form it eventually took, but its founding was followed in less than half a century by the Declaration of Independence. It is also noteworthy that the co-author of Carolina's constitution, John Locke, could also claim, if he chose, a hand in the Declaration, which owed something to his philosophy.

The first settlement in Carolina went back to 1564, when three shiploads of French Huguenots, sponsored by Admiral Coligny, founded Fort Caroline. But they had happened on what the Spanish called Florida, an elastic geographical entity with no defined northern boundaries, and the Spanish promptly massacred them. The Spanish commander, Menendez de Avilés, took the precaution of explaining that this act was directed not at Frenchmen as such, Spain being at the moment at peace with France, but at heretics. This was in the tradition of the great European witch hunt in which heretics were regularly identified as witches, both being apostates from the true faith. After the massacre the Spanish built a fort at St. Augustine from which to patrol the coast.

Two decades later the English, thanks to the exertions of Sir Walter Raleigh, made their first settlement. The spot chosen was Roanoke Island, hard by the great natural bastion of Cape Hatteras, breeder of storms and contrary winds. Again the Spanish defeated the attempt, though this time indirectly. They tried to take a greater island, England itself, and in the distraction of standing off the invasion, Roanoke Island could not be visited, let alone supplied. When relief finally came there was left of the colony only shards, and a mysterious signpost, "Croatan," the name of a local Indian tribe. What became of the colonists, including little Virginia Dare, first white child born on American soil, no one ever learned. The lost colony became legend, a subject for poets, and for nearly a century it remained the last concerted attempt to colonize Carolina.

In 1629 there was a near miss. Lord Baltimore hoped for land there, but Charles had already granted a patent to Sir Robert Heath. A year later a ship set out for Carolina, carrying French Huguenots. It was the *Mayflower*, not impossibly the same that had landed the Pilgrims far north of their intended destination, for it repeated the performance. The passengers were landed in Virginia; they sued and collected £600 in damages, but they never reached Carolina. After this mischance Sir Robert did nothing with his patent except to block off the territory for nearly four decades from serious settlement.

Some Virginians did press south to form a few communities along Albemarle Sound. Once some New Englanders, always land-hungry, made a "discovery," but not liking it went home again. Responsible settlers would not come in numbers while the land titles were still uncertain, and so for a long time one of the finest stretches of the coast was known only to seafarers. Those who were called privateers (when they held a royal commission and restricted their activities to attacks on enemy shipping) and pirates (when they dispensed with such technicalities) became intimately acquainted with the multiple inlets and snug harbors that lay between St. Augustine and Cape Hatteras, and embarrassingly continued to profit by this knowledge even when at long last the colony of Carolina took root. But they were only hit-and-run visitors, not settlers, and since they kept no records, were not even proper "discoverers."

Meanwhile events were taking place in Barbados and Bermuda and in England itself that would determine the fate of Carolina.

2

The settlement of Bermuda had roughly coincided with that of Virginia; the settlement of Barbados, far south toward the Spanish Main, close to the northern coast of South America, with that of Massachusetts Bay. It was from a brief venture in Barbados that Henry, son of the elder John Winthrop, had been recalled to participate in the founding of Massachusetts, where his adventure was still briefer. Soon after the wreck of the *Sea Venture* on Bermuda reefs in 1609, a permanent settlement was made there and prospered well.

The islands had a particularly intimate relation to majesty; they were considered the king's "foreign domains" rather than part of the kingdom of England. During the rebellion, and especially after the regicide, Barbados and Bermuda refused to recognize Parliament and proclaimed the fugitive Charles II as their monarch. In the former colony Cavaliers acted against Roundheads in their midst by seizing their estates and packing them home to England.

It was the arrival in England of exiled Barbadians clamoring about their wrongs that impelled Parliament to send commissioners to "reduce" the colonies, including Governor Berkeley's Virginia. Thereafter political neutrality prevailed; Cavaliers and Roundheads suffered each other with no further tumults. When in 1660 Charles II was indeed proclaimed king, the loyal looked to him for due reward.

They were bitterly disappointed. Charles indeed distributed baronetcies with a lavish hand, thirteen in Barbados alone. But he left undone that which they most craved; he did not repeal the Navigation Act. Inspired by Cromwell as a punitive measure, this act forbade trade with any foreign nation without special dispensation. Since it was on such trade that the prosperity of the Sugar Islands depended, repeal was the bounty most desired. But the act had proved itself as a source of revenue, and an impecunious monarch in debt to his friends, whose mistresses had expensive tastes, had no intention of abandoning it. Instead of easing the burden he increased it by levying a permanent tax of four and a half per cent on all produce of the islands. The proceeds were earmarked partly to finance the settlement of rival claims to Barbados by the Earls of Marlborough and Carlisle, and partly to enrich the Crown.

In their unhappiness loyal Barbadians began to look elsewhere. Some of them would soon have been bound to do so in any case. Their island was small, sugar plantations required vast acreage, and the tendency had been the creation of a few great estates to the detriment of small planters. Hardly three decades after the first settlement there was no room to expand, and the same was true in Bermuda, where some were saying, "This island is become a prison." Restless islanders, including two of the newly elevated baronets, looked north to the neglected expanse of coast that lay between St. Augustine and Virginia, and made "discoveries."

In this they were aided by the fact that in England King Charles was indebted to a group of personages too distinguished to be awarded such small change as baronetcies. Earldoms were bestowed on some of this kind, and then Charles gave eight of them something more substantial, the proprietorship of the Palatinate of Carolina. He did so first in 1663 and again in 1665, having in the meantime taken the precaution of canceling the patent so long and uselessly held by Sir Robert Heath.

None of these eight men ever saw their palatinate. Unlike Penn, to whom England was a place of exile after he had visited his colony, they were content to direct colonial affairs by remote control. They were men of picturesque history. Edward Hyde, Earl of Clarendon, was grandfather to two future English queens, William of Orange's Mary, and Anne. William, Earl of Craven, old now, was still famous for his youthful exploits in love and war. The great Gustavus Adolphus had commended his courage in battle (by a pat on the shoulder) and he was reputed to have won the heart of the lonely daughter of James I, Elizabeth, Queen of Bohemia.

Sir William Berkeley of Virginia and his brother John were proprietors; at his coronation Charles had made a point of honoring the former by wearing a robe of silk produced at Greenspring. Others were Sir George Carteret, naval officer who had held the Isle of Jersey for Charles, Sir John Colleton, one of the new baronets from Barbados, and two who had played a dual role during the civil war.

George, Duke of Albemarle, was the famous General Monck who had subdued Scotland for Parliament. After the death of Cromwell he had made amends by taking the initiative in recalling the royal exile, and for this service his majesty had made him duke. Anthony Ashley Cooper, Lord Ashley until Charles made him Earl of Shaftesbury, had also been on the welcoming committee at the Restoration, after playing it both ways during the interregnum. Eventually he would forfeit Charles' trust and end his life in exile. A man of great ability, who would rise to Lord Chancellor before his decline began, he became leader of this group and directed the full force of his intellect and his energies to seeing that this time a Carolina patent would not lapse for want of attention.

It was Ashley's doing that Carolina was given a constitution composed by a philosopher. John Locke, then in his early thirties, was a member of his household, and in accepting the assignment must have felt himself the superior of Plato, whose republic existed only on papyrus. Or perhaps he felt nothing of the sort. Plato presumably had a free hand in composition; Locke was under the direction of his patron. A phrase in the preamble to the

Fundamental Constitutions came oddly from the pen of one whose later writing would inspire the Massachusetts Adamses and the Virginian Thomas Jefferson. It was "that we may avoid erecting a numerous democracy."

To this end a local nobility was created which, rather than the "commons," would control the provincial "parliament." Charles had empowered the proprietors to raise a colonial aristocracy on the condition that titles be distinguishable from those in the English hierarchy. So landgraves and caciques were set up in Carolina; the former title, with which went double the amount of land, 48,000 acres, was derived from old German courts; caciques were what Indians in these parts called their chiefs. The honors were to be the exclusive prerogative of Carolina residents; whoever was sent as governor would automatically become landgrave. In practice, however, the proprietors found the quaint titles of utility in seeking favors from their friends; in time there were not a few London landgraves, including John Locke, in recognition of his labors.

The proprietors also established a hierarchy among themselves; the eldest should be palatine, and there were rules of succession. Each was to possess 96,000 acres; other lands were divided into counties, subdivided into baronies and manors. In each county three-fifths of the land was available to common settlers. Many, however, would necessarily settle on the baronies, where they would become leetmen in the tradition of medieval England "under the jurisdiction of the respective lord . . . without appeal from him."

There were eight Supreme Courts, each with its specific function, legislative as well as judicial, and all subject to the Palatine Court in England. Trial by a jury of freeholders was set up in the lesser or precinct courts, but the accused could have legal counsel only as an unpaid kinsman could provide it. The biennial parliament would contain a freeholder elected in each precinct, but these "commons," meeting in the same body and outnumbered by their betters, the governor, the landgraves, and the caciques, would be under due control.

Freedom of religion was conditionally permitted; a freeholder was required only to believe in God and join in the public worship thereof, a provision that admitted Jews. The Church of England was, however, recognized as "the only true and orthodox faith" in that it alone could be supported by public funds.

The government of no American colony had been so elaborately designed while the country was still in the hands of the original caciques. The nearest analogy would be Penn's far more liberal constitution, but Penn would come to his colony and revise on the spot such details as proved unrealistic. The original Carolina proprietors, sitting in state in London, never saw their colony, though one or two of their successors did, and governed in august psuedo-majesty from afar. In practice, however, some adjustments were made by their deputies, the governors.

The constitution was to be ratified by the freemen of the colony; it never was. And though Carolina was founded, acquired distinctive character and even prosperity under this regime, it prospered much better when it finally got rid of the Fundamental Constitutions, the Lords Proprietors, the landgraves, caciques, and all.

3

In its infancy the colony had no less than three Charlestons. The first was founded mostly by Barbadians at Cape Fear in 1665, but it did not last. The proprietors, who then saw their Palatine Court as a kind of land office, had not yet made sufficient financial investment to give their colony real support. Spain and England were at war, and even in the territory that was to become North Carolina the colonists were apprehensive of attacks from St. Augustine or Cuba. They abandoned their settlement in 1667.

By 1669 the constitution was ready and the proprietors had assessed each other £500 apiece to charter three ships, purchase supplies, and begin in earnest. This time the intention was for Port Royal, but when in 1670 the prospective settlers, much diminished, having suffered storms and shipwrecks on the way, reached Carolina, they avoided the place. Reports that the Spanish had stirred up the Indians in that area proved to be true.

What the Spanish could do with Indians under their influence was long to prey on the minds of Carolinians, and these were disinclined to risk the fate of the Huguenots. They accepted an Indian invitation to settle at Albemarle Point (not to be confused with the North Carolina Albemarle, just north of Roanoke Island) and there founded their second Charleston.

A decade later they removed their capital to the third and permanent Charleston, at the junction of the two rivers that they named Ashley and Cooper for the most active of their proprietors. Like Philadelphia, by then in process, it was a planned city, with streets intersecting each other at right angles, and, more than any other colonial city, Charleston was to become not only the capital but the very heart of the young colony.

These settlers lacked a Bradford to record their intimate experience. Of the Cape Fear colony there is only one good story, the fate of a supply ship from Barbados, whose captain was so bedeviled by contrary winds that he went mad and jumped overboard. The vessel was then brought safely to port "by the knowing and prudent conduct of a child," whose name is not on record.

There was a somewhat similar nautical exploit connected with the second Charleston. John Coming, nettled by being accused of cowardice when he lost a vessel on the bar, demonstrated his courage by crossing the Atlantic in a longboat.

Coming had been first mate on the *Carolina*, which with the *Port Royal* and the *Albemarle* had set out from England in 1669. The 121 passengers on his ship included two whose descendants would figure in Carolina history: Stephen Bull, and Captain Florence Sullivan, who gave his name to Sullivan's Island in Charleston Harbor. At least five passengers were women (though when a founding father bears the name of Florence it is difficult to be sure) and sixty-three were servants, some of them picked up in Ireland.

The ships came the long way around under the direction of Joseph West, a decent, able man, who was to serve Carolina thrice as governor. At Barbados other colonists were recruited and supplies assembled. A half-dozen sows and a boar, whose progeny would soon overrun much of Carolina, were added to the manifest. Seeds and roots for experimental planting were taken: cottonseed, indigo, and roots of ginger, cane, and vine, carried in tubs of earth.

The fleet reached Barbados in October; in early November a hurricane damaged all ships and wrecked the *Albemarle,* which had to be replaced by a sloop. At Nevis one Dr. Henry Woodward joined the colonists. He had been left behind on an earlier discovery to remain with the Port Royal Indians to learn their language and ways. His presence here was due to his capture by the Spanish, from whom eventually he had escaped. He was an invaluable recruit; in him the colonists would have an interpreter in their dealings with the Indians, and his work would be important in establishing the fur trade, which would be the first source of Carolina prosperity.

En route to Bermuda, the *Port Royal* was lost. Losing contact with her sister ships, she tried to reach the Bahamas, only to be grounded. The master, John Russell, managed to hire a sloop from nearby Providence to get some of the company to Bermuda, but many had died as castaways, some elected to remain at Providence, and one couple took passage to New York.

In Bermuda the colonists were given their governor. Sir John Yeamans, who had been in nominal charge at Cape Fear, filled in a blank commission in favor of a Bermudian, William Sayle. He was aging, in failing health, and a Puritan, a circumstance that offended much of the company; but before he died in 1670 to be temporarily replaced by the always dependable Joseph West, he had settled his company at the second of the three Charlestons, and after more than a century of false starts, Carolina had properly begun.

4

The new homeland was a far cry from the rocky coasts of New England, the palisades of the Hudson, or the meadows and groves of Pennsylvania. Its vegetation most nearly resembled Virginia's in its cypress swamps, its live oaks, but only southernmost Virginia had the ghostly drippings of Spanish moss from the trees.

It had what Virginia had and more. Palmettos bristled up from the swamps, which harbored the mailed alligators, clumsy and not too dangerous on land, but vicious if encountered in black water, and given in the mating season to roars "like the bellowing of a beef creature." There were fireflies, common to all colonies, but here extraordinarily luminous, lighting up the undergrowth like errant stars. There were the mocking birds echoing the melodies of all feathered kind. There were turtles and tortoises, very good eating these, and on the shore there were sponges and sometimes ambergris.

The climate was warmer than Virginia's. Livestock, in short supply at first, much of it procured at great expense from the north, needed little care and no fodder against the winter. Indeed, the cattle, multiplying in the wild, soon became a pest. For some reason the colonial parliament in Charleston required planters to fence in their lands instead of stockholders to fence in their cattle, and this was a great labor and expense to those who complied and a tribulation to those who did not.

There was no real starving time in a country where three crops could be harvested in one year. There was the usual trouble in acclimating English grains to so exotic a soil, and some protest against the proprietors' sending most of the first fruits for trade with the Sugar Islands. On the other hand, the proprietors were not niggardly with supplies until the colony could produce, the colonists quickly learned the merits of maize, and later experimented with rice seed from Madagascar.

Most remarkable of all, there was at first no "general sickness" on the scale experienced elsewhere. Even the short-lived Charleston at Cape Fear had enjoyed prevailing good health; and though by 1680 the second Charleston at Albemarle Point was removed to what was considered a more healthful spot at Oyster Point, there had apparently been no unusual mortality. "Seasoning" was hardly heard of at first, or was dismissed with the remark that settlers who took ordinary care of themselves speedily recovered. People from Barbados were already seasoned. The puzzling fact that later Carolinians had to take to the sea islands or the pine barrens to escape the fever in summer is sometimes explained by the coming of the Africans. There is a theory that the Carolina mosquitoes did not carry malaria until they tasted the infected blood of a labor force brought directly from the Guinea coast.

Even the Indians lived differently than their brothers to the north. Near the coast their compact communities of round houses thatched with palmetto more nearly resembled African villages than the longhouses and wigwams known to John Smith. And though leathers of deerskin were put to use, deer being abundant in the forests, their women affected a style which would have surprised Pocahontas: moss robes, fashioned from the gray trailings of Spanish moss that curtained the coastal swamps.

Local Indians were friendly at first; it was one of their caciques who had urged the merits of the ultimate site of Charleston upon the settlers. Later, trouble would arise from two causes. One was the planters' craving for cheap labor, which made them disregard the proprietors' express prohibition against enslaving the Indians. The other was the proximity of the St. Augustine Spaniards, who had their own Indian alliances, and used these to make trouble for Carolina.

The earliest years in the colony were nebulous; traditionally, many early settlers were more interested in trade than in planting. But the colony took root and grew. In 1680 when Oyster Point became the third and final Charleston, only thirty houses were built. Two years later there were a hundred, and though most were wooden, the colonists were learning to make good brick; the population of the colony was already twelve hundred. Some who had come as servants had acquired land and cattle and servants of their own. By the turn of the century the population was in the neighborhood of ten thousand, more than half of it Negro. The communities were scattered along the tidal rivers in spite of the handicap imposed by the proprietors' engrossing of large tracts for their own baronies.

Emigrants had been coming steadily from England and the Sugar Islands; Dorchester, Massachusetts, had exported a small congregation in the 90s, troubled, some said, by the prevalence of witch-hunting in the Bay Colony. And the Huguenots, balked so long in their efforts to settle Carolina, had at last obtained a foothold.

5

No one deserved Carolina more. The massacre of 1564 had not deterred them from trying again in 1629, when Cardinal Richelieu was making their life miserable in France. The nautical inefficiency of the *Mayflower's* master did not prevent their attempt again in 1680 when the Lords Proprietors gave them express permission to settle. After 1685, when Louis XIV, le Roi Soleil, went counterclockwise to the European trend toward freedom of conscience by revoking the Edict of Nantes, they came in numbers. France lost the substance of its middle class, as well as some families of aristocratic lineage, and America was the gainer. Boston got its Fanueils and Reveres, and Carolina got whole parishes.

The beginning was not easy. Some had escaped Louis' dragoons with hardly more than the clothes on their backs. Some got to the French border disguised as peasants, carrying what property they could in oxcarts. A few reached Carolina with means; more, including some whose descendants would become first families in fortune and prestige, had nearly nothing. "I have been six months together without tasting bread," Judith Manigault would reminisce in later life, "working the ground like a slave." She had been born to the family of Citon, which had to abandon its Languedoc home with all its furnishings. By bread she probably meant the European kind; friendly Indians had taught the use of maize in corn pone. She had "worked like a slave" with her first husband, the weaver Noe Royer, to help him clear his plot on the Santee. Judith's elder brother endured the hardships in the unfamiliar climate only eighteen months before he died of fever.

The Huguenots founded the St. Denis quarter, named for a French Protestant victory in 1567, and in time occupied much of Craven County. An observer wrote of them as "temperate and industrious," and said that though they had little to make do with, they "outstripped the English who brought with 'em larger fortunes . . . though less endeavor to manage their talents to the best advantage. They live like one family, each one rejoicing at the progress and elevation of his brethren." It might have been, word for word, a description of the Quakers then cheerfully living in their caves on the banks of the Schuylkill.

But the Huguenots were not immediately popular. Their natural cohesion, their program of mutual aid struck some Englishmen as clannishness. When in 1692 Craven County sent to parliament at Charleston representatives bearing names like Alexander Thésée Chastaigner, Paul Bonneau, René Ravenal, there was protest. "Shall the French who cannot speak our language make our laws?" But the enmity was probably less intense than that among Carolinians of English origin by virtue of their affiliations as Roundheads or Cavaliers, a matter which presently led to head-breaking and one attempt to exclude dissenters from the franchise. The Huguenots were assimilated into the community life after 1696 when a law admitted such as took the oath of allegiance to full citizenship. Soon Carolina was proud of a group that included such distinguished names as Ravenal, Laurens, Legaré.

In time the phrase became "rich as a Huguenot" and was applied to Judith Citon Royer. She who had begun by working like an African field hand to help her first husband break ground, became the mother of the wealthiest merchant in Charleston. That was after her second marriage, to Pierre Manigault, whose brother Gabriel had come with sufficient capital and know-how to set up a distillery. The son of Judith and Pierre, named for his uncle, married into the provincial aristocracy; his wife Ann was daughter of John Ashby, a cacique.

The Gabriel Manigaults lived in colonial opulence, derived not only from the family distillery but from trade with England and Barbados in the two Manigault ships, the *Neptune* and *Sweet Nelly*, and from the Cooper River plantation, Silk Hope. Possession of the latter proved how high the Huguenots had risen, for it had been founded by Governor Nathaniel Johnson. On it Johnson had experimented with the culture of silkworms, fed on Carolina mulberries; little slave children tended the worms for him, and at one time he realized as much as £400 a year from his silk. Manigault allowed the experiment to be continued, but it was not the real source of his profit from the plantation. Rice had become the staple crop, and later he turned to the even more profitable production of indigo.

By the time of Judith's second marriage in 1699 Carolina was no longer a place where, as in New England, a penniless young couple could make a modest substance by planting a few acres. Madagascar rice did well in the cypress swamps, but only when levees were built to control alternate flooding and draining. Such construction required capital and a large labor force. The trend was already to large estates, like the tidewater plantations in Virginia, and the labor force was African. By the time of his death Gabriel Manigault possessed 270 slaves, mostly grown by natural increase from an original purchase of eighty-six.

6

Immigrants from Africa were not unknown in any colony, barring perhaps obscure little New Hampshire. Planters in Virginia and Maryland had long come to rely on slave labor. But the situation was unique in Carolina in that here the South's most peculiar institution was not evolved over decades but existed full-fledged from the start. Barbadians brought with them both slaves and a slave code. The numbers were few at first, but as the colony found its staples more were imported. The founding of Carolina roughly coincided with the opening of the great century of the slave trade that was so vitally to affect the future of both Africa and America. By 1700 the Africans were beginning to outnumber the whites.

A new country needed labor above all else, and here the Africans best served. The white servants brought on the first emigrant ships could not be held after their terms expired, and in the meantime such as absconded could merge indistinguishably with the rest of the population. Indians, who to the proprietors' displeasure were sometimes pressed into service, could escape to their own people. Africans escaped too, but they had no natural sanctuary.

In white communities they were marked by their color. Indians friendly to Carolinians were cautious about harboring them. They were welcomed only by the Spanish, and St. Augustine was a far journey.

As laborers they were superior to both Indians and whites in that they were better versed in the agricultural way of life than the one and better adapted to the climate than the other. It would be said that whites could not survive hard labor in Carolina, in spite of the general good health of the earliest settlers. When Africans were set to work on the rice plantations in the steaming, watery lowlands, they suffered heavy mortality. But they could be replaced.

The institution grew, hardly remarked except by outsiders. The Barbadians were used to it and saw nothing remarkable; the rest were too beset with their problems to make sociological notes. It was not until after the turn of the century, when the Society for the Propagation of the Gospel sent out missionaries, that the situation came in for disinterested scrutiny.

The missionaries came to bring the gospel to the Indians, and to the whites, who outside of Charleston and one Huguenot parish and the little Dorchester meetinghouse at Summerville, went largely unchurched. In 1706 Francis Le Jau came to Goose Creek to assemble a congregation, and at once became involved in the problems of the slaves.

It was still early days in Carolina. There was here little of that rapport between slave and master that would later impart a quality of intimate humanity to phases of the relationship. Here the slaves were a wild lot, hardly broken to their fetters, and some masters were driven by their fear of them to brutality. Le Jau was divided between his horror at such cruelty and what seemed to him the total depravity of the slaves. In his experience the women were universally promiscuous.

Having no acquaintance with Africa, Le Jau could only consider this as African original sin. He was in error. A stable African community deplored promiscuity, especially on the part of females, and dealt with it ungently. But these immigrants were thousands of miles and many years removed from their own ways.

Forcibly uprooted, thrust pell-mell among Africans of different and often hostile tribal origin, they had no means of preserving their culture; the American-born had no inkling that they had any. The destruction of native taboos was further complicated by the importing of an excessive disproportion of males. From natural appetite, from the unavailability of any other means of mating, except with an occasional Indian woman, promiscuity was forced upon the women, and so came the disorderly beginning of an Afro-American matriarchate.

Le Jau perceived nothing of this. He saw only that here were precious souls to be saved, and he labored to do so. It was discouraging work. Once, having tutored a talented youth to the extent of enabling him to read his own Testament, he was appalled at what came of it. The young man found his way to the Book of Revelation, which had elements of mysticism that appealed to many Africans, and prophesied and expounded visions in a way that made the good pastor's blood run cold.

He had even more difficulty with the masters. Some were friendly to his proposal to catechize and instruct their people; others recoiled. A young man said point-blank that he would come no more to the Lord's table if his slaves were permitted to share it with him. A woman, when asked permission to convert her slaves, was aghast. "But then, shall I have to meet them in heaven?" she inquired.

Carolina would do better than that, but not so soon in Goose Creek.

7

The turn of the century, a man-made convenience of casual astronomical significance, often suggests disaster to searchers for signs and omens. In the Bay Colony, humbled by the loss of its charter, ravaged by the effects of the Salem witchcraft, there was a disposition to equate the year 1700 with Doomsday. Harvard-bred ministers, searching their Bibles as earnestly as Le Jau's proselyte, came in their turn upon the Book of Revelation, and by learned computation found proof. Almost anything can be proved by the Book of Revelation.

If Carolinians undertook such computations they kept quiet about it. A portent had been sighted as early as August 1682 when Thomas Newe saw Halley's comet. If anyone interpreted this as a warning, it would be his home folks in England, for Newe never wrote again. He took a fever and died of it, without ever receiving the "good French hat, the fine thread to make lace," the shop books for which he had been urgently writing.

If any Carolinians expected a holocaust in the waning days of the century, they were soon justified. The good health record was broken in 1697 when smallpox became epidemic; by the following March, Governor Joseph Blake reported to the proprietors that up to three hundred had died of it. When warm weather came, the virulence of the disease abated among the settlers, but spread to the Indians. Mrs. Affra Coming reported that one whole nation had been wiped out, the few survivors flying in panic, leaving their dead to the buzzards.

At the height of the epidemic, earthquake and fire struck Charleston, destroying according to Mrs. Coming a third of the town and leaving fifty families homeless. In the fall of 1699 Charleston made its first acquaintance with the full force of a hurricane. The seas rose and swamped the town, driving people to their second stories. Luckily, few houses were swept from their foundations, but the *Rising Star,* anchored off the bar with refugees from a colony that the Spaniards had recently plundered, was destroyed with all but such passengers as happened to be ashore at the time. The Reverend Mr. Archibald Stobo, having been invited to preach at a Charleston church, had left the ship with his wife and a few friends. When the storm subsided they found James Island strewn with the bodies of their friends and spent a grim day giving them burial.

While people labored to repair the ravages of the hurricane, a new pestilence struck, the more terrifying because they did not know what it was, though they identified its probable provenance as shipping from Barbados. Probably this was the yellow fever, which struck Philadelphia at about the same time. It did not kill quite so many as the smallpox, only 160 in Charleston, and seems not to have spread to the country, but the effect was demoralizing in that parliament was in session, and nearly half its members died of the infection. Other officials also died, among them the redoubtable Chief Justice Edmund Bohun.

If 1700 did not bring Doomsday, it brought a close approximation.

Aside from such acts of God, Carolina was preoccupied with three major problems: piracy, the unsleeping threat from the Spaniards, and difficulties in adjusting to remote control from the proprietors through John Locke's Fundamental Constitutions.

Piracy was in some ways the least of their trials; in fact, they were accused of practicing it themselves, or at least of giving aid and comfort to such pirates as made port in Charleston. There was an approximate truth in the charge, made among others by Edward Randolph, Inspector of Customs, who visited Charleston in 1699, and there were reasons. One was the great difficulty in distinguishing between outlaws and the lawfully commissioned privateers. Even royalty did not always so distinguish. Charles II had knighted Henry Morgan for his raids on Spanish shipping and later made him governor of Jamaica, though inasmuch as England was then at peace with Spain, Morgan's work had been piratical.

In a colony so remote that it was seldom informed as to whether the mother country were at peace or war and with whom, any captain who preyed on foreign shipping, especially that of the dangerous Spanish, was considered a privateer until proved otherwise, and was welcome to outfit and provision his craft in Charleston. It was not until after the turn of the century that Carolinians wiped out a nest of pirates at Cape Fear.

After a disastrous attack by the Spanish, responsible Carolinians nearly undertook piracy on their own. This was in 1686 when three galleys from St. Augustine descended on settlements on the Edisto and destroyed a Scotch community planted at Port Royal three years earlier by Lord Henry Cardross.

When survivors reached Charleston, the news stirred the city to action. They stopped only to compose an appeal to the proprietors to present their plight to his majesty, and then went to work. Governor Joseph Morton, whose house on the Edisto was one of those sacked, his council, and parliament united on a plan to destroy St. Augustine. Two vessels were outfitted, four hundred men recruited for the task force, and they were about to sail when they were stopped by a ship from Barbados.

It bore a dignitary who they now learned had just been made landgrave and commissioned as their governor in the room of Morton. It was James Colleton, brother of one of the proprietors, and he would hear nothing of an expedition whose success might have facilitated the progress of Carolina. Spain, all appearances to the contrary, was at peace with England; an expedition against the Spaniards would be piracy, and he would hang the pirates.

The new governor would have been hard put to it to hang so many, and within three years the colonists would send him packing. At the moment, however resentfully, they were impressed enough to wait on the reply of their memorial to the proprietors.

It was not sympathetic; the proprietors said that the disaster at Port Royal was the colonists' fault for encouraging pirates. In spite of the fact that the royal charter, in recognition of the dangers besetting so remote a colony, had given the proprietors' representatives express authority "to make war and pursue the enemy . . . even without the limits of the said province," they now declared that Governor Morton and all his colleagues might "have answered with their lives" had they moved against the Spanish.

The proprietary arbitrariness had its own cause. Their lordships were exposed to the displeasure of James II, who, intent on keeping peace with Spain, was threatening to revoke their charter. They could not know that James's intransigence was about to provoke the revolution of 1688 and bring Mary, granddaughter of one of them, and her husband William to the throne.

Carolina gave Governor Colleton two more years than England gave James, though they were embroiled from the start. The governor negotiated with St. Augustine and obtained reparations of a sort, but refused to consult what he called "the commoners" in Charleston's parliament while he did so. Members of the assembly were already embroiled on the question of their civil liberties, whether these derived from the charter or the Fundamental

Constitutions, and if the latter, whether they derived from the form issued in 1669, which the proprietors had subsequently disallowed as an imperfect copy, or a later form contested by the colonists.

In the end Colleton attempted to govern without reference to parliament. He labored to collect the quitrents, no more popular in Carolina than in Pennsylvania; tried to cut off private trade with the Indians, still the chief source of colonial profit until the rice plantations could be more firmly established. When finally he undertook to govern by martial law, naïvely disregarding the fact that the militia he summoned for the purpose consisted mostly of his enemies, the colony was saved from anarchy only by the arrival of a proprietor, who took office on the grounds that any senior proprietor on the spot automatically became governor.

The newcomer was Seth Sothell, who having bought the proprietorship of the Earl of Clarendon, had come over to govern Albemarle, in what was soon to become North Carolina. Albemarle had cast him out; news of the Glorious Revolution was encouraging the expulsion of any number of officials unpopular in the colonies. Sothell, banished by little Albemarle, helped Charleston in its turn to banish Colleton, and governed not too badly until London sent yet another replacement.

The proprietary government of Carolina survived the tumult in England. It was not until 1719 that it came under the Crown; and what had been in New England the supreme humiliation was for Carolina a decisive step into stability and progress. It was lucky in its Crown governors, and henceforth turned with relief from its ersatz nobility, its landgraves and caciques, titles which toward the end were put up for sale.

Yet even under the proprietors and their somewhat dizzying succession of governors there had been progress in what now was to be South Carolina. It had voted by ballot from the first. At the height of the years of disaster it had started both a postal system and a public library. The former was set up in 1698 when Francis Fidling of Charleston was authorized to collect letters from incoming shipmasters, post a listing at his house, and charge one-half royal postage to the claimants. At the same time the library was set up under the charge of an Anglican minister in his rectory. By 1703 it was sufficiently well stocked to justify parliament to appropriate £5/15 to pay Edward Moseley for making a catalogue.

There was an awakening of interest in education, in which Carolina had lagged behind the New England colonies and Pennsylvania. It had so far nothing like Boston's grammar school, there were no legislative acts as in Pennsylvania requiring parents to instruct their children, and Carolina was in no haste to establish the counterpart of Harvard to train its own ministry. As in earliest Virginia, the first settlers had come more as "adventurers" than planters and few had brought their families with them.

By 1708, however, the population was estimated at twelve thousand, and families of ten to a dozen children were not uncommon. The "common sort" set their young to work by the time they were eight; the gentlefolk, especially those in and about Charleston, where the population was still concentrated, engaged tutors for their young, and this would remain the fashion on the larger plantations, as in Virginia.

But there was an impulse to make education more widely available, as evidenced by wills designating legacies to be used toward the founding of a free school, and in 1710 the legislature appointed commissioners to receive such bequests. A year later the Society for the Propagation of the Gospel responded to an appeal from the colony by setting up a school under William Guy. Most of the scholars paid their tuition, but a few were admitted free.

What was life like in the colony? One observer speaks of uncarpeted floors, unplastered walls exposing the rough texture of the wood, rush-bottom chairs, and bedtime at eight. Others testify that in such estates as Silk Hope people lived grandly.

Charleston, busy market town of the colony, had taken its place among the little metropolises of America. Ships came from the Islands, from Virginia, from London. Homes were clustered mostly along the Cooper between Meeting Street and the bay. It was fortified with bastions, palisades, and a half-moon called Johnson's Raveline which had a drawbridge. It had at least one "large and stately" church, built of black cypress on a brick foundation; this was St. Philips, which then occupied the site of the present St. Michaels. The Huguenots also had a church in town, and came to worship on Sunday, resentful that in spite of the distance they had to go the Lords Proprietors made them worship at the same hour as the English. There was also a Baptist church, and toward the Ashley a Quaker meetinghouse.

Estates had also been planted out of town on the neck between the rivers. John Archdale, another proprietor, this one a Quaker, who briefly governed the colony after one bout of turbulence, was lyrical in his account of the overland approach to these places through stands of pine, cedar, and cypress. "Out of Charleston for three or four miles, called the Broadway, is so delightful a road and walk of a great breadth, so pleasantly green that I believe no princes in Europe by all their art can make so pleasant a sight for the whole year."

1

O<small>N</small> January 13, 1733, the frigate *Ann* dropped anchor off Sullivan's Island, and its 125 passengers jostled for a place at the bulwarks for a look at Charleston. They had made a lucky voyage, less than two months out of Gravesend. Here was America, and it looked good.

It was not as it had been a century ago in the Bay Colony, when even the stouthearted had quailed when they saw the straggle of shacks called Boston. Charleston was no longer a dream, a promise of a town. Even from a distance it had distinction in its substantial buildings, many of rosy brick, placed gable end to the streets as in old New Amsterdam. The white steeple of St. Philips rose above the deep purple of the pantile roofs, and in an offshore wind they could catch its ring of bells.

The harbor was full of coming and going: a ship or so in from the islands or from England; sloops, barges, dugouts down from the waterside plantations on the Cooper, the Ashley, the Santee. It was not with the *Ann's* passengers as it had been with the first-comers; here was the visible substance of what they could hope for if they applied themselves; here were inns to receive weather-beaten bodies.

Not that they got to the inns. This was not their destination. Their stay was brief, and it was well that they were kept aboard, for what they could see from afar was too tempting. There were some who, wearied of the job of building a city of their own, would ask themselves why take so much trouble when here was a fine one ready-made, and these would watch their chance to run for Carolina.

In the meantime the longboat had been lowered, a handsome personage had been rowed ashore, and Charleston was turning itself inside out to give the illustrious James Oglethorpe a royal welcome. He sat in the Governor's Council and received its praises; he was wined and dined. He was promised all good things for his planting on the Savannah, and the promises were not empty. Through the town, up and down the rivers, good citizens were circulating to enlist aid for the new colony.

Private citizens collected among them £1000; one group of well-wishers arranged to transport a hundred head of cattle, another group, a herd of sheep; the governor promised seven horses. A drum was donated, a silver boat and spoon to be given the first child born in Georgia. William Bull prepared to join Oglethorpe to help in laying out the town lots. He and Joseph Bryan had twenty servants dispatched to the Savannah to contribute a month's labor to the work of clearing and building; six sawyers were sent. Presently the Carolina Assembly would vote supplies of cattle, rice, scout boats, the loan of fifteen rangers to serve Oglethorpe, and eventually a total of £10,000 in aid.

Such enthusiasm, such wholehearted generosity, was something new in the history of American colonizing. Not thus had Virginians welcomed the Dutch to New Amsterdam or the Calverts to Maryland; the Dutch had extended no right hand of fellowship to the Swedes on the Delaware. The usual response to a new colony had been a warning, "Watch it. That's ours." Yet here was Carolina joyously, eagerly pressing upon a handful of settlers the whole rich territory south of the Savannah.

The generosity was not disinterested. Though Carolina had now planted Beaufort, near Port Royal of tragic memory, it still lived in dread of the St. Augustine Spaniards, their piracies and Indian alliances, their organizing of runaway slaves into military units. The founding of Georgia under one of England's most able military men would end all that.

And so it did. Oglethorpe and Georgia would, after a perilous time, justify this faith. In the meantime Carolina did not grasp the significance of the principles on which Georgia was being founded; when very soon it did so, there was an abrupt cessation of public appropriations and private gifts of livestock and drums and silver spoons.

2

Idealism had figured in the founding of many of the colonies, from Plymouth to Pennsylvania, but Georgia was the first founded explicitly for charity's sake, with the purpose of enabling the English poor to become self-supporting on lands of their own without having to spend their best years in servitude to pay costs. The paupers sent to Georgia had free passage, free land, and until they could make the land yield, free rations.

It was the one colony that prohibited slavery, the one temperance colony. Temperance, not abstinence. The trustees of Georgia knew better than to forbid Englishmen their ale, and were at pains to send the supply ships well stocked. What they forbade was strong drink, especially rum. Besides these philanthropical motives was the one that had so stirred Carolina, the aim of providing a line of defense both against the Spaniards and the French, who were now pressing eastward from their posts on the Mississippi.

The charter granted by the Privy Council to the twenty-one trustees provided something analogous to a proprietorship; it was completely unlike in that profit-taking was forbidden. The trustees were not even salaried, and must present a yearly accounting of any monies they collected. Subscriptions were taken on the basis of £20 to plant an adult and £10 to settle a child. Parliament itself contributed £10,000, thus for the first time reversing the policy by which the expenses of colonization had been left to private enterprise.

Emigration was not restricted to the pauper class. Though the trustees rejected one wealthy applicant, saying that it was not their purpose to make the rich richer, they did sell land to freeholders able to pay their way. Such holdings were limited to five hundred acres. Land speculation such as had been involved in some of the patroonships of New Netherland was not to be permitted, or the creation of anything like the Carolina landgraviates, or the vast estates in Virginia.

It was for this reason that slavery was prohibited. As a group the trustees were no abolitionists, though Oglethorpe soon became one. English intellectuals had not yet got around to giving active attention to the plight of the African slave. When Georgia was founded, the great century of the slave trade had already run a third of its course. But barring a few Quakers and some of the German settlers of Pennsylvania, the humane gave no more thought to what was going on than they did to investigating practices in those abattoirs which provided their Sunday joints of good English roast beef.

If the trustees had no humanitarian interest in the welfare of the African slaves, they did have a realistic grasp on their effect on the white worker. Slavery debased labor and made it impossible for the white laborer to compete. He cost too much, and there was no holding him to the soil when his time was up. What was worse, indentured laborers, freed from their bonds, had almost no place to go in colonies like Virginia, much of Maryland, and Carolina. On such scant acres as they might acquire they could not hope to compete with the monopolistic plantations.

What the trustees hoped for in Georgia was the creation of a yeoman class rooted in small farms like those of New England. For all that New England and Georgia were poles apart, they might have succeeded but for circumstances. Some were beyond their control; some were due to defects in their own planning.

Beyond their control was Georgia's position just across the Savannah from Carolina, which had had a slave economy from the start and took it ill when it discovered that the trustees really meant their prohibition of slavery, and exerted pressures which in time became irresistible. Also beyond their control was the proximity of the Spanish and their Indian allies. This meant that the one real leader of men they found for the colony, Oglethorpe, had to concentrate on the southern border, and spend his time negotiating with the Indians and containing the Spaniards. In the end he was brilliantly successful, but in the meantime the settlers on the Savannah languished for want of dynamic leader-ship.

It should have been in their power to give their colony some measure of the self-government which, rather than subsistence farming as such, had made New England so successful. Instead their preliminary plan was to entrust the rule of each settlement to three appointed bailiffs. In Savannah the chief bailiff was Thomas Clauson, who being also the storekeeper, could exert his will by bestowing or withholding rations. No use to accuse him of malfeasance or of appropriating public property to his pri-vate benefit, because when such charges came to court, Clauson heard the case and rendered judgment.

They might also have given thought to the practical problems facing a hitherto landless people, some of whom had spent years in debtors' prison, when they were cast up on strange shores and told to dig in. They had taken pains in selecting the paupers, in-terviewing each head of family, making sure that each was honest. But they rejected not only those with criminal taint but those who had any prior experience in husbandry or prospects of supporting themselves in England.

Such emigrants, as distinct from the freeholders, needed more than free transportation, a year's supply of rations, and a fifty-acre lot to start the new life. Especially those drawn from the city streets needed training and guidance, and no farm agent was sent to help them. Nor would expert counsel have availed such as in the haste of first settlement received their fifty acres—which in England sounded like such largess—in pine barrens where no amount of hewing and grubbing would produce a crop. Worse, their lots were inalienable; settlers were supposed to stay where they were put, with no swapping, no moving about in search of greener pastures.

The wonder is not that so many of the pauper class dismayed the trustees by proving as improvident in the new world as in the old, but that any prospered at all. Some did, but they are name-less; the trustees collected no case histories. Others abandoned their briery plots to try their luck at selling their services in little Savannah, or absconded to the amenities of Charleston. The ab-

sconders came back, for there was no work for them there, and
no stores from which they could draw rations.

3

After being feted in Charleston, Oglethorpe had been given the
king's pilot to guide the *Ann* down the coast to Port Royal. There
the passengers were transferred to smaller vessels and taken to
new barracks at Beaufort, while Oglethorpe and William Bull
went ahead to reconnoiter a proper site on the Savannah.

Bull pointed it out at once: the flatlands on a bluff above the
tomato-colored river. There was one drawback; some Yamacraw
Indians had a village there, and saw no reason why they should
remove. Oglethorpe, however, had as deft a hand in dealing with
the Indians as Penn himself. It was not with him a matter of being
instructed by the inner light; he belonged to the Enlightenment
rather than to the period of religious ferment that had preceded
it. Far from yearning to redeem these heathen from darkness, he
liked them immensely as he found them, and had a gift for making friends.

At the Yamacraw village he was also lucky, for here lived "the
Georgia Pocahontas." This was the Creek wife of Colonel John
Musgrove, a Carolina trader. Her Creek name had been Consa-
ponakessa, but she had been christened Mary during a brief stay
at a Carolina mission. Now in her early thirties, she spoke English
and all local languages. She had no occasion then or thereafter to
save the life of a white man; the Yamacraws were not so hostile,
and Mary was too efficient an intermediary. She became Oglethorpe's interpreter, and it was through her that he convinced the
Indians that the white men came only in friendship and induced
them to make a provisional treaty until the consent of their nation
could be obtained.

The settlers were sent for and encamped in four large tents
until the townsite could be laid out. The Indians exerted themselves as Charleston had to make a ceremony of welcome. Cock-
neys who until recently had never been beyond the sound of the

Bow Bells watched a medicine man dance toward them, waving a fan of white feathers hung with little bells, and saw local royalty condescend to enter Oglethorpe's tent for gifts and refreshment.

First impressions are all-important. These settlers would live to experience fear and one hysterical stampede, but not because of the Indians. Whenever thereafter red men descended on Savannah, whatever their numbers, whatever paint they wore, the English would not take to cover. On the contrary, they would eagerly gather around to enjoy what was their nearest approach to a circus.

During Georgia's first summer an unexpected group of immigrants reached Savannah, forty Jews, mostly Portuguese, who had raised funds by their own efforts. They came independently, having bypassed the trustees, who were accordingly wroth, and ordered Oglethorpe to expel them. It was not their intention, they wrote, "to make a Jews' colony of Georgia."

The immigrants, however, preceded the instructions by some months, and Oglethorpe liked them. The colony had been founded on the basis of complete religious freedom except for Papists, and these were no Papists. He found the Jews worthy, industrious, and knowledgeable, and was especially grateful for the services of a Dr. Nunis, who at once busied himself attending to the sick. The trustees, it would seem, had given insufficient attention to the medical needs of the colony. When they heard of the doctor, they directed that he be given a suitable gratuity, but repeated that the interlopers should receive no allotments.

Most of them did move on to Carolina, disillusioned by the lack of opportunity here, especially in the matter of civil rights. Nevertheless, they left their mark on Georgia. The Temple of Mickva Israel was founded in Savannah, and at least three families remained, the Sheftalls, the Minis, and the De Lyons. Abraham de Lyons became vigneron of the colony.

When Oglethorpe left at the end of 1734 to report to the trustees and prepare a greater migration, Savannah was a healthy settlement of forty wooden houses. The streets had been laid out at right angles, a square named for South Carolina's Governor Johnson, a storehouse built at the river landing, a battery to command the sea approach; and a ninety-foot lighthouse, the tallest on the American coast, was under construction at Tybee Island. There were also lesser settlements; three families on Thunderbolt, others at Hampstead and Highgate.

Oglethorpe had concluded a vital treaty with the Yamacraws. Chief Tomochichi had not only ceded to the English a great swath of land between the Savannah and Altamaha rivers, but had bound his people to form no alliance with the Spanish or the French. It was no empty formality, for the ninety-year-old red chief and the highborn Englishman, whose line went back to Edward the Confessor, liked each other at first sight, and only death would interrupt their friendship.

Tomochichi, accompanied by a retinue, went to England with Oglethorpe to be regaled by English royalty. Such visits, which antedated Pocahontas, were popular in England. Like the Romans of old, the English liked to see their tributary peoples marched through the streets, but not as captives—rather as honored guests, to be greeted with bonfires and the ringing of bells, shown the sights, showered with gifts. Estichi, a handsome youth who attended Tomochichi, carried home a gold watch. Several years later, when it went out of order, he entrusted it to a "packhorse man" to be brought to Charleston for repair. When the trader returned without it, the youth killed him, a rare event in these parts, which shocked the Indians even more than the whites.

4

In 1735 Oglethorpe led to Georgia the first wave of its "great migration." Besides the paupers and the freeholders, he had with him a "praying company," including young John and Charles Wesley, who had not yet got around to founding that special form of dissent known as Methodism, but were earnestly working on Oglethorpe to elevate his colony by making public his personal profession of faith. Oglethorpe bore their importunities with humor, remained their lifelong friend, but he did not comply.

More important than the Wesleys, who remained only two

years, were European immigrants, the Lutheran Salzburgers from
the Tyrol, a few of whom had arrived earlier, and German Moravians. In spite of some illness, the Moravians were so stout of
faith that when in a Sabbath service a great sea broke through
the hatchways and deadlights and nearly swamped them, they
never lost a beat in the psalm they were singing.

The Salzburgers delighted in their landfall. "While we lay off
the banks of our dear Georgia in a very lovely calm and heard
the birds singing sweetly, all was cheerful aboard," one of them
wrote. They were something of a problem to Oglethorpe. When
he showed them the land he had allotted them they politely de-
clined it and insisted on scouting for their own choice. They settled Ebenezer at a confluence of two creeks about thirty miles
up the Savannah, not far from Purysburg, South Carolina, recently founded by Huguenots. Three years later Oglethorpe was
annoyed to learn that this land no longer suited; they were petitioning to found a new Ebenezer downstream a bit at Red Bluff.
"They leave a sweet place where they have made great improvements to go into a wood," remarked Oglethorpe in disgust, but
deeming them "only ignorant and obstinate . . . without any ill
intention," he gave in.

Obstinate they were, ignorant they were not; they had brought
with them a knowledge of husbandry and a will to work that
made them the most successful of the early settlers, and their community a close approach to the trustees' ideal for Georgia. They
still had problems; Oglethorpe was exasperated at a call to intervene in a dispute between their aged storekeeper, a Mr. Vat, and
the youthful leader Baron von Reck. Dispute or no, the new Ebenezer flourished, and the old served the colony as its official Cow
Pen.

After 1738 when Oglethorpe, who now went by the courtesy
title of general, led a group of sturdy newcomers far south to
found Frederica (taking Mary Musgrove with him) the problems
of Savannah and Ebenezer, old and new, concerned him seldom.
They shortly became the concern of William Stephens.

5

In 1741 Stephens was sent to act as chief magistrate in Savannah and as Secretary of the Colony. Georgia needed a secretary, for though Oglethorpe was capable of vigorous expression, he had no patience with paperwork and had ill luck in finding secretarial assistance. Charles Wesley had briefly and resentfully so served him at Frederica. When it was borne in on the youth that the general interpreted his title as Secretary for Indian Affairs as an excuse for assigning him all his correspondence with the trustees, he quit. At Savannah he picked up his brother, who had got involved in a mild scandal with a girl, and went home.

Stephens was a born secretary. He did not so serve the general, whom he hardly knew by sight, but he indefatigably cast up accounts, applied himself to voluminous correspondence, and for the benefit of the trustees kept a journal. From him they had a lively day-to-day picture of what was going on.

They knew that of a hot evening the young men of Savannah liked to shuck their clothes and take to the river. The deep channel ran close to the shore, which was a peril to nonswimmers, and the river was infested with alligators, a peril to everyone. One youth was found drowned with his arm torn off, and the debate waxed hot as to which came first, the varmint or the drowning. But while the youths debated, they shoved and splashed each other in the water.

The trustees heard how Founders' Day was yearly celebrated and the cost of the biscuits and beer which Stephens provided on these occasions. They heard of the three pines under which Oglethorpe had negotiated his first Indian treaty, and which were piously preserved until lightning blasted them. Stephens reported the work on the Tybee Beacon which he had to finish, and the repairs to its foundation when storms shifted the sand. When it was necessary to buy good horses from Carolina to enable the keeper of Old Ebenezer Cow Pen to round up the cattle in the woods, Stephens explained why.

When a brush fire, such as was regularly set in the spring to clear the undergrowth, got out of hand and threatened Savannah, he gave full report. When followers of the Methodist George Whitefield, who had visited the colony and set up an orphanage there, made trouble with the Anglican rector, when respectable men went over to the Moravians, when "ignorant" Methodist preachers drew the congregation away from the Establishment, Stephens told the story, and remarked that it sometimes seemed to him that the colony's freedom of religion applied to everyone except "the poor Church."

Apologetically he confessed the expenditure he had been put to to equip the courthouse, which was also the church, with a new roof and colonnades. The trustees could believe their faithful secretary that the improvements were unavoidable. Not only had hard rains threatened to bring the old roof down on everyone's ears, but without the handsome colonnade the summer heat baked everyone who went in, whether to attend court or divine service.

He described successes and failures in the experimental gardens over which he watched with loving care. The trustees had hoped that in latitudes as southern as Georgia all sorts of exotics could be grown: limes, lemons, oranges, spices, drugs. Whatever roots and seeds they sent, Stephens had planted, and he sedulously studied the results.

He reported the work of Abraham de Lyons, the colony's vigneron. Here as elsewhere the wild grape was abundant; when the first settlers came the fruit grew so high that it was often necessary to fell a tree to get at it, and too often it was found that the birds had got it first. De Lyons was pruning, taming, cultivating, and enriching the vines with grafts from old-world vineyards. He was exhausting his substance, running into debt to get roots from Portugal. He pressed his wine, and Stephens tasted it and found it good. But for all the vigneron's selfless devotion, he never produced it in such quantity that the trustees would realize their dream that England would send to Georgia instead of the Canaries for its sack.

He reported on the silk culture. Mulberries grew in Georgia; silk had been produced on a small scale in both Virginia and

Carolina; here it was hoped the scale would be large, and England need no longer depend on the Piedmont and Italy for raw silk, and the Georgia producers would grow rich. If the trustees objected to seeing the rich grow richer in their colony, they had no such prejudice against their paupers. They imported white mulberry when it transpired that the native mulberry was black, its leaves too tough for the worms, and sent a Piedmontese expert, one Nicholas Amatis, to take charge.

Stephens never met Amatis, who long before he came had defected to Carolina in anger at his lack of religious privileges. Somehow, in spite of their ban on Papist settlers (they were afraid they might combine with the Spanish and French) the trustees had picked a Catholic for this job. The story was that when he was refused a priest during an illness, he destroyed some of his machinery and went off, leaving the Georgia silk industry in the hands of his servants, Mr. and Mrs. Jacques Camuse. When Stephens got there, Mrs. Camuse was in sole charge.

In Stephens' journal Mrs. Camuse had the prominence of a queen. She was harder to please than George's Queen Caroline; "intolerable" was sometimes the diarist's word for her manners, and he suspected her of hitting the bottle. Once she made a great to-do about a horse and wagon that hadn't been delivered as promised, and Stephens had to remind her that they had been ready for months, that she hadn't bestirred herself to pick them up. So much depended on her that he studied her royal humors like a sycophant, marking with touching joy those days when she was affable, and when she promised to take two or three young girls as apprentices in the mystery of her craft. This was a rare concession, for Mrs. Camuse was bent on keeping her craft just what the craftsman called it, a mystery. She was on salary, and demanding fringe benefits, like provision for her old age.

The hard-working Salzburgers duly raised mulberries and had some success with the silkworms. Stephens was gratified when visitors from Carolina dropped in to see how Savannah was doing and told him that it had been a mistake to give so much acreage to rice, for which the European price had lately fallen, and that they were thinking of taking up silk culture. Substantial amounts of silk actually were sent to England, but never in such quantities as to menace the monopoly of the Piedmontese. And the cost in relation to the supply was astronomical. Georgia proved that silk could be raised but that it was hardly worth the trouble.

Unlike the bachelor Oglethorpe, Stephens had a wife and family in England. Presently two of his sons joined him, and the younger, who shared his father's pleasure in husbandry, was a credit to him. Thomas, the elder, for a long time was not; he fell in with some subversive Carolinians.

Georgia's honeymoon with Carolina was over long before Stephens came. It ended when Carolinians learned that the trustees meant business in prohibiting rum and slavery. The egregious bailiff Clauson had caused the first rift when he inspected Carolina river craft and staved all the rum barrels he found. Since the Savannah was as much Carolina's as Georgia's, this was considered an outrage.

Then Oglethorpe insisted that all traders with the Georgia Indians be licensed. The prosperous Carolina trade had extended to these Indians long before Georgia had been thought of, and rum had always been a most profitable commodity. The climax was the discovery that though Carolinians were free to buy Georgia land, they would not be allowed to bring their slaves to till it for them. When some families tried it, they were sent packing.

Enforcing the prohibition of rum was a hopeless task; the stuff was bootlegged. Its clandestine availability in Savannah was one reason why some settlers deserted their pine barrens to try for work in town. Georgia Indians also still got it; young Estichi had been under its influence when he accused the trader of stealing his watch.

Slaves were less easily bootlegged, and the German settlers, especially the Moravians, were nearly unanimous against the institution. There was vacillation among other religious groups. First George Whitefield opposed it, and then he began to think about the advantages slavery conferred upon the poor ignorant Africans in rescuing them from heathenism. Planters grew restless at the difficulty of finding men to cultivate their soil, knowing

that they were readily available from Carolina. There was talk
that the good Lord never designed the white man for hard labor
in this climate. Pressures were brought to bear on the trustees, one
in the person of young Stephens, who went to London to present
complaints against his father.

It was a grief to the older man, who in truth repined at being
unable to find enough laborers for the experimental gardens or
his own little plantation at Bewlie, but he was too loyal to join
the protest. He went his quiet way, a kindly, honest man, florid
of countenance and portly of build, but active for all that. He
had none of Oglethorpe's fiery qualities of leadership. He was
by nature a "moth of peace."

Suddenly, when he had been in office not quite two years,
the tumults of war were upon him.

6

Frederica, which Oglethorpe planted on St. Simon Island, just
south of the mouth of the Altamaha, was to be as impermanent
as Jamestown. Once it had served its purpose, its settlers would
drift away, and the town would fall into ruin until a later generation came to erect a memorial to its heroic past. Its function
was to serve as supply base for the forts Oglethorpe erected
against the Spanish.

Many of the settlers whom Oglethorpe had brought to Georgia
in 1735 were destined for this area. The three ships the *Prince of
Wales*, the *Two Brothers*, and the *Peter* stopped at Peeper's Island at the mouth of the Savannah to give the passengers a chance
to refresh themselves. Men found amusement by cutting down a
great tree to get at an eagle's nest; women took advantage of a
fresh-water pond to perform the rite that always marked the end
of an Atlantic voyage; they did their washing. They were caught
at it in "a smart shower of rain which wetted our good women to
the skins before they could get aboard."

Then came a moment of decision. No certified pilots were available to guide the ships down the coast, and the captains wouldn't

risk the journey without them. The alternative was to transport
the passengers in pirogues, which meant six to fourteen days in
open boats with no cover from the rain and no better sleeping
quarters than the frosty ground. Oglethorpe presented the difficulty and offered a choice. Those who shrank from such hardships
might have land on the Savannah.

This was a hardy lot; many said that they had expected nothing better. Only some Moravians elected to stay behind, and this
because they heard that there might be fighting to the south and
their religion forbade them to take up arms; they went to Ebenezer. The rest embarked in a fleet of pirogues and scout boats,
reached St. Simon Island by mid-March, and set to work with a
will. A passenger on a schooner that followed with supplies was
amazed when he overtook them on March 23 to find Frederica
well under construction.

A battery already commanded the river from a half-finished
fort, within which a three-story storehouse was going up. The lots
had been laid out, and each family was camped in the back of his
own in a "bower" of palmetto leaves. These shelters would serve
until wooden houses were built on the front of the lots; they were
picturesque and snug, for the palmetto thatching made them
"tight in the hardest rains."

The work had been done under the supervision of Oglethorpe,
who had divided the men into working squads. One had the job
of cutting "forks, poles and lathes, another set them up, a third
fetched palmetto leaves, a fourth thatched, and a Jew workman
bred in the Brazil and come from Savannah taught them to do
this nimbly and in a neat manner." A start had also been made in
planting potatoes and Indian corn.

The construction well started, the general left with his friend
Tomochichi to investigate the fluid Georgia-Florida boundary. His
method was simple. The old chief pointed out what land was his,
and all that land the general claimed for Georgia. Thus he came
to the St. Johns River, across which, only a mile away, lay St.
Augustine. The Creeks resented the Spanish, and Oglethorpe had
to restrain them from making a quixotic raid. He notified the
Spanish governor and the trustees that he would keep a guard

on the bank of the St. Johns to prevent his Indians from attacking. The Spanish, especially in the home office in Madrid, did not appreciate his solicitude. There was talk of their taking the whole coast, straight up to Port Royal. The trustees were alarmed by Oglethorpe's contention that St. Augustine itself should be English since Sir Francis Drake had once occupied the spot; they ordered the general to get out of the St. Johns River and leave boundary negotiations to London. In October, Oglethorpe achieved a treaty with Governor Francisco del Moral Sánchez, whereby each agreed to keep his Indian allies from molesting the other. Though this treaty set no limits on the Florida bounds, Madrid was incensed by it, sent for Sánchez, and hanged him.

Oglethorpe also went home, in 1736, and had his troubles there. He succeeded in getting a grant from Parliament of £20,000 to defend his colony, but he had powerful opposition from Prime Minister Robert Walpole and from those who wanted peace with Spain at any price. It was 1738 before he could return; this time he remained four years, until his job was done.

Next year the War of Jenkins' Ear broke out. Neither Jenkins nor his ear, of which the Spanish had allegedly robbed him, were of importance, but the phrase made a better rallying cry than more recondite causes known to the Foreign Office. Oglethorpe declared Georgia's war on the Spanish as soon as he had the news, and in 1740 with the aid of a naval blockade and some help from South Carolina, invested St. Augustine. But he couldn't take it; he had to withdraw, and the next attack came from the Spanish.

In the summer of 1742 their ships advanced in overwhelming force, not only from St. Augustine but from Cuba. Oglethorpe heard of it in time to call for help from Carolina, but he didn't get it. Charleston excused itself on the grounds that it needed its forces to hold off the French, though these at the moment were not on the march. There was no holding off the Spanish fleet; one by one the little outposts fell until an advance guard of the enemy was within a mile of Frederica. From any military standpoint the town was indefensible, yet here the stand must be.

7

It was the last Sunday in June when first news of the danger
reached Savannah. The work on the courthouse had been completed, and Stephens had attended divine service there. It had
gone well; no Methodist enthusiast had interrupted the ritual as
sometimes happened, and the rector had administered Holy Communion from a table which was turned one way for the magistrates and the other for sacred office.

It was in this peaceful context that a friend burst in on Stephens
with frightening intelligence. In the bay he had met with an "express" from Oglethorpe, bound "with utmost expedition for
Charleston," and learned that the Spanish had mounted a full-
scale invasion. There had already been an engagement on Cumberland Island with the general participating "in the utmost peril
. . . when the smoke and fire was so thick 'twas not possible to
see what success attended it."

It was so late in the evening when Stephens heard this that he
decided to give the town a good night's sleep before he had the
drums beaten to sound the alarm and muster the militia. By
Tuesday, June 29, he had the fifty-six Savannah freeholders and
the men from Highgate and Hampstead drawn up before him
on the Parade. With them came volunteers from the trustee's
"Dutch servants"—apparently they were German-Swiss—whose in-
dentures would expire in December. He found them "hearty and
resolute" and gave them an officer who spoke their language. He
directed the distribution of arms, ordered a guard set up at
Thunderbolt to watch the sea lanes and fire the cannon in case
of danger. He revoked all permission to travel up the Savannah
except for craft bound for Fort Augusta.

All this went well. The muster had been performed with alac-
rity. But now Stephens faced the first signs of panic. Men were
demanding the means of sending their families to safety, among
them some of the troublemakers who had conspired with his son
Thomas against him: "that arch politician Duchee," William

Woodruff, and a character whom Stephens regularly referred to as "that poor silly man John Pye."

Stephens said no. Man of peace that he was, he had Spartan notions. The presence of the women and children would, he reasoned, give the men incentive to fight; also there was a chance that in conducting wives to safety, some men would stay with them. The delegation responded to these sentiments abusively, and presently spirited their families away without leave. Stephens, now busy placing an abandoned ship called the *Caesar* downstream at Mile Point to serve as battery, was too busy to watch them.

Daily he prayed for word from Oglethorpe. On July 2 an express finally reached him from Frederica, but its news was nearly a month old, the letter having mysteriously come to him roundabout via Purysburg. As of that date the general was not yet under attack; he had only heard that Spanish reinforcements were on their way from Cuba. He was instructing Stephens to take precautions.

By July 9 Savannah was in an uproar, "what I once hoped I never should see here," as Stephens put it. Bad news had come. On the seventh Stephens had a letter only five days old reporting that the Spanish fleet had anchored off St. Simon Island in overwhelming strength. A day later an orphanage official had encountered in the Narrows a boat from Frederica containing some women being sent to safety by the general's orders—"so they said" —and a report that more than thirty Spanish vessels had bypassed Fort Simons and that the general was retreating to Frederica.

Stephens beat up another alarm and addressed his militia. If the general could hold off the Spanish nothing worse was to be expected here than minor raids; if the worst happened and Savannah must be evacuated, the retreat must be orderly; he himself would be the last to go.

"I feared I saw diffidence among some," remarked Stephens of the reception of this speech. By Friday, July 9, the "diffidence" was in full cry.

Savannah had until now known nothing of raids and massacres. There had never been anything to fear from the Indians. There had been no slave insurrections here as in Carolina, because there were no slaves. Potential enemies like the French and Spanish seemed far away. The nearest French post was at Mobile; closer was the remarkable Jesuit father Christian Priber, who was working among the Cherokees, but he hadn't yet been caught at it. The Spanish threat had so far been bluster; there had been uneasiness in 1740, but then the English were the aggressors.

Now the Spanish were on the march, not only from feeble St. Augustine but from terrible Cuba, and their reputation was hideous. From Carolina Huguenots, Georgians probably heard traditions of the ghastly fate that had befallen their early settlement. The Spanish would rape and torture and kill by slow degrees, and under their tutelage the Indians would not function as entertainers. There were also Africans with the Spanish, runaways from Carolina, eager to avenge themselves on any English they could find.

Now it was not only the men who besieged Stephens; suddenly the women were after him. They ran shrieking through the streets, their children clinging weeping to their skirts. And Stephens surrendered his Spartan notion of keeping the whole town together.

As morale builders, families thus distraught were worse than useless; to look at them one would suppose they were caught in the sack of Troy. If Stephens had to send men to reinforce Frederica (such orders were on the way), no command or persuasion was likely to induce them to leave with such terror behind them.

For two days he applied himself to rounding up enough boats to get the women out of town. Most went to Abercorn or Ebenezer, but some insisted on getting into Carolina, either Purysburg or Captain MacKay's plantation. Stephens took satisfaction in noting that these lost face with those who elected to remain in Georgia. He was frightened enough to pack up all the Trust's books and papers and to send them for safekeeping to Ebenezer, and to bury "the lumber," whatever that was.

On Thursday, July 15, Stephens beat the drums again to call for volunteers for Frederica. "Our streets were now grown very thin." Nevertheless, in response to the danger and to his offer of ten shillings apiece "to drink the king's health," thirty responded, and were off next morning. With them went a young minister, Thomas Bosomworth, on his way to meet Oglethorpe, and the "Georgia Pocahontas," who still served the general as interpreter. (Bosomworth would become her third English husband and ruin her reputation by impelling her to do what the Virginia Pocahontas had never done, set a price on her services.)

Two days before panic struck Savannah, the battle of Bloody Marsh had ended forever the danger from the Spanish. While Oglethorpe readied himself for the improbable task of defending Frederica, two lieutenants from a regiment of Scotch Highlanders that he had settled at Darien prepared an ambush among the palmettos at the edge of a marsh where a Spanish detachment had stacked their arms and settled down to rest. When the camp was quiet, the Highlanders charged, and it was all over with the Spanish.

It should not have been, and it was some time before Oglethorpe could know that he had won his war. The loss of two hundred at the marsh did not impair the tremendous numerical superiority of the invaders. But the commanders from Havana and St. Augustine had fallen into dissension, Bloody Marsh damaged morale, and a dispatch that Oglethorpe planted in the pocket of a French spy he had captured and sent back gave misleading information about the forces at Frederica. From then on, though skirmishes continued, they were only to protect the Spanish withdrawal down the coast to Florida and Cuba.

On July 23 Oglethorpe was able to proclaim a "public thanksgiving to Almighty God for His great deliverance."

"Wonderful, even beyond our imagination," said Stephens when he heard of Bloody Marsh. He was still trying to find more recruits for Frederica, "but most of our young people being already gone hither . . . what levies [we] got now seemed like the last gleanings." He hoped to hear that the Spanish fleet had been destroyed by naval units from Charleston, but Charleston had not bestirred itself and this news never came.

By late July the women and children were returning to Savannah, all but those belonging to a man who had proclaimed "Georgia to be a lost colony," and who now said that the general's reports of so improbable a victory "were nothing else but a pack of falsehoods." Life went on in Savannah, but not quite as usual. Crops had been neglected, and the exhaustions of anxiety and flight had left a mark. There was sickness all fall, almost what Plymouth had called a "general sickness."

Georgia survived and achieved its destiny. Seven years after Bloody Marsh the trustees admitted slavery. Their charter had only one more year to run, and they were weary of coping with the pressures.

The Moravians packed up and went to Pennsylvania. The Salzburgers, though not without some searching of conscience, accommodated. The former were quickly replaced. The "Dorchester congregation" moved again, this time to a great tract that they named Midway, bringing with them many slaves; down from both Carolinas, down even from Virginia came the land hungry.

Now the colony departed in full from the ideals of its founders. Acreage was no longer restricted; rice and indigo plantations became big business. Slave labor, which already in Carolina included men skilled at blacksmithery, carpentry, carriage- and harness-making, supplanted white labor and drove the poor farther into the pine barrens. Planters overextended themselves and ran into debt, and that which had inspired the migration to these parts in the first place was established in Georgia: the debtors' prison.

Good William Stephens lived long enough to benefit by slave labor at his beloved Bewlie, but not to observe the long-range results. The stresses of the Spanish war had been followed by the invasion of the Thomas Bosomworths; the "Georgia Pochontas," who now called herself "the Creek queen," returned to Savannah demanding a small fortune and some of the sea islands for her services to Oglethorpe. "This very land is mine!" she shouted, stamping on it.

Stephens, now in his eighties, was a tired man. The grateful trustees retired him on full pay and he lived at Bewlie with his now reconciled son Thomas. "I have done eating and drinking in this world," said the old man one August day in 1752, thrusting aside his dish of tea. Next day, as his son affectionately reported, "without pain or sickness, priest or hobgoblin, in peace he resigned his soul to the great God who gave it."

8

Oglethorpe also lived into his eighties, vigorous to the last, and to him was given what had been given no other founding father; he celebrated the independence of his colony from British rule.

He had gone home in 1743, once he was satisfied that the Spanish were securely contained. His work was done, and he could no longer afford the luxury of life in Georgia. The trustees had supported him ill in his most critical years; he had spent £90,-000 of his own fortune on Frederica.

The necessity had arisen from the offense he had given by his casual ways of keeping records and accounts. From the first, his method of dealing with the time lag occasioned by the breadth of the Atlantic had been to draw bills on the trustees whenever he needed funds, without stopping to ask their leave or presenting an itemized account afterward. From the view of a busy man faced with on-the-spot decisions, this was an admirable system; but it inconvenienced trustees who had to account for every penny they laid out. Exasperated by being so cavalierly bypassed, they finally refused to honor such bills, and Oglethorpe drew on his own estate.

In England he recouped by marrying a well-endowed spinster. It wasn't necessary, for eventually Parliament repaid him, but the marriage of convenience was a happy one. Now in his late fifties, Oglethorpe had only one high adventure ahead of him, and it did not add to his fame. He took the field against the Stuart Pretender, Bonnie Prince Charlie, and through mismanagement or bad luck just missed a golden opportunity to take him. His family had been ardently Jacobite; his birth had been a sore inconvenience to his mother, who was up to her ears in conspiracy at the time. Thus when the Pretender escaped, Oglethorpe was suspect and he was court-martialed. He came off well, but the incident ended his public career.

Yet his happiest years were just beginning. While Georgia turned to slavery, its founder gave himself to the cause of abolition. Even during his Georgia days he had found time to rescue from Kent Island, Maryland, an enslaved Fulani prince and return him to his own people. Now he looked forward to ending slavery itself.

Interested in literature, he took the pains to call on a young Scot named James Boswell, whose work he admired, and through him he entered the circle that revolved around the great Dr. Johnson. Its ladies loved him; "a preux chevalier, heroic, romantic, and full of the old gallantry," one of them wrote, though by that time the indignities of age had cost the general his teeth.

When the third George impelled the colonies to revolt, including the one that the second George had founded, Oglethorpe's sympathies were with the American patriots. He lived to celebrate the outcome. In his eighty-ninth year, just a month before his death, he overwhelmed the first American ambassador to the court of St. James, one John Adams, by presenting himself for a courtly call of congratulation. The year was 1785; the last of the founding fathers had lived to see the colonial adventure come full circle.

Postlude

So the story ends in a new beginning, the creation of the United States of America, a great work still in progress.

Are we finding what you prayed for, William Bradford, John Winthrop? Have we found the way to the freedom of faith that you proclaimed, Roger Williams, Lord Baltimore, William Penn? Have we preserved the beauty of the land to which you eloquently responded, George Percy, David de Vries? Have we dealt justly with your people, Pocahontas, daughter of Powhatan, Mary Musgrove, Creek "queen," who took three English husbands? Or with yours, whose labors established our foundations, Domingo Angola? And are you content, James Oglethorpe, you who alone among the founding fathers lived to see the nation you helped create? If we have not yet realized your hopes, your prayers, take heart, for beyond us lies yet a newer beginning.

NOTE ON SOURCES AND SUGGESTED READING

IN accumulating the materials for this story I am indebted to the staffs of the Saugus and Lynn Public Libraries, (particularly Miss Ludovine Hamilton of the latter) and of the Boston Athenaeum, especially Mrs. Philip Johnson. Generous help has come from Joey Grunow, Barbara Morse, and Ann Pantalone. Miss Ola Elizabeth Winslow has often generously interrupted her own work to discuss a moot point. I thank my editors, Lewis Gannett and George Shively, for their guidance, and above all I thank Lucy and Pyke Johnson for suggesting that I undertake this most wonderful of assignments.

One pleasant and profitable mode of historical research is the visiting of sites and reconstructions of old villages and ships. There is no better way of getting the feel of the original *Mayflower* than by prowling through the *Mayflower II* at Plymouth, a reconstruction based on the most careful research, and no mock-up, but a living ship that has proved its seaworthiness by crossing the Atlantic.

The same is true of Pioneer Village in Salem, Massachusetts, with its dugouts, wigwams, pit saws, colonial garden plots, its reconstruction of the little mansion in which John Endicott welcomed the gentlefolk of the *Arbella* and where Lady Arbella herself resided briefly. The village affords invaluable insight into the conditions of first settlement not only in New England, but in colonies as far south as the Hudson, and quite possibly the head of the Chesapeake. Pioneer Village once had a mock-up of the *Arbella*, but it was badly damaged in a hurricane, and the wherewith being unavailable to restore it, it had to be destroyed.

Plymouth has also rebuilt old Plymouth Plantation, and in Pilgrim Hall it offers a wonderful collection of the furniture, tools, bits of armor, and other keepsakes that actually belonged to the Pilgrims; it also has the hull of the sloop *Sparrowhawk*, wrecked in Bradford's time. Saugus, Massachusetts, has one of the most remarkable reconstructions of all this period in the forge, water wheel, and outbuildings of the Saugus Iron Works, which John Winthrop, Jr., helped establish. All these are built on the original site, and there is also an original building, the beautiful home of the Iron Works manager, furnished in period.

Virginia has rebuilt old Jamestown with its star-shaped fort and its three little ships, but I have not seen it. I was lucky enough to watch the reconstruction of Williamsburg rise bit by bit on its old foundations; but colonial Williamsburg belongs to a period that was just beginning at the point where my story ends.

GENERAL SOURCES

My bible has been the documents in the multiple volumes of Scribner's *Original Narratives of Early American History* (New York, 1907–12), general editor J. Franklin Jameson, reprinted in 1959. I have also kept constantly by me Carl Bridenbaugh's *Cities in the Wilderness* (New York, 1955), for its intimate detail on early days in Boston, Newport, New York, Philadelphia, and Charleston. Another favorite because of its fine reproduction of early portraits has been James Thomas Flexner's *American Painting: First Flowers of Our Wilderness* (Boston, 1947).

For an overview of the colonial period I found helpful George Bancroft, *History of the United States of America*, Volume I (New York, 1884); Lyon Gardiner Tyler, *England in America, 1580–1653* (New York, 1904); Thomas Jefferson Wertenbaker, *The First Americans, 1607–1690* (New York, 1927); Daniel J. Boorstin, *The Americans, the Colonial Experience* (New York, 1958). A recent, readable (but occasionally inaccurate) sketch of founders from Sir Walter Raleigh to James Oglethorpe is Denis Meadows, *Five Remarkable Englishmen* (New York, 1961).

And no one prospects far in American history without heavy reliance on the *Dictionary of American Biography* (Oxford).

EARLY VIRGINIA AND MARYLAND
(Chapters II, III, V, VIII, XV)

For early Virginia history my favorite source was Lyon Gardiner Tyler, *Narratives of Early Virginia, 1606–1625* (New York, 1907); it is one of the most painstakingly edited of the "Original Narratives" series. George F. Willison, *Behold Virginia; The Fifth Crown* (New York, 1951), is a popular modern interpretation. John Fiske, *Old Virginia and Her Neighbors* (New York, 1897), is pleasant reading. Wesley Frank Craven, *The Southern Colonies in the Seventeenth Century* (University of Louisiana, 1949), is a scholarly study that goes far beyond Virginia. Alfred J. Mapp, *The Virginia Experiment, the Old Dominion's Role in the Making of America, 1607–1781* (Richmond, 1957), is of value. I drew on Richard Lee Morton, "Colonial Virginia," Volume I, *The Tidewater Period* (Oxford, 1960), for Bacon's Rebellion. An example of a historical novel so carefully researched as to rank as history is David Garnett, *Pocahontas, or the Nonparell of Virginia* (London, 1933).

For Maryland, the relevant "Original Narratives" volume is Clayton Colman Hall, *Narratives of Early Maryland, 1633–1684* (New York, 1910). A good general history is Matthew Page Andrews, *The Founding of Maryland* (New York, 1933); special studies of Claiborne and the Kent Island affair are John H. Latané, *Early Relations between Maryland and Virginia* (Baltimore, 1895), and J. H. Claiborne, *William Claiborne of Virginia* (New York, 1917).

NEW ENGLAND
(Chapters I, IV, VI, VII, IX, XIV)

The story of the voyage of the *Arbella* is based on John Winthrop's journal as found in the Massachusetts Historical Society, *The Founding of Massachusetts, a selection from the sources of the history of the settlement, 1628–1631* (Boston, 1930). I also used Robert C. Winthrop, *Life and Letters of John Winthrop* (Boston, 1868).

The Plymouth chapter is based on William Bradford, *Of Plymouth Plantation, 1620–1647*, Samuel Eliot Morison, ed. (New York, 1953). I also used Samuel Eliot Morison, *The Story of the Old Colony of New Plymouth* (New York, 1956) (especially good on nautical details of the *Mayflower's* voyage and social life of the settlement), and George F. Willison, *Saints and Strangers* (London, 1946).

For a general history of Massachusetts in this period, my favorite is the oldest: Thomas Hutchinson, *History of the Colony and Province of Massachusetts-Bay*, Lawrence Shaw Mayo, ed. (Harvard University, 1936). A rather cursory modern review is Henry F. Howe, *Massachusetts, There She Is, Behold Her* (New York, 1960).

There is first-rate material in Charles Francis Adams, *Three Episodes of Massachusetts History* (Boston, 1893) (I drew on this for my account of Anne Hutchinson), and in Samuel Eliot Morison, *Builders of the Bay Colony* (London, 1930). Documents are available in several publications of the Massachusetts Historical Society: *The Planter's Plea, or the Grounds of Plantations Examined and Objections Answered* (Boston, 1930), and Francis Higginson, *New England's Plantation, and Journal of His Voyage to New England* (Boston, 1930). The "Original Narratives" series includes Edward Johnson, *Wonder Working Providence, 1628–1651*, J. Franklin Jameson, ed. (New York, 1910). The classic of Connecticut history is Benjamin Trumbull, *A Complete History of Connecticut* (Hartford, 1797).

In centering the Rhode Island story on Roger Williams I made much use of Ola Elizabeth Winslow, *Master Roger Williams* (New York, 1957). George Locke Howe, *Mount Hope* (New York, 1959), has a lively account of King Philip's War.

NEW YORK, DELAWARE, PENNSYLVANIA
(Chapters X, XI, XII, XIII)

J. Franklin Jameson, ed., *Narratives of New Netherland, 1609–1664* (New York, 1909), contains the documents. Detailed general histories of New Netherland are Mrs. Schuyler van Rensselaer, *History of the City of New York in the Seventeenth Century* (New York, 1909); E. B. O'Callaghan, *History of New Netherland, or New York under the Dutch* (New York, 1846); Ellis Lawrence Raesly, *Portrait of New Netherland* (New York, 1945).

For the benefit of the unwary I add that Washington Irving, *Diedrick Knickerbocker's History of New York*, whatever its merits as satire, is neither history nor even good historical fiction.

Two first-rate studies of the Delaware colony are Christopher Ward, *The Dutch and Swedes on the Delaware* (Philadelphia, 1930), and John H. Wuorinen, *The Finns on the Delaware* (New York, 1938).

The documentary sources for the whole region are in Albert Cook Myers, ed., *Narratives of Early Pennsylvania, West New Jersey and Delaware, 1630–1707* (New York, 1912). I drew on this for most of the eyewitness material in Chapter XIII, though Sally Brinkley's charming letter is from Isaac Sharpless, *A History of Quaker Government in Pennsylvania* (Philadelphia, 1898). A fine social study is Thomas Jefferson Wertenbaker, *The Founding of American Civilization, the Middle Colonies* (New York, 1938). I also made use of John Fiske, *The Dutch and Quaker Colonies in America* (Boston, 1899); Catherine Owens Peare, *William Penn* (London, 1959); Sydney C. Fisher, *The Quaker Colony* (New Haven, 1920).

CAROLINA AND GEORGIA
(Chapters XV, XVI)

A detailed account of the two abortive Carolina colonies, the Huguenot settlement, and the lost Colony of Roanoke is in Harold Lamb, *New Found World, How North America Was Discovered and Explored* (New York, 1955). The original documents of the permanent Carolina settlements are in Alexander S. Salley, Jr., *Narratives of Early Carolina* (New York, 1911). The best general history is Edward McGrady, *History of South Carolina under the Proprietors, 1670–1719* (New York, 1897); for material on the Huguenots there is Arthur Henry Hirsch, *The Huguenots of Colonial South Carolina* (Durham, 1928).

A sentimental but readable Georgia history is the Rev. William Bacon Stevens, *History of Georgia* (New York, 1847); more modern interpretations are Thomas L. Stokes, *The Savannah* (New York, 1951); Albert B. Sayre, *New Viewpoints in Georgia History* (Athens, Georgia, 1943), gives a scholarly account of the work of the trustees. An authoritative study of the principal founder is Amos Aschback Ettinger, *James Edward Oglethorpe, Imperial Idealist* (Oxford, 1936). Many of Oglethorpe's letters are in the *Collections* of the Georgia Historical Society, III, 1873. There is lively material in William Stephens, *Journal*, E. Merton Coulter, ed. (Athens, Georgia, 1959); Francis Moore, "A Voyage to Georgia Begun in the Year 1735," Georgia Historical Society *Collections*, I, and the Rev. R. A. Strobel, *The Salzburgers and Their Descendants* (Baltimore, 1855).

INDEX

Atlantic

Wells
Dover
York
Kittery
Portsmouth
Plymouth
Provincetown
E COD
NEW HAMPSHIRE
CONNECTICUT R
Springfield
MASS.
Boston
Taunton
Providence
CONN. R.I.
New Haven
New London
New Amsterdam
Ft. Orange
Isopus
HUDSON R
Newark
NEW JERSEY
DELAWARE R
Chester
Eltsborg
Burlington
Philadelphia
Ft. Christina
Casimir
KENT ISLAND
St. Mary's
CAPE HENLOPEN
Swanendael
PENNSYLVANIA
SUSQUEHANNA R
MARYLAND
POTOMAC
CAPE CHARLES
Kecoughtan
CAPE HENRY
ALBEMARLE SOUND
YORK R.
JAMES R.
Williamsburg
Jamestown
Ft. Monroe
ROANOKE R.
V I R G I N I A

Scale of Miles
0   100   200   300

map by palacios